Studies in American Popular History and Culture

Edited by
Jerome Nadelhaft
University of Maine

A Routledge Series

Studies in American Popular History and Culture

Jerome Nadelhaft, *General Editor*

The Farm Press, Reform, and Rural Change, 1895–1920
John J. Fry

State of 'The Union'
Marriage and Free Love in the Late 1800s
Sandra Ellen Schroer

"My Pen and My Soul Have Ever Gone Together"
Thomas Paine and the American Revolution
Vikki J. Vickers

Agents of Wrath, Sowers of Discord
Authority and Dissent in Puritan Massachusetts, 1630–1655
Timothy L. Wood

The Quiet Revolutionaries
How the Grey Nuns Changed the Social Welfare Paradigm of Lewiston, Maine
Susan P. Hudson

Cleaning Up
The Transformation of Domestic Service in Twentieth Century New York City
Alana Erickson Coble

Feminist Revolution in Literacy
Women's Bookstores in the United States
Junko R. Onosaka

Great Depression and the Middle Class
Experts, Collegiate Youth and Business Ideology, 1929–1941
Mary C. McComb

Labor and Laborers of the Loom
Mechanization and Handloom Weavers, 1780–1840
Gail Fowler Mohanty

"The First of Causes to Our Sex"
The Female Moral Reform Movement in the Antebellum Northeast, 1834–1848
Daniel S. Wright

US Textile Production in Historical Perspective
A Case Study from Massachusetts
Susan M. Ouellette

Women Workers on Strike
Narratives of Southern Women Unionists
Roxanne Newton

Hollywood and Anticommunism
HUAC and the Evolution of the Red Menace, 1935–1950
John Joseph Gladchuk

Negotiating Motherhood in Nineteenth-Century American Literature
Mary McCartin Wearn

The Gay Liberation Youth Movement in New York
"An Army of Lovers Cannot Fail"
Stephan L. Cohen

Gender and the American Temperance Movement of the Nineteenth Century
Holly Berkley Fletcher

Gender and the American Temperance Movement of the Nineteenth Century

Holly Berkley Fletcher

Routledge
Taylor & Francis Group
New York   London

First published 2008
by Routledge
270 Madison Ave, New York, NY 10016

Simultaneously published in the UK
by Routledge
2 Park Square, Milton Park, Abingdon, Oxon OX14 4RN

Routledge is an imprint of the Taylor & Francis Group, an informa business

© 2008 Taylor & Francis

Typeset in Adobe Garamond by IBT Global

All rights reserved. No part of this book may be reprinted or reproduced or utilised in any form or by any electronic, mechanical, or other means, now known or hereafter invented, including photocopying and recording, or in any information storage or retrieval system, without permission in writing from the publishers.

Trademark Notice: Product or corporate names may be trademarks or registered trademarks, and are used only for identification and explanation without intent to infringe.

Library of Congress Cataloging-in-Publication Data

Gender and the American temperance movement of the nineteenth century / by Holly Berkley Fletcher.
  p. cm. — (Studies in American popular history and culture)
  Includes bibliographical references and index.
  ISBN 0-415-96312-5
  1. Temperance—United States—History—19th century. 2. Sex role—United States—History—19th century. 3. Gender identity—United States—History—19th century. 4. Women--Suffrage—United States—19th century. 5. Men—United States—History—19th century. I. Fletcher, Holly Berkley.

HV5229.G46 2008
178'.1097309034—dc22   2007029538

ISBN10: 0-415-96312-5 (hbk)
ISBN10: 0-203-93257-9 (ebk)

ISBN13: 978-0-415-96312-1 (hbk)
ISBN13: 978-0-203-93257-5 (ebk)

To my husband, Kevin

Contents

List of Figures	ix
Acknowledgments	xi
Introduction	1
Chapter One Self-Made Men: Temperance, Identity, and Authority in Antebellum America	7
Chapter Two Temperance Counter-Cultures and the Coming of the Civil War	30
Chapter Three "Let Patriots Join Hands:" The Civil War and the War on Alcohol	58
Chapter Four Crusading Women: The Creation of a New Temperance Icon	79
Chapter Five A "Knitting Together of Hearts:" The Crusader, the WCTU, and the Building of a Temperance Coalition	102
Notes	125

Bibliography 169

Index 187

List of Figures

Figure 1.	*King Alcohol and his Prime Minister*	10
Figure 2.	*Tree of Temperance*	12
Figure 3.	A certificate of membership for temperance societies	17
Figure 4.	Frontispiece of the *Western Temperance Almanac for 1835*	27
Figure 5.	*The Great Republican Reform Party, Calling on their Candidate*	57
Figure 6.	*Woman's Holy War*	76
Figure 7.	*The Ohio whisky war*	87
Figure 8.	*The Temperance Crusade, or Four Hours in a Bar Room*	89

Acknowledgments

I have needed and accepted much help in the process of this work, and therefore I have incurred huge debts to a great many people, too many to mention here individually. I wish to offer humble, collective thanks to all those who assisted this project (such as it is)—colleagues, professors, editors, students, archivists, librarians, friends, family, and, yes, therapists—in ways both great and small, occupational and voluntary, professional and personal.

More specifically, I am grateful to the members of my graduate committee at the University of Oklahoma—David Levy, Robert Griswold, Catherine Kelly, and Lesley Rankin-Hill—and especially to my graduate adviser, Robert Shalhope. His impeccable instruction, considerable wisdom and clear perception have honed my skills enormously and have bailed me out of numerous scholarly jams. But his steadfast support of and interest in me as a person has made him my true mentor and friend; it is in this capacity that I have most treasured his assistance.

I am also extremely indebted to H. Wayne and Anne Morgan, whose generosity funded the bulk of my research through a fellowship they established for the University of Oklahoma's History Department. I must also thank the helpful staffs of the Berea College archives, the Cincinnati Museum Center library, the Ohio Historical Society library, the Western Reserve Historical Society library, the American Antiquarian Society, and the Library of Congress Manuscripts Division. Their assistance and advice have been invaluable.

I am blessed with a host of family and friends who have given me the strength to see this work through and who, thankfully, have filled my life with much more than this work. I credit my college mentor and later colleague at Hardin-Simmons University, Paul Madden, for giving me a love of history and a belief in myself. My graduate school family—Charlie and Angie, Lorien, Brett and April, Jeff, Dan, George, The Sisterhood—has been my greatest professional asset and inspiration; their friendship has certainly been my richest reward. Special thanks go to Sarah Eppler Janda and Lorien Foote, who, in addition to being dear friends, read the entire manuscript and provided many helpful suggestions. My parents, sister, and extended family have constantly encouraged me with their words, active support, and prayers. Finally, and most especially, I want to thank my husband, Kevin, whose love, friendship, empathy, and good humor fuel everything I do and fill my life with great joy.

Introduction

Before the 1970's, the temperance movement received little attention from historians, who largely dismissed it as, in the words of Richard Hofstadter, "a pseudo-reform, a pinched parochial substitute for reform."[1] Hofstadter's assessment was despite the fact that temperance was the largest and longest-sustained reform effort of the nineteenth century and culminated in an amendment to the Constitution. But beginning in the early 1970's, scholars altered their perceptions. Temperance began to take its place alongside abolitionism and women's rights as a legitimate reform and one that could perhaps tell historians the most about the time in which it thrived. Scholars shed light on the movement's inner workings and the motivations of its membership, as well as its relationship to the larger culture—an America becoming an industrialized, urbanized nation with a sizable middle class. Yet despite the increased attention temperance has received in the last three decades, historians have not exhausted its potential as a tool for understanding nineteenth-century American culture, nor have they mastered the intricacies of the reform as a movement and an ideology. Temperance historiography has not yet been adequately synthesized with the most recent trends in historical inquiry, nor has the movement itself been properly and fully situated within the social and intellectual history of the nineteenth century.

Scholars have generally organized the movement into several phases, each one distinct in its leadership, membership, and character. Before the 1820's, elites, whose goal was to reduce alcohol consumption rather than to eradicate it, largely comprised the movement. The middle classes, under the influence of evangelical Christianity and the pressures of an industrializing economy, then appropriated temperance in the antebellum era, and gradually teetotalism rather than moderation became the standard. Men dominated the movement, though women assumed a visible but passive role. In the 1840's, the reform underwent another transition, as large numbers of working-class Americans for the first time became involved through the Washingtonian movement. Women assumed a more active role in the 1840's and 1850's, even though the increasingly political path middle-class reformers took during these decades hampered their efforts. The Civil War diverted almost all attention from the movement; it did not re-emerge with any force until the 1870's, when women directed temperance work to a great extent under the auspices of the Woman's Christian Temperance Union.[2]

In their study of the antebellum temperance movement, historians have reached a consensus that regards temperance as a response to industrialization and the resultant transformations of American society. Most scholars acknowledge that, after 1820, the majority of temperance reformers were middle-class and that there were definite connections between temperance and the construction of a middle-class culture.[3] They recognize, too, a religious impulse behind temperance (and antebellum reform in general) that emanated from the millennial Christianity of the Second Great Awakening and emphasized individual perfection and salvation as the basis for social redemption.[4]

In studying the post-Civil War movement, historians have examined the connections between temperance and feminism, female reform and female consciousness in the context of the WCTU. While scholars generally recognize the organization served as a vehicle for expanding women's public roles and linking temperance to women's rights, they disagree on whether the organization truly challenged traditional gender ideology. Ruth Bordin, Barbara Epstein, Janet Giele, Suzanne Marilley, and others argue that the WCTU can be considered a "feminist" movement because it expressed antagonism to men and raised members' consciousness of the disabilities and exclusions faced by women. But all agree that the WCTU represented a more "domestic" feminism than that of radicals like Elizabeth Cady Stanton in that it centered on issues related to women's traditional roles and interests as wives and mothers.[5] Other historians have largely discounted the feminist content of the WCTU. Lori Ginzberg, Louise Newman, and others view the WCTU as a wholly conservative movement that bolstered class and racial/ethnic solidarity.[6]

While scholars of temperance have made significant progress in explaining the cultural relevance of the antebellum movement and the WCTU, their most glaring omission has been the failure to establish a connection between them. Jack Blocker, who has written the most comprehensive study of the full span of temperance, gives the issue fairly shallow treatment. He describes the movement as "cycles of reform" but does not adequately show continuity and change within temperance over time, nor does he link the movement's progression to larger forces in American

Introduction

culture and thought. Jed Dannenbaum's study is better; he demonstrates the WCTU's roots in women's antebellum involvement, especially with the growth of male prohibitory work in the 1840's and 1850's. Since society excluded women from political participation, they began to carve out their own niche within the movement, a process that culminated in the WCTU.[7] But Dannenbaum's study only begins to explain how the antebellum temperance movement, dominated and led by men, gave way to the WCTU's starring role in the reform by the 1870's.

This inquiry demands not simply an examination of women's role within the movement over time or a description of how the external forms and structures of temperance changed, but a thorough look at the ideas, assumptions, arguments, and debates that comprised temperance over the course of the nineteenth century. More specifically, it demands a fuller employment of the tools offered by recent social and intellectual histories of the nineteenth century that assume ideas and identities are dynamic, cultural constructs instead of fixed, isolated entities. Intellectual historians increasingly combine their study of formal ideologies with that of "discourse," the social and political function of those ideas and the language that expresses them.[8] In particular, historians have become increasingly interested in the discursive construction of definitions and structures pertaining to race, class, and gender. Scholars additionally regard these categories of identity as ideologies themselves, likewise defined and redefined in a social setting rather than existing as static, objective, or monolithic categories rooted purely in biology or economics.[9]

The field of gender history in particular offers modes of inquiry essential to an understanding of the temperance movement. Within the last twenty years, historians have begun to take a holistic approach to gender that examines both masculinity and femininity and views them as dynamic and interacting social and political categories. Numerous studies have illuminated the processes by which male and female identities and roles have been constructed in relationship to each other and to men and women of other races, ethnicities, religions, and classes.[10] The application of this kind of gendered approach to temperance is still in its beginning phases. Historians have been especially late to arrive at an examination of the confluence between temperance and masculinity, which is essential to understanding both the movement's central concerns and one of its central features in the nineteenth century, its apparent gendered evolution.

Two recent works of note demonstrate the exciting possibilities gendered history holds for temperance and vice versa. Bruce Dorsey's book on the relationship between gender construction and antebellum reform finds the temperance movement during this period fraught with questions and conflicts surrounding male identity. He locates within temperance competing discourses based on race, class, and generational conflict. He also demonstrates the connection between this struggle to define masculinity and female roles within the movement.[11] Likewise, Elaine Frantz Parsons has examined temperance in terms of the gendered discourses surrounding the individual's power of volition and the state's power of redemption. She argues that the figure of the drunkard cast serious doubt on male independence and necessitated the rescue of men, first by women, then by the government. She links women's increasingly public and political role in temperance to this progression of thought.[12]

While these works advance a more sophisticated cultural and ideological examination of temperance, they only begin to mine the reform movement of its rich resources. More specifically, they do not fully integrate their histories of temperance into the enormous changes experienced by the United States in the nineteenth century. Since temperance was the largest and most sustained reform movement in American history, it holds enormous potential as an indicator of cultural change. Dorsey's study demonstrates the importance of antebellum temperance for male identities and how temperance illuminates the complexities of those identities, but his work is confined to the antebellum period. He makes little attempt to explain how and why the meaning of temperance changed in nineteenth century or how this transition shaped and was shaped by evolving gender roles and definitions. Parsons' work, on the other hand, covers the span of the nineteenth-century movement and addresses the question of its shifting gendered components. But she tends to view gender in isolation and therefore does not adequately describe the movement's evolution in terms of larger cultural change, particularly pertaining to the ways in which gendered ideas and identities interacted with those of race and class.

More specifically, these studies do not examine the nature and extent of the Civil War's impact, a subject of much historical interest. Historians have debated whether or not the war created a new reform culture based on efficiency, science, and state power that replaced the antebellum one of emotion, idealism, and individualism.[13] They have also discussed the war's impact on female reformism as part of the transformation of American reform. Most historians agree that women's public roles expanded after the Civil War, but they disagree on whether this resulted from a continued belief in female morality, from a stronger identification with men based on class, or from racial and ethnic realignments within American political culture.[14] Lastly, historians have examined the war's ramifications for the dialogue on racial equality, whether it continued after the war or was consumed within the cultural drive for national unity and new political concerns, such as the mounting divide between labor and capital.[15]

This study attempts to build upon these discussions and developments to create a narrative of temperance in the nineteenth century that portrays the reform as a mutable and complex set of ideas, assumptions, rationales, and sources of identity, shaped and claimed by diverse, often competing groups and individuals over time, in different contexts, and for different purposes. It will also aim to illuminate the reciprocal, symbiotic relationship between temperance and its cultural context through an examination of the dominant images and cultures—the icons—of the movement, the "self-made man" in the antebellum period and the "crusading woman" in the Gilded Age. The origins and functions of these icons not only help explain the progression of the temperance movement, they reveal much about the political culture of the nineteenth century, particularly as pertains to the ongoing discourses of race and gender and the Civil War's impact on that discussion. Throughout the nineteenth century, temperance served as a language for exploring other matters of concern; the cultures surrounding these icons and those that contrasted with them provide a window into this exploration.

The study follows a loosely chronological approach, since one of its central goals is an examination of change over time, of the gendered evolution of the movement's dominant, visible culture. Chapter one explores the gendered, class, and racial origins and complexities of the movement's antebellum icon, the self-made man. An examination of this icon reveals the antebellum movement to be chiefly concerned with the issues of white, middle-class male identity at a time when those notions were in flux. Temperance became a medium for participants to explore the anxieties of the changing economy and to reaffirm male independence and authority in relationship to women and African Americans. Temperance during this period was a deeply personal issue that focused primarily on the individual and the family.

Chapter two examines cultures and impetuses within antebellum temperance that contrasted with the dominant culture of the self-made man in terms of class, gender, and/or race. The Washingtonian movement challenged the middle-class movement's concept of male independence, while women's rights supporters, African Americans, and abolitionists challenged the dominant culture's concept of white male authority. In the process, these latter three groups threatened to embroil the temperance movement in the mounting conflict over slavery. The chapter ends with an examination of the World's Temperance Convention of 1853 that demonstrates the polarization of the antebellum movement within the larger debate over gender and racial equality.

Chapter three addresses the impact of the Civil War on the temperance movement with regard to the decline of the self-made man and the rise of the crusading woman. The war, and new political and social realities in its wake, altered the meaning, context, and ideology of temperance. The war worsened the political and cultural fortunes of the movement and weakened the discursive alliance between temperance and masculinity. The war also transformed the cause into a wholesale political fight, while simultaneously casting doubt on the fitness of the male body politic in waging that battle. Stemming from these other developments, the war produced a reconfiguration of women's functions for the movement.

Chapter four examines the construction of the crusading woman as a new icon for the movement. Whereas other histories have emphasized the temperance crusades of the 1870's as a purely women's movement, this chapter argues that both men and women created the image of the Crusader in order to benefit the cause politically and to reconnect with the movement's antebellum heritage of moral suasion. This chapter also depicts the complexities and tensions within the Crusader image, particularly with regard to its relationship to women's rights.

Chapter five demonstrates the function of the crusading woman in the era of the Woman's Christian Temperance Union. Though individuals within the WCTU and elements of its reform program visibly diverged from the Crusader image, the organization and the temperance movement as a whole deliberately maintained that image because of its political importance. Under its guise, the WCTU became a means of building consensus where the movement faced disagreement and of building a broad political coalition in support of prohibition.

This study pursues two related arguments in the course of this narrative. First, it argues that the gendered evolution of the temperance movement was more symbolic than real. The two icons of the movement in the nineteenth century masked the complexity and diversity of temperance during the entire period with regard to race, class, and gender. The self-made man did so as a statement of the exclusivity and authority of white, middle-class manhood. The crusading woman did so as a pragmatic means of building a political coalition. Second, a study of the existence, creation, and function of these icons is nevertheless important for understanding the evolving meaning and context of temperance and its employment of gender. Through an examination of the self-made man and the crusading woman, temperance becomes a story of how the debate on racial and gender equality became submerged in service to a corporate, political enterprise and how male and female identities and functions were reconfigured in relationship to each other and within this shifting political and cultural landscape.

Chapter One
Self-Made Men
Temperance, Identity, and Authority in Antebellum America

When historians have considered the antebellum temperance movement, they have often described an icon of antebellum America itself, the self-made man. He was white, upwardly-mobile and individualistic. During the day, he competed in a market economy to get ahead, and at night, he returned home to a domestic, feminine oasis from the capitalist fray. A total abstinence lifestyle was a natural choice for such a man. The temperance movement made alcohol a readily identifiable source of failure, which soothed the anxiety surrounding a man's personal fortunes and eased his conscience regarding those who enjoyed none of their own success. He could assure himself that he would not slip into poverty if he simply abstained and that those who did slip must have done the opposite. The total abstinence lifestyle also made him a model father and husband in the sentimental, middle-class home.[1]

Although temperance literature from the time bears out this interpretation, it also speaks to the complexities and tensions within the character of the self-made man.[2] Certainly, the dominant image of the movement during these years was white, male, and middle-class; the overall message of the antebellum movement was one of male achievement, authority, and mastery. But the deeper story of the relationship between temperance and the self-made man was one of class, gender, and racial identities in flux. In antebellum America, temperance became a way of discussing these issues and constructing these identities.

Temperance, in its original form, was not an antebellum creation. Reformers first touted the idea that alcohol was a major problem in the nation's culture as early as the 1780's. With the necessity of virtuous citizens for the new republic and rising alcohol consumption, it is not surprising that Americans' awareness of the issue increased in the wake of the American Revolution.[3] In 1784, they saw the first scientific evidence that alcohol could potentially destroy human health and happiness when Dr. Benjamin Rush published *An Inquiry into the Effects of Spiritous Liquors on the Human Body and Mind*. The next few decades witnessed the birth of dozens of temperance organizations, led by society's elites and dedicated to promoting moderation in drink, both for its members and the larger society.[4]

The formation of the American Temperance Society in 1826 marked a changed direction for the movement and the start of its life as the most widespread and enduring reform movement in American history. The ATS loosely coordinated temperance activity throughout the country, sending out paid agents as traveling lecturers, printing and distributing temperance literature, and encouraging the establishment of temperance societies. The results were spectacular; by the next decade, the ATS boasted five thousand state and local societies and more than a million members, each of whom had taken a pledge of total abstinence from most forms and usages of alcohol.[5]

By the time the ATS transformed temperance into a mass movement, the nation was in the throes of "the market revolution," the economic shift to a capitalist economy and the concomitant social and political shift towards greater individualism and democracy.[6] As part of this larger transformation, the Second Great Awakening provided an important spiritual impetus for the antebellum movement. Temperance easily melded with the Awakening's democratic impulse, as it created extra-denominational rituals that served as alternatives to the authority of established churches. And the message of antebellum revivalism provided a powerful religious impulse behind temperance, particularly as it emanated from millennial hopes for American society. In Lyman Beecher's *Six Sermons on Temperance*, delivered in 1825 and credited as a precipitating event for the formation of the ATS, he singled out alcohol as "the sin of our land" that threatened to "defeat the hopes of the world."[7] As it encroached upon the lives of individual citizens and turned them into loathsome, irrational, and poverty-stricken drunks, alcohol threatened to stunt the political, economic, social, and moral progress of the nation, defeating all utopian possibilities. Like other perfectionist reforms that emanated from religious trends, temperance linked individual perfectibility to that of society. If individuals purged their own lives of alcohol's detrimental effects, the nation, and even humanity as a whole, might be elevated.[8]

Although temperance had this broader, cultural component, in the antebellum years, it was deeply and preeminently personal for its participants. Scholars agree that temperance was particularly dear to the burgeoning middle classes. Those classes appropriated the movement from its earlier elitist leadership and re-made it into an individual pursuit of total abstinence, which, *writ large,* would eventually and completely eliminate alcohol from national life.[9] The middle classes employed the movement to shore up their own position in society and to negotiate their own class identity—neither of which were certainties. As historians have most recently demonstrated, the middle classes often moved back and forth on a broad trajectory between poverty and wealth, employee and employer, manual labor and professional work. In addition, far from being unapologetic creations and beneficiaries of capitalism, the middle classes often expressed, in word and behavior, mixed feelings about the culture of the market; they at once strived to succeed within it and disapproved of its core values. Temperance discourse revealed the ambivalence and contentiousness of middle-class culture and aided its resolution.[10]

On a purely practical level, total abstinence from alcohol was a defensive strategy against the threat of poverty—a constant theme in antebellum temperance literature. A leading temperance newspaper of the 1830's so believed in the success reaped from abstinence, it called temperance societies "savings banks" and claimed their members were "making money. . . . Every citizen is cordially invited to share the gains with us."[11] Horace Greeley, a temperance advocate throughout his career, saw such principles operating in his own family; he attributed his parents' "pecuniary ruin" to their use of "ardent spirits and tobacco—very moderately, they think, but greatly to their injury, I know."[12] Temperance fiction often exploited the fear of poverty in promoting total abstinence. "History of Peter and John Hay" narrated the experience of two brothers living the liberal American dream, who eventually became "slaves of intemperance," lost all, and died horrible, drunkards' deaths.[13] *The Story of James and Mary Duffil: A Tale of Real Life* (and most other temperance stories) had only a change in cast.[14] Such temperance tracts struck at the heart of middle-class fears by warning, "If you are determined to be poor . . . to starve your family . . . to blunt your senses, be a drunkard, and you will soon be more stupid than an ass. . . . You [will] be dead weight on the community."[15] A man who failed to provide for himself and his dependents was "useless, helpless, burthensome and expensive."[16]

As these examples reveal, the middle-class fear of poverty was not simply a terror of individual failure but a betrayal of community.[17] Peter and John, for instance, were not self-made but instead attained success "by wisely improving the fruits of their father's labors."[18] And though middle-class promotion of temperance has often been portrayed as a shrewd, if unconscious, business tactic for securing a disciplined, productive work force, there is just as much evidence that middle-class Americans employed

10 Gender and the American Temperance Movement

Figure 1. *King Alcohol and his Prime Minister* (1820's-1880's). The stream of moderate drinkers on the left becomes the graves of drunkards in the foreground and the "Alms house" and weeping, poverty-stricken family on the right. Library of Congress, Prints and Photographs Division, LC-USZ62-90655.

temperance to further communal values, not just individual gain.[19] Consider, for instance, a tract entitled "The Well-Conducted Farm," which told the story of a Massachusetts farmer who forbade his workers to drink. The tract certainly boasted that the farm made more money. But it also claimed, "The men appeared, more than ever before, like brethren of the same family, satisfied with their business, contented and happy."[20] The story demonstrated a longing not just for individual wealth and success but for more republican ideals of community and virtue, values that eroded under the onslaught of individuals striving to succeed.[21]

Reformers sometimes revealed a deep distress that economic progress in some cases came at the price of these values. Nowhere is this attitude, and middle-class ambivalence about the market, more clearly evident than in the depictions of those who made their living from the sale and manufacture of alcohol. Rumsellers and distillers were entrepreneurs themselves and, in a sense, models of middle-class striving and success. In temperance literature, the rumseller was often a pillar of the community, a deacon or at least a church member. Reformers expended great effort to lift the veil of respectability from these men and to expose them for what they believed they were, those who sacrificed the good of society for their own wealth. They had particularly strong words for those who called themselves Christians, claiming that if they could see their trade through the eyes of God, they "would sooner beg your bread door to door, than gain money by such a traffic. The Christian's dram shop! Sound it out to yourself. . . . It is doubtless a choice gem in the phrase-book of Satan!"[22] It was unfair that the drunkard bore all the shame of intemperance, while "men will bow to [the rumseller] and seek his acquaintance, though he has proved to one person, if no more a *robber* and a *murderer!*"[23] Indeed the "hardihood, effrontery, and shameless audacity of Rumsellers is unparalleled by any other class of the vile and abandoned on earth."[24]

The attacks by middle-class reformers on middle-class rumsellers potently revealed the tensions within middle-class culture. Even while temperance discourse proclaimed the cause would aid pecuniary success and even portrayed it as a moneymaking enterprise, it expressed discomfort with the pursuit of material gain at any cost. Rumsellers disgusted temperance folk because they epitomized the values of the marketplace in a society that tried to temper cultural change with the preservation of republican values; they revealed how tenuous the balance was between material and moral progress. Dealing in alcohol offended because "its sole reason is *to make money*. It is not because it is supposed that it will benefit mankind. . . . It is an employment which tends to *counteract the very design of the organization of society.*"[25]

Figure 2. *Tree of Temperance* (A.D. Fillmore, 1855). This engraving demonstrates how temperance harmonized the disparate values of the market and community. On the one hand, the tree includes fruits such as "Economy" and "Industry," and in the distant background a steamboat and locomotive are pictured. On the other hand, the tree produces "Brotherly Kindness," "Philanthropy," and "Righteousness," and the foreground features a church and people in idyllic relationship. Library of Congress, Prints and Photographs Division, LC-USZ62-54497.

Such objections to the capitalist enterprise of the alcohol industry can be interpreted in two ways. On the one hand, one might argue that middle-class reformers employed alcohol as a scapegoat that allowed them to ignore the larger problem of the market's impact on social values. But one might also argue that temperance reformers leveled a meaningful social critique of unrestrained capitalism. Either way, however, temperance discourse in this instance speaks to the nuances of middle-class culture and its relationship to the market revolution. It also helps explain the appeal of temperance for the middle classes, as it at once warded off poverty and emphasized the sin of pure material pursuit. At both ends of the spectrum, individual behavior affronted the values of community. Middle-class Americans, by choosing to abstain, might set a powerful example and "change the habits of a whole nation."[26]

The tension within middle-class culture between the competing values of the market and a republican social order was often expressed in gendered terms and contained gendered dimensions, as those competing values became sexualized in the antebellum mind. Historians have all but dismantled the notion that nineteenth-century men and women resided in "separate spheres" by demonstrating the involvement of even middle-class, white women in politics and business. Contrary to earlier historical interpretation, as the household economy eroded (which in itself occurred unevenly and over a protracted time span), women of the new middle classes were not quarantined to isolated, domestic enclaves. In truth, the middle-class home was no oasis from the market; it was the scene of market consumption and oftentimes business transactions (such as boarding arrangements), both conducted chiefly by women. Nor were women confined to the home. They attended political rallies and parades, sat in the galleries of Congress, ran benevolent organizations as businesses, and sold their handcrafted goods at fairs. Even women in wealthy, hierarchal, southern households engaged in these activities and served an economic function within the home, such as the management of domestic slaves.[27]

Although gendered spheres were not strictly geographic or actual, antebellum Americans did hold to the idea that men and women embodied different qualities and values. Barbara Cutter has recently argued that Americans of all classes and races associated men with the values of the market—greed, selfishness, ambition—and women with morality, virtue, and self-sacrifice. Women's function was to temper male behavior and values and lend them, in the words of Brian Roberts, "a veneer of respectability," both in public and in private.[28]

Implicit in this segregation of values was an assertion of male independence and female dependence at a time when patriarchy was disintegrating. In the eighteenth century, the ideal male was the independent householder, free from market entanglements and at the apex of a hierarchy of dependents. As the market revolution eroded the independence of patriarchal households, as well as the authority of patriarchs within them, and made an increasing number of men into wage-workers, the gendered association of work and engagement in the marketplace with masculinity and domesticity with femininity eased the anxieties associated with this transition. The insistence on female dependency and confinement, even in the face of its fiction, helped retain the *idea* of male independence and male authority within the actuality of their erosion. Indeed, as Brian Roberts has noted, the idea of "a lone male provider" made men's paid labor seem "heroic;" without men as breadwinners, women might starve to death.[29]

Temperance was instrumental in upholding the notions of independent masculinity and male authority, as it reinforced the idea of male independence and provision for dependent women.[30] Alcohol undermined a man's ability to fulfill the role of breadwinner by decreasing the likelihood of his success in the marketplace. The fear of financial failure had class dimensions, but perhaps its gendered implications loomed even larger. Strong drink robbed men of full use of the mental faculties so crucial in a competitive marketplace and thereby endangered male independence. This mental degeneration was often described in feminine terms that underscored the conflation of failure and dependence with a loss of manhood. Francis Wayland, president of Brown University, explained in an 1832 address the progressive mental degeneration produced by alcohol, beginning with "feverish excitement" and ending with "stupid vacuity." None of these states was "suitable to the best exercise of human intellect," and indeed, in each the drinker was "under the influence of a partial, a self-inflicted, but to all practical purposes, real insanity."[31] Not coincidentally, physicians at the time often used similar language to describe "hysteria," a typically female disorder.[32] At times, reformers employed language that was explicitly gendered; one temperance article likened the drunkard's state to a "Sybriatic effeminacy, a submission to bondage."[33] The latter metaphor alluded to slavery as well, thereby reinforcing the gendered loss of independence produced by alcohol with racial imagery. This emasculated mental and physical state translated into a similar economic one, the failure of a man to provide for his dependents. In one temperance tale, a drunkard's wife, the quintessential victim of the male failure to provide, asks, "How hard is it for a man to thrive with all his industry and wits about him. Then how can it be done by one who is stupefied and palsied by hard drink?"[34]

But alcohol destroyed masculinity in more ways than one. Not only could a man's bibulous demise occur through his dependency and failure to provide—his being made feminine—it might also arrive through a kind of hyper-masculinity, the over-inflation of "male" qualities, and the destruction of any sort of morality and humanity. Alcohol "blast[ed] every noble and manly feeling of the human heart," it "relax[ed] honorable and honest principles" and "moral sensibilities."[35] It transformed "the once kind husband, affectionate father or dutiful son" into a "morose, peevish, unfeeling, unreasonable, implacable, unmerciful" figure.[36] The drunkard's debacle went beyond gender to humanity itself. Alcoholics were "frenzied at the suspicion of insult . . . revengeful until death, at the least indignity," their appetites "roused to ungovernable strength by the remotest object of gratification."[37] Alcohol turned a man into "a ferocious beast, and our only security is to flee from him or chain him."[38] As with his economic failure, a man's moral decay consumed his family members, and his home became "the abode of discord, and strife, and misery" until "all that is lovely in domestick [sic] virtues . . . is smitten."[39]

The depiction of alcohol in temperance literature as both a feminizing agent and one that magnified masculine traits to the point of inhumanity speaks to the contradictory nature of middle-class male identity and the gendered bifurcation of values. Men were at once thought to embody the values of the marketplace—independent but selfish striving—and expected to be affectionate members of virtuous homes. Antebellum culture simultaneously exalted the man cultivated by virtuous women and the self-made man, the man who successfully took on a competitive, democratic society and rose to its top, like the heroic but ill-bred and unrefined symbol of his age, Andrew Jackson.[40] It is not surprising, then, that middle-class men sought ways to reconcile these competing claims by seeking activities that reaffirmed them both. Mark Carnes and Mary Ann Clawson demonstrate how middle-class men in antebellum America turned to fraternal ritual to bolster masculinity in the face of the domesticating influences of the female-dominated home and evangelical Christianity. The fraternal ritual reasserted male presence in both these arenas by invoking fatherhood in an exclusively male setting and emphasizing Old Testament patriarchs rather than Christ. Female opposition to fraternal organizations only strengthened their value to the cause of male gender identity. In the lodge, men could create a male culture that did not endanger male roles as husbands and fathers in the sentimental family but rather co-existed with those roles peaceably. In a way, fraternal orders were a safe, middle-class version of the working-class saloon.[41]

Like fraternal orders, temperance organizations served a positive function for male gender identity. A temperance lifestyle in itself amalgamated and promoted the two basic aims of middle-class manhood—success in the marketplace and domestication at home. Sobriety went hand-in-hand with hard work, clear thought, and competitiveness in the business world. At home, it accompanied virtue, beauty, gentility, and provision for one's family. Temperance work and membership in a temperance organization likewise combined male needs by allowing men to promote personal behavior pleasing to feminine sensibilities in a setting that gave women a scant role. Not only were most antebellum temperance societies segregated along gender lines, temperance work included activities—oratory, publishing, and by the 1840's, legislative petitioning—that remained largely beyond the bounds of the prescribed roles for women. Nor did middle-class reformers conceive of women as objects of reform; the American Temperance Society estimated that women only consumed one-sixth of the alcohol imbibed by the nation as a whole, a statistic that did not seem to warrant any special effort to reach female drinkers.[42] Therefore, the antebellum temperance movement existed principally as a male province, led and dominated by men.[43] This is not to say, however, that American women remained aloof from the movement; quite the opposite, they joined temperance organizations in droves by signing total abstinence pledges alongside, and oftentimes ahead of, their male family members. Women comprised anywhere from thirty-five to sixty percent of the antebellum membership of the ATS and its successor, the American Temperance Union.[44] But women found that once they entered the temperance fold, male reformers seemed to believe women's passive presence was their primary contribution.

However, male leaders highly valued women in that capacity because of the enormous moral authority society ascribed to women in antebellum America.[45] Women were thought to embody virtue, morality, self-sacrifice—the values of the home—and to bring those values into any realm they entered. As Jan Lewis and Elizabeth Varon have shown, nineteenth-century Americans believed that even the male-dominated world of politics might benefit from a feminine presence; women gave moral sanction and legitimacy to political life and culture.[46] For the antebellum temperance movement, too, women played an important role in a male-dominated culture. On a practical level and in a direct sense, female aid gave temperance forces an edge in what was seen as a moral conflict. Women were the secret weapon of the temperance movement; bring them in, and the foe would fall. Without them, men fought a losing battle. In 1834, the executive committee of the ATS passed a resolution stating "that the influence of woman is essential to the triumph of every great and good cause; and should that influence which God has graciously given her, be ... exerted in favor of the Temperance reformation, its triumphs would be certain and complete."[47] One temperance paper insisted, "*female influence* is that formidable battery that *vice* most dreads, that Satan and his

Self-Made Men

Figure 3. A certificate of membership for temperance societies (lithograph by Thomas Sinclair, 1840's). A man signs the pledge at the offering of two male reformers and at the urging of his wife and child, demonstrating how temperance served as a male domain that still had the sanction of female morality. Library of Congress, Prints and Photographs Division, LC-USZ62-90146.

children most fear!"[48] If the Prince of Darkness himself trembled in the presence of woman, she must have been commanding indeed.

Beyond their promotion of victory for the cause, women played a key role in the employment of temperance in defining gendered identities. Just as temperance literature instructed men that alcohol brought with it a loss of manhood, it told women that their failure to the cause would deny their moral authority and thus result in a loss of womanhood. In 1833, the New York State Society for the Promotion of Temperance (an auxiliary of the ATS) made a plea for female assistance that insinuated if women ignored their duty to temperance, they risked their femininity: "We ask nothing impracticable or unreasonable, when we call upon the females in our land. . . . Elevation of character . . . on which woman must ever depend for permanent dignity and valuable power [is] . . . incompatible with a supine disregard to the great moral revelations of the day." A woman who refused their request "should not hope to be distinguished for great or splendid qualities."[49] In other words, temperance was as essential to femininity as it was to masculinity.

Women's failure to the cause might be more severe than simply the withholding of their support; they might actively harm the cause out of a selfish and foolish concern for social standing. Here temperance discourse exposed a contradiction within antebellum gender ideology. It simultaneously exalted women as morally superior and frivolous and as both defining and defined by social mores. Female power was undisputed if properly cultivated, but women became notoriously distracted from this task by "the 'thousand caprices of fashion.'"[50] "Fashion" could dictate serving wine while entertaining, an imitation of the rich that temperance reformers deplored. They blamed "the social glass," "the most insidious and mischievous guise which [intemperance] assumes," for leading many otherwise respectable middle-class men down the path to alcoholism and ruin.[51] Women implicated themselves when they did not "banish . . . wine from their tables," or "abandon . . . expensive and sumptuous entertainments, and many similar indulgences . . . [that] impair something of the force of Christian example."[52] Most often criticism centered on women's thoughtlessness, but at times it became more harsh, making women seem malicious, willing to sacrifice all that is good because "it is the fashion."[53]

The belief that woman could be a weapon either for or against the cause prompted temperance reformers to persuade women to participate "in all suitable ways."[54] But male reformers defined "suitable" in very narrow terms. Besides simply attending temperance meetings, the primary role of women in the cause was as mothers. Because antebellum efforts, particularly before the 1840's, put heavy emphasis on prevention, children became a focal point of the work. If reformers could "produce upon [children's] minds a strong impression of the dangerous tendency of even a moderate use of ardent spirits," the march of alcohol would be arrested and the nation redeemed within a generation or two.[55] The ATS started children's clubs and, in 1832, sent temperance constitutions to every household in the nation, thereby hoping to create homes devoid of liquor.[56] Women were important to this effort, since they already held responsibility for the moral instruction of children.[57] Temperance reformers firmly asserted that "the influence of the mother's habits over the physical, . . . moral and intellectual character of the children seems to be of a more decided nature than that of the father."[58] Women were bound to exercise this authority in a proper way. A temperance tract reminded them, "You are to become the mothers of our future heroes and statesmen. . . . You have the future of our beloved country in your hands. . . . [Do] not . . . put the cup to the mouth of your offspring," not even medicinally.[59] For temperance reformers, though they sincerely believed mothers were paramount to their efforts, employing the family as a venue for their work partially solved the dilemma of assigning women a significant role. In the home women "could . . . go hand in hand with [men] without the least impropriety," and better still for the movement, "*all* the influence of other sex . . . would be brought to bear directly upon the subject."[60]

In a related role in the battle against alcohol, women were symbolic casualties of war. Temperance discourse underscored not only female moral authority but its counterpoints, female dependency and male power. In temperance narratives, alcohol represented an invasion of the cold, outside world into the domestic sphere in the absence of a male defender; women were helpless victims, unable to contend with the enemy. Ardent spirits "pour[ed] . . . streams of agony and despair, into the once happy and cherished circle of domestic peace and love."[61] Male temperance writers and lecturers incessantly employed the pathetic image of the drunkard's wife to garner support for their cause, both within society as a whole and among women themselves. That of all the "bitterness and anguish intemperance infuses into the cup of human sorrow, woman drinks its very dregs" was accepted fact.[62] Pathetic accounts, all claiming truth, of women killed or made destitute and broken by their drunken husbands filled the pages of temperance literature. The ATS report for 1832 told the story of a man who had beaten his wife to death while she breast-fed their child. The authorities found the woman "still holding the clinging babe to her bosom, with a maternal fondness that neither cruelty nor death could overcome."[63] Other tales told of men who drank themselves to death or incapacity, leaving their wives and families to starve. In *The Story of James and Mary Duffil*, James eventually drank away all the family owned. When the bar owner claimed the Duffils' farm, James returned home in a rage, physically throwing his wife and children out into the cold night. Mary, with "supernatural strength," spent the entire night trying to shield her children from exposure. By the next morning, one had died, and she and the other children went to live in the poor house.[64] Such stories dramatically contrasted male power and female dependence; the destruction of masculinity, either through the feminizing loss of livelihood or the dehumanizing loss of feeling, necessarily endangered female survival.

The dichotomous portrayal of women, as victims and moral authorities, and the passive and circumscribed yet lauded and actively solicited role of women in the movement demonstrated how temperance served male gender identity as it related to that of women. The movement allowed men to be both the heroic, masculine protectors of and providers for weak, defenseless women and the domesticated, respectable beneficiaries of female morality.

The positive function of temperance activity for male identity as well as its ambivalence towards female influence characterized an early episode in the career of George Barrell Cheever. As a young Congregationalist minister in Salem, Massachusetts, he became an uncompromising foe of alcohol who seemed to gravitate toward controversy. In 1833 and again in 1835, a Unitarian deacon and distiller in Salem named Stone sued him for libel over Cheever's thinly veiled references to him in sermons and in a popular temperance tract that portrayed distilling as demonic work. Cheever served a one-month prison sentence when he lost the 1835 suit in court. He also suffered a violent attack by "a ruffian Irishman," whom Cheever suspected Stone had hired.[65]

While Cheever became a sensational martyr in reform circles, his mother was unimpressed, despite her own support for temperance.[66] From the start of the controversy until its finish, she repeatedly expressed her disapproval of her son's outrageous tactics. In 1833, she wrote to him with the concern that his "*zeal* should carry you beyond the bounds of *prudence*" and cautioned him from future controversy.[67] About his famed tract, she said, "I regret you ever wrote it. . . . If you repeat these offenses too often you will harm your influence. I cannot bear to have you called an imprudent minister."[68] In fact, the only unequivocal praise George received from his mother during the controversy stemmed from his "meek endurance" of the beating, since he had so manifested "the temper of Christ."[69] His mother commended him only for his most effeminate action, lying down during a physical confrontation, while she criticized his more manly verbal attacks on the deacon-distiller.

His mother's anxiety no doubt had an impact on Cheever; since the death of his father when Cheever was a boy, his mother's influence must have weighed heavily.[70] Though he completely ignored her advice, Cheever's letters to his mother nonetheless consistently expressed deference to her influence and admiration for her faith and piety. He explained that the "path of duty" dictated that he disregard her "maternal reproofs," but he thanked her for them and prayed "the Lord give me grace to benefit by them; for if I do not deserve them exactly the way you suppose, I do in many other ways abundantly."[71] These remarks demonstrated a desire to display his mother's influence and an acknowledgment of their common beliefs, even as his actions showed some degree of rebellion.

But despite Charlotte Cheever's disapproval, George obviously relished the attention his actions garnered and seemed enamored of his own misfortunes. He was particularly impressed by "the agitation I have produced among the . . . sewing circles. What a fine thing it is to be of so much importance."[72] He told his brother Henry that he found his imprisonment to be "not a little romantic, to wander at night through the gloomy grated entries," and claimed the small jail in Salem was actually "as strong as the Bastille, all solid rock and iron."[73] For a young man such as George Cheever, the whole controversy was a great and noble adventure, an almost cosmic struggle in which he played a starring role. He told the court during his appeal of the Stone case that he sought "the favor of the court upon manly ground," that he fought "for the sake of freedom in the proclamation of truth" on behalf of "the mothers that have been broken-hearted, the wives that have been made widows, the children that have been made fatherless."[74] Cheever saw himself as a hero, a true man, and the savior of helpless women. That his mother disapproved of his fight only seemed to reinforce this. Cheever's experience exemplified a negotiation of independent, assertive, heroic manhood and conformity to womanly virtue. That his cause was temperance is not surprising. The temperance movement had special appeal for middle-class men; it was a cause that allowed them to be the gallant saviors of the home and the nation without sacrificing personal respectability. It was a life at once on the battlefield and in the parlor.

In more concrete ways, too, temperance addressed the needs of male identity and authority. The temperance movement not only strengthened male identity and the idea of male independence, its shift to legal reforms sought to augment male independence and authority in actuality. By the antebellum period, patriarchy was threatened not only in economic terms, as the independent household became a thing of the past but in legal terms as well. Specifically, marriage laws gave women more status as individuals within the home, and drunken husbands were one of the strongest arguments in favor of this trend. When temperance reformers turned to prohibition, it was with male authority in the home in mind.

In its first decade, the American Temperance Society's methods were largely of the "moral suasion" variety. Through oratory and literature, reformers of the 1820's and 1830's aimed their efforts at trying to convince Americans to give up alcohol voluntarily. The ATS employed agents to go on speaking tours and urge people to sign temperance pledges, and temperance societies all over the nation started newspapers, each issue of each one presenting the argument for total abstinence.[75] The aim of the ATS was therefore: "By the diffusion of information, the exertion of kind moral influence, and the power of united, and consistent, example, to effect such a change in sentiment and practice, and drunkenness and all its evils will cease."[76] This was in keeping with the optimism of antebellum reform in general. Society was perfected as each individual made a conscious decision to perfect himself and enlisted others to do the same. In the early stages of the movement, reformers dismissed legal measures as irrelevant; the movement sought "to change the habits of a whole nation—habits that have grown inveterate by long usage," a task that required acting upon the hearts and minds of citizens, not forcing them into submission through law.[77] As one temperance newspaper stated, "It is the boast and glory of the temperance cause, that its only weapons are those of truth and love."[78]

But this attitude would soon change. By 1833, the ATS had already stated that its next goal was to attack the laws that authorized the liquor traffic. The organization planned to do so in an apolitical way, however, by addressing "legislators as individuals" instead of approaching legislatures as governmental bodies[79] The ATS tread lightly, as the move toward legislative action was potentially controversial. President Justin Edwards wrote to his friend and fellow reformer Gerrit Smith and explained that in introducing the issue, "I have avoided, as you will see, using the words 'prohibiting the sale of spirit.'"[80] Most reformers were not quite ready for prohibitory measures. Not only would they mean the expansion of government's reach, they gave a negative cast to the prospects of antebellum reform.

Nonetheless, as the movement moved into the 1840's and 1850's, legislative strategies gained more prominence, even while reformers continued "to operate by light and love, through sound argument and kind persuasion, on the people."[81] By 1838, Massachusetts, Tennessee, and Connecticut had restricted the sale of alcohol after massive petitioning and demonstrations by supporters.[82] By 1840, the American Temperance Union resolved that "the enactment of a law entirely prohibitory must be the necessary result of a public sentiment on this subject."[83] Petitioning for various legislative measures, including the repeal of excise laws (which, in the minds of many reformers, sanctioned the traffic) and efforts to encourage men to vote for temperance candidates, became commonplace. Then, with the 1850 passage of the Maine Law, which banned the manufacture of alcohol and restricted its sale, and subsequent labors for like legislation in other states, the temperance movement moved unabashedly into the work of legally ridding the nation of alcohol. In 1852, Edward Delavan, ATU official and president of the New York State Society, reported to Gerrit Smith that at a recent convention, "The cry was *'the Maine Law or nothing.'*"[84]

This shift in temperance methods and ideas took place within a larger political and legal context. The coalescence of the Whig Party reflected and forwarded the notion of an activist state for the promotion of social stability and harmony. Like the reform movement with which it often overlapped, the Whig Party pursued order and moral progress to offset the potentially chaotic and disruptive changes of industrial development. In both Whig and temperance ideologies, social and moral conservatism could co-exist with economic innovation. Both groups arrived at the activist state as the key to this balancing act. In contrast to the Democrats, who believed government interference necessarily meant privileging certain groups, Whigs contended that government had an obligation to intervene in society in order to balance interests.[85] Closely related to this political change were developments in American legal thought. Historians have charted how the evolution American law paralleled larger cultural and ideological change. By the antebellum period, the law, which had been seen in the eighteenth century as a mechanism for promoting the public good, instead became an arena for competing individuals and interest groups.[86] Although temperance reformers argued the laws they sought were for the protection of the whole community, temperance legislation fits well within these legal changes. Reformers represented a distinct interest group within American society and sought the sanction of law to bolster their position.[87]

But most important for understanding the temperance movement's shift to legal measures, and for demonstrating the centrality of gender in temperance ideology, were developments in the area of family law. In the liberal, individualistic world of antebellum America, relationships between people became increasingly contractual. Therefore, it should not surprise that marriage began to be viewed in contractual terms as well, and the law began recognizing that women had some rights within the marriage agreement. If a husband did not function as an adequate protector, provider, and legal representative, the law might intervene on a wife's behalf. In this way, judges and courts began to replace the patriarchal authority of husbands within the home in the nineteenth century, and the legal arena became one in which families aired private matters. This new view of marriage had radical implications, upon which reformers had begun to seize by the 1830's and 1840's. The idea of marital "unity," and coverture itself, came under heavy fire. Coverture assumed a husband would act on behalf of his family's well being; but what if he did not? What if he were a philanderer, an abuser, a drunkard? Some reformers began arguing for everything from property rights for women to liberalized divorce laws, the most radical redress of marriage.[88] Once these issues came into play, the entire ideology of gender became vulnerable; if wives were equally contracting individuals within marriage, were they not such outside of it as well? The ideological constructs of separate spheres, coverture, and sexual difference itself might all come into question, and even the chimera of patriarchy might be destroyed.

Temperance was at the heart of these debates and developments in family law. Intemperate husbands were easy targets for marital critics and divorce proponents, and intemperance was one of the few acceptable causes for divorce in those states that allowed it.[89] The drunkard's wife was a common archetype not only for temperance reformers but for more radical ones as well. The latter seized upon temperance literature's portrayal of alcoholism as the ultimate breach of the marital bargain and shaped the conservative images of helpless women into calls for radical reform, including easier divorce and women's recognition as citizens under the law. But such measures encountered widespread opposition, not just among social conservatives but among some women's rights reformers. The latter believed that easy divorce would backfire in a society where women had little economic opportunity and legal protection. Marriage was still the best option most women had in securing a livelihood for themselves and their children. Such reformers often turned their efforts to securing laws that would regulate male behavior—such as outlawing drink altogether.[90]

This was also the route most male temperance reformers took by the 1850's. In temperance literature, it is clear that a primary motive behind agitating for the Maine Law was to address the problem of delinquent husbands. John Marsh wrote forcefully in 1851 in support of the Maine Law, asking "Who suffers like woman?" and entreating his readers to look closely into the American family: "There sits the young husband and father with her to whom he swore protection. The poison is in his veins. His wife is alarmed. But ah! Little does she know of her fate."[91] The connection between prohibition and defending the existing familial order was made most explicit in the debate over the Maine Law in the New York legislature in 1853. At one point, a supporter of the measure explained that under the current laws, "an innocent woman, wedded to a drunken husband, is bound to his odious carcass in indissoluble ties." But instead of arguing those ties be loosed, he "appealed to the young men, into whose hands the interest of this society is being placed, to sustain [the Maine] law."[92] Legal prohibition was not only temperance reform for its own sake; it was a way of strengthening the idea of male authority within American homes and, by extension, male identity as it was rooted in that authority.

In the 1850's, as debate over prohibitory laws went on in most northern states, the temperance movement received a powerful reminder of why such efforts were necessary. From Connecticut to Ohio to Michigan came reports of bands of women mounting protests, some accompanied by vandalism, in saloons and distilleries. These were not riff-raff or radical feminists either but women who were "all married . . . and of respectable standing in society."[93] In most cases, they simply presented petitions to the owners of the establishments asking them to close their doors or issued "strong remonstrance . . . against the destructive tendency of the business."[94] But at other times, they destroyed property and dumped barrels of whisky into the street.[95] In some cases, they were successful in closing the establishment. On at least one occasion, in Fairfield, Connecticut, police arrested the women on charges of rioting. The judge in the case acquitted them, however.[96]

The response to these events by male temperance reformers demonstrated their awareness of what was at stake. They surprisingly expressed no disapproval, even though the behavior of these women was decidedly unorthodox. They seemed to excuse their impropriety because of "the bitter sufferings and wrongs inflicted through rum-imbruted men."[97] Because the women acted out of helpless desperation—because they reinforced the notion of female dependency—they earned the support of male reformers. "To our mind, there can be presented no scene of such touching interest as this," one temperance paper explained, "Of retiring, gentle, loving women being forced to come forth from their desolate homes to plead with the men who have ruined their dearest relatives, blasted their brightest hopes."[98] Here was proof that the Maine Law was necessary, that women would become distressed to the point of such drastic action. Indeed, the women called attention to the failures of men as protectors and the failures of the movement to redress wrongs done to women. They did "what men . . . should have saved them the trouble of doing . . . to knock in the heads of the rum barrels, and empty the poisonous contents into the street."[99] The underlying message in this interpretation of the events was that women's survival and happiness rested completely in the hands of men; they were completely dependent on men. In fact, these women, though disguised as victims, were actually taking matters into their own hands, fighting for their own rights and protection. But male reformers heard a cry for help—help that men could provide using their legal and political might.

Not only was temperance important for the negotiation of the gender identity and for bolstering the gendered authority of participants, temperance discourse spoke to issues of racial identity and authority as well. The idea of independence and individuality was not just a gendered concept, it was a racial one, and male independence contrasted not only with female dependence but also with that of black slaves. Temperance literature often portrayed the drunkard, one who had lost his independence, as not only feminine but colored. Like a slave, a drunkard had "surrendered his liberty, and that to the worst of all masters."[100] The drunkard lost his manhood through the loss of independence, but he also lost his whiteness in physical appearance. One historian has noted that temperance narratives repeatedly mentioned alcohol's discoloring effects. Usually, the literature described the alcoholic's skin as red or "flushed," bringing to mind the nineteenth-century image of the Indian.[101] But sometimes his skin more closely resembled that of a black slave. One recovered drunkard described his face at his nadir as "dirty and brown."[102] In either case, the coloring of the drunkard's whiteness was the diminishing of his manhood. Antebellum Americans viewed both black slaves and Indians as "children," dependents needing the care and living under the authority of white men.[103]

Temperance engravings employed race as a potent, visual warning of alcohol's effects. "Grog shop" scenes, often juxtaposed with peaceful domestic images on the pages of temperance newspapers, frequently included the presence of a black man amidst the devastation. One such engraving featured a white man leaning on a barrel with vomit pouring from his mouth, another white man passed out on a bench, and still another in a fist fight with a black man. The picture presented was one of social chaos, violence, and the absence of human dignity. That a black man would be featured, particularly consorting freely with whites, is instructive. He represented the loss of manhood, the breakdown of social mores, and the resultant disorder.[104]

Not surprisingly, the racial aspects of the temperance movement are particularly apparent when examining the movement in the South.[105] Though the movement never attained the kind of popularity there that it did in the North, the association of temperance with male identity and authority also had resonance in the South, though for different reasons. While northerners grappled with industrialization, urbanization, and new, liberal values, southerners worked to bolster their own society against the constant dangers inherent in the institution of slavery. This work took on new importance in the antebellum years, especially with the rise of the abolitionist movement in the 1830's.[106] The threat of slavery's collapse and concomitant social chaos seemed more possible than ever before. In

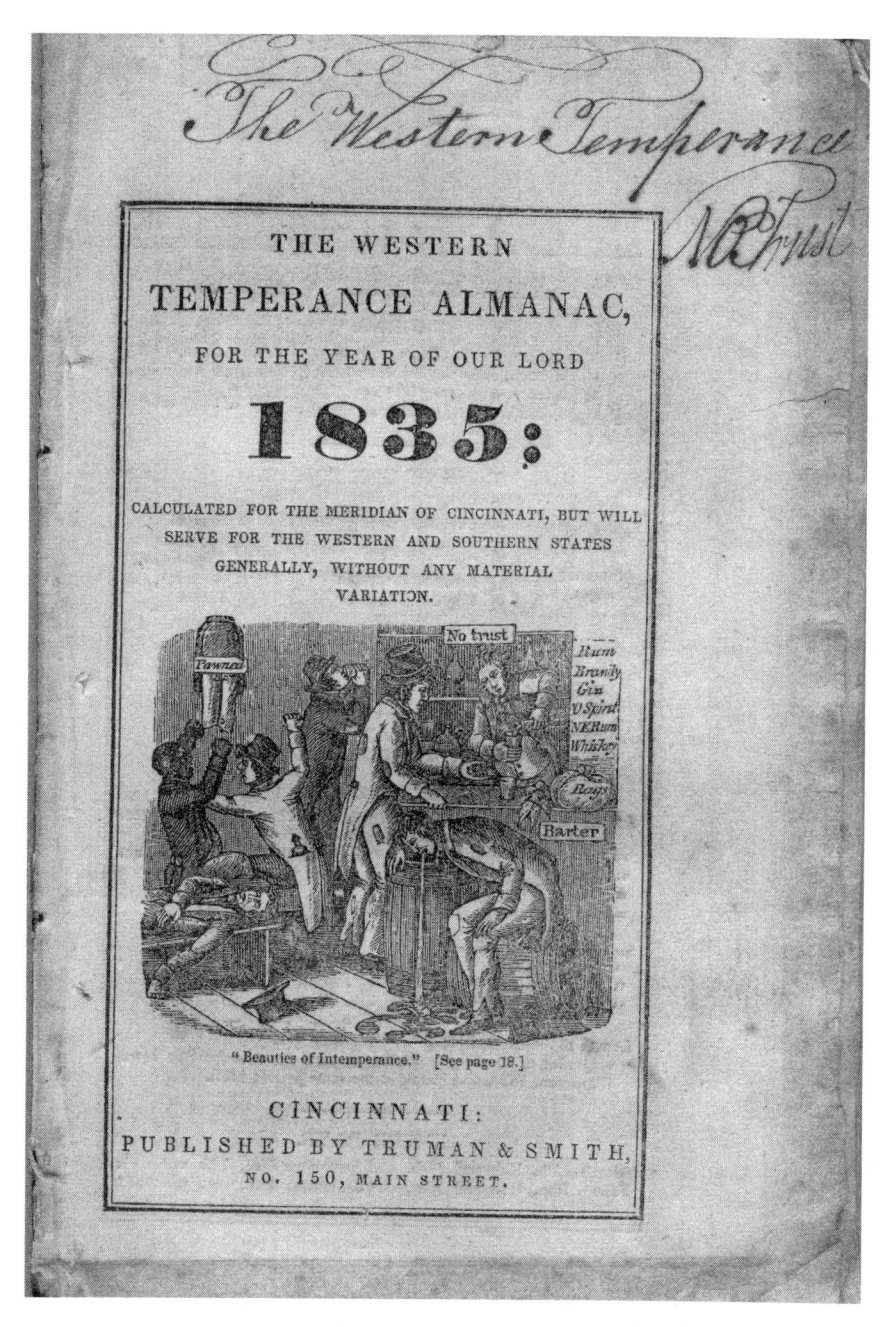

Figure 4. Frontispiece of the *Western Temperance Almanac for 1835* (Truman and Smith publishers). American Antiquarian Society, Worcester, Massachusetts.

the minds of southerners who supported temperance, pursuing a sober South was a practical, preventive step. Alcohol threatened to dissolve and weaken patriarchy, which was the very glue of southern society. Masters, whether they lorded over hundreds of slaves or simply a wife and children, regulated and controlled households of dependents, the most basic unit of the southern economy, polity, and social structure. If drink incapacitated masters, their dependents were left dangerously unchecked, threatening the racial and gendered order.[107] Intemperance eroded the efficacy of masters in controlling their slaves, the economic benefits of slavery, and the moral justifications of it. It is no wonder that southern temperance societies attracted slaveholders in significant numbers in the 1820's and 1830's.[108]

Southern temperance literature spoke to the issue of race indirectly and the issue of slavery directly. It confronted white men with the racial implications of the loss of their manhood. The mark of manhood, North and South, was independence and authority over dependents, but in the presence of slavery, this belief had particular salience. Independence was the basis of both patriarchy and citizenship. Without it, the master was ruled and protected by his wife or slave, as was one drunken white man in a southern temperance anecdote. When the tables turned in this manner, "then does the slave learn to despise his master: and then does he learn that he can strike with impunity a white man." The ramifications of this scenario struck terror in the hearts of white southerners. The white man's drunkenness threatened his citizenship, and by extension the political fate of the nation. White American men could rule themselves and others because they were free "from grievous oppressions." If they became "slaves of intemperance," the entire "country is enslaved."[109]

Southern temperance literature dealt more explicitly with alcohol's impact on slaves themselves and on the institution of slavery. Temperance reformers particularly questioned the paternalistic practice of giving alcohol to slaves as part of the yearly Christmas feast and urged masters to "Celebrate Christmas day with cold water."[110] The negative repercussions of drunken slaves far outweighed the benefits of paternalism. On an economic level, drink made for unruly, sickly, and inefficient workers. But more pernicious was how alcohol might brutalize the master-slave relationship. "The severity rendered necessary to control drunken slaves, whose moral sense has been destroyed and passions inflamed," exaggerated the negative aspects of the institution and made paternalism a more flimsy justification for it. The South Carolina Temperance Society estimated that "three-fourths of all the punishment our slaves receive . . . is rendered necessary from the brutalizing effects of the spirits they drink."[111] A policy of total abstinence would make slaves easier to control, masters kinder and gentler patriarchs, and the institution of slavery safer from moral attack.

In both the South and the North, then, temperance was intertwined with the concerns of male identity and authority at a time when both faced new challenges. In the North, middle-class men employed temperance to explore their ambivalence to the market, to bolster their sense of independence, and to protect their position in their homes. In the South, men came to the movement out of a racial and gendered fear for patriarchy, the basis of southern male identity and for southern society. In both regions, the dominant image of temperance that emerged was that of the self-made man, the capable master of himself and others. He was indeed the icon of the antebellum movement, the most visible representation of it. He served on behalf of temperance, attracting millions of American men to the cause. But temperance served on his behalf, too; the discourse of temperance uplifted the notion of his dominance and independence, even as it revealed his doubts, uncertainties, and weaknesses. Other reformers in antebellum America, who were not self-made men or who acted on behalf of those who were not, would seize upon these latter themes, employ temperance for their own ends, and create their own temperance cultures.

Chapter Two
Temperance Counter-Cultures and the Coming of the Civil War

> "Millions of slaves sighing for freedom; the greatest soul of Womanhood crushed and degraded; outcast children and drunken parents, should not be left to suffer. . . . I have a bright ideal for the Future . . . that each man and each woman may give to his own intellectual, moral and physical nature the fullest development."
>
> —Lucy Stone to Henry Blackwell, 1853[1]

Lucy Stone's words to her husband clearly demonstrate that the culture of the self-made man existed alongside other temperance cultures and visions in the antebellum movement. Stone viewed temperance not in terms of white, middle-class male achievement, identity, or authority but in terms of the exclusivity of that world in its denial of independence, individuality, and opportunity to those outside its boundaries. For Stone, temperance underscored the dignity and rights of all human beings, not that of a single group.

Stone's words also highlight the intersections between the antebellum reform cultures of temperance, abolition, and women's rights. Within the temperance movement, the influence of the latter two reforms proved to be incredibly divisive. This was the case on both an ideological level, as racial and gender equality countered patriarchal assumptions, and on a practical level, as the American Temperance Union tried to maintain national unity as the Civil War drew near. An examination of the feminist and abolitionist employment of temperance illuminates how temperance became an arena for debating the gendered and racial structures of society and how the movement was embroiled in the emerging divide between North and South. In this political climate, the icon of the self-made man became a lightning rod for conflict instead of a unifying symbol.

The ways in which temperance fit within this larger dialogue also demonstrates the diversity and elasticity of temperance ideology. In other words, different groups and individuals conceived of temperance in different ways and to different ends. Even taken as an insular reform, temperance was no singular movement of white, middle-class men. The working-class Washingtonian movement comprised a notable departure from the mainstream. In particular, the Washingtonians demonstrated new ways of thinking about gender roles and definitions within the context of temperance. Although there is no evidence that the Washingtonians directly influenced or contributed to the brewing conflict over gender and racial equality, within temperance and without, they subtly subverted the culture of the self-made man and illuminated the complexities of temperance discourse.

Historians have documented well the roots of the Washingtonian movement in the late 1830's, when the temperance movement, as well as the American economy, entered a period of decline. Disputes over the extent of teetotalism and the use of legislative action were partly to blame. In addition, the dire economic situation resulting from the Panic of 1837 depleted the American Temperance Union's coffers.[2] It was at this point, in 1840, that six working-class Baltimore alcoholics pledged to each other they would quit drinking. With unemployment on the rise, they viewed it as a practical step toward greater personal security and never intended to begin a mass movement of abstinence among working-class men and women. Within six months, however, twenty thousand people formed fifty new "Washingtonian" temperance societies, injecting the temperance movement as a whole with new life—and infusing it with new ideas and directions that challenged the iconography of the self-made man.[3]

The Washingtonians were primarily artisans on the upper end of the working class; the culture of their movement differed considerably from that of their middle-class counterparts.[4] Like the ATS/ATU, Washingtonian societies appointed agents who went on nation-wide speaking tours, exhorting people to sign total abstinence pledges. But all Washingtonian agents were reformed alcoholics, and their stump speeches were tales of their own dramatic "conversions." As a result, Washingtonian meetings took on the appearance of religious revivals of the most emotional sort. At one meeting in St. Louis, "the whole audience was overcome. . . . The house resounded with shouting and clapping" when a "confirmed drunkard" came forward to sign the pledge.[5] Whereas clergymen led the mainstream movement and acted as its agents, Washingtonian agents were untrained and uneducated laymen who gave their movement a decidedly democratic feel. Though their meetings manifested a kind of religiosity, the

Washingtonians adhered to "neutrality" in spiritual matters and steered clear of doctrinal or theological statements. This was much to the dismay of mainstream, middle-class reformers, especially the clergy among them, who explicitly linked temperance with Protestant Christianity. Middle-class reformers also resented the Washingtonians' opposition to the legislative work that had come to dominate the mainstream movement.[6]

On a deeper level, the Washingtonians created a culture of temperance—and of masculinity—that was at odds with the middle-class version. Whereas mainstream reformers flocked to the temperance movement to ensure their continued success, the Washingtonians arrived out of an already-realized failure. Whereas middle-class men pledged temperance as an individual endeavor of self-mastery and achievement, the Washingtonians did so as a communal exercise of mutual encouragement and support. And whereas self-made men exalted their own independence, reformed drunkards admitted their continued dependence, now on their community instead of on alcohol.

The Washingtonian view of the drunkard highlighted the working-class movement's unique culture. The biggest change the Washingtonians wrought on temperance activity was to shift its focus to the alcoholic, to recast him as a victim rather than a villain, and to act on a belief that he could be reformed with the help of friends. At Washingtonian meetings, "the drunkard unexpectedly found himself an object of interest. He was no longer an outcast."[7] The Augusta, Maine *Washingtonian* noted the differing approaches of the new movement and the mainstream movement, with regard to drunkards. Of the mainstream movement's tendency to bind "the seller and the drinker together, and [exclude] them both from the society and patronage of the community," the *Washingtonian* declared, "a greater system for making hypocrites and drunkards could never have been invented."[8] The Washingtonian motto, "Never forsake a brother," manifested itself through kind pleading, consistent encouragement, and material aid.[9] "Tell them what useful men they might be, what good citizens they might make, and how happy they can make themselves as well as relatives," one paper exhorted, "Treat a drunkard well and you can reform him."[10] In order to start anew, the reformed drunkard required food, medicine, and especially clothing; "he had need to lay off his 'filthy rags' for a 'teetotal dress' before he could seek employment with any hope of success."[11] These working-class reformers "actually *washed* the filthy, clothed the naked, fed the hungry and provided lodging for the houseless inebriate," if he would sign the pledge.[12] A pledge of sobriety, instead of marking a man as "self-made," integrated him into a community of aid and comfort. The source of self-possession was the mutual support of the group.

Conversely, the group culture formed around the individual experiences of its members and, more specifically, around the collective and sentimental enterprise of telling and hearing those experiences.[13] Attendees at Washingtonian meetings heard personal, seemingly spontaneous tales of drunkards' doleful lives and their glorious redemptions. Speakers formed an emotional bond with the audience; tears flowed freely. John Hawkins, one of the movement's founders, reported that at one "experience" meeting, "more tears were never shed by an audience in one evening.... Old gray haired men sobbed like children, and the noble and honorable bowed their heads and wept."[14] Whereas middle-class reformers spoke "from the head rather than the heart," Washingtonians spoke a language to which the lowly alcoholic could relate and respond, one of personal experience and empathy.[15]

Given that much of the audience and all of the speakers at such meetings were men, Washingtonians presented not just their own version of temperance but unique ways of linking it to male identity. The Washingtonian's manhood was decidedly sentimental, emotional, and affectionate. It was communal more than competitive. These men related to each other outside the realms of the political, the commercial, or even the intellectual, as they were more interested in the telling of personal narratives than the construction of convincing arguments. As the mainstream movement shifted its focus away from moral suasion to legislative action, the Washingtonians continued to shun all tactics except love, care, exhortation, and "brotherly kindness."[16]

Washingtonians appreciated the unique culture they created. Despite gestures from middle-class reformers to unify the two groups, Washingtonians insisted upon maintaining their own identity simply because it was one other temperance men did not share. "We are a class of men who have associated together heretofore; we have taken the social glass together.... We have now ... reformed together," while mainstream reformers "have never used intoxicating drinks.... They take pride in saying they have never had an inclination to drink. Then what possible service can they be to us?" Though Washingtonians bore no ill-will toward the "old temperance men," many thought it best to "let each of us move in our own particular spheres."[17] The use of the gendered word "sphere" is interesting; it suggests that the differences between the Washingtonians and other temperance men did not arise simply from class, tactics, or prior experience but from gender identity. Washingtonians were not the "self-made men" of the ATS/ATU, individuals striving for greater mastery and personal success; they were a community of men, leaning on each other, encouraging each other, bearing each other's burdens.

The Washingtonian movement, though predominantly a male movement, incorporated women in significant ways into its larger community of support. In many respects, however, the gender ideology of the Washingtonian movement differed little from its middle-class counterpart. Women retained immense moral authority in both. In fact, an article appearing in the *Worcester County Cataract*, a Washingtonian paper, in 1843 on women's obligation to the temperance movement was a verbatim reprint of a speech given by reformer W.K. Scott nine years earlier. Both listed reasons why women should be involved: "They control the fashions of the day. . . . The sphere of life in which they move, and the peculiar duties they are called upon to perform, render them more susceptible to feelings of humanity. . . . They can do more than men to prevent the formation of intemperate habits in the young. . . . The heaviest calamities occasioned by intemperance fall on them."[18]

In other ways, however, Washingtonian temperance was far more open to the presence, influence, and activism of women than was the middle-class version. A middle-class gender ideology that enshrined women as moral authorities combined with an emphasis on material aid gave Washingtonian women, or Martha Washingtonians, greater importance within the working-class movement and more opportunities for active participation.[19] The first Martha Washingtonian society began in New York in May 1841. Soon dozens dotted the nation. Women joined by signing a total abstinence pledge and paying small monthly dues. These dues went toward buying second-hand clothing, medicine, and lodging for reformed drunkards and their families or for the families of alcoholics who had yet to reform.[20]

Performing charity work comprised the bulk of the women's activities. This work became their exclusive domain, while Washingtonian men focused their energies on speaking and soliciting new members. Men and women went together into the poorest neighborhoods, "visiting," inviting people to their meetings, checking on those who had signed the pledge already, and assessing physical needs. Then, the women assumed responsibility for meeting those needs. This might mean taking in a homeless woman and her children, as one Martha Washingtonian directress did,[21] or mending items of clothing for dispersal among the "half-clad reformed inebriates" so they might have something to wear on job searches.[22] The Washingtonians, male and female, had limited means themselves but made up "the deficiency of funds in the labor of their hands."[23] The object of material assistance was not only "to aid the poor, simply because they are poor," but to make the work "a powerful lever in their hands for raising the individual with whom they communicate to better *habits* and to an improved state of mind and feelings."[24] Moreover, unlike "many persons of wealth [who] impart pecuniary aid as a *condescension*," Martha Washingtonians approached their work with great empathy.[25] They were not much higher on the socio-economic ladder than the recipients of their charity, just more "respectable" in terms of their behavior.[26]

In addition to affording material help, women in the Washingtonian ranks were the missionaries of the temperance gospel to their own sex. Much more so than the mainstream movement, the Washingtonians realistically acknowledged that, despite women's overall moral superiority, not all of them fulfilled the potential of their gender. Reports of drunken women made frequent appearances on the pages of the movement's newspapers. The *Samaritan and Total Abstinence Advocate* out of Providence, Rhode Island estimated that there were "hundreds of vicious females . . . in our community who need to be reclaimed."[27] The *Michigan Temperance Journal and Washingtonian* included a report from New York "that the drunken females who have come under the official cognizance of the police during the week—God only knows how many there are whose cases have not been reported—number *only* one hundred sixty-six!" The paper concluded, "If women will get drunk, it's all their own fault," indicating that Washingtonians no less than other temperance workers held women to higher standards.[28]

It was up to the Martha Washingtonians to help them live up to these standards. This was work only women could do successfully because of their "tender, sympathetic bearing toward the sorrowing, suffering and disconsolate."[29] Many female reformers had been rescued from drunkenness themselves, and they offered their alcoholic sisters their "friendship and confidence."[30] Their methods produced successful results, even with the most "filthy and degraded" women. One Martha Washingtonian took in a woman found in a debilitated condition on the streets of New Haven; three months later the reformer had made her over into "the image of respectability."[31]

Washingtonian men were similarly "domesticated" by women, just as middle-class men were. But in the Washingtonian movement, the *process* of female influence gave women more opportunities for publicity and power. As the culture of the working-class movement embraced a mutual dependence between members, it also affirmed male dependence on women. Women played a major role in the conversion of male drunkards, particularly their husbands. Sometimes wives publicly pleaded with their husbands at experience meetings; one woman did so "with an earnestness that seemed all unconscious of the crowd," an act that moved other men to follow her spouse to the front.[32] Once these men entered the temperance fold, women kept them accountable. They did so primarily by providing entertainments that served as alternatives to and distractions from the temptations of the saloon. The Fourth of July was the big Washingtonian event of the year, marking not only the nation's independence but that of members from alcohol. But the celebration also displayed reformed men's *dependence* on women for their sobriety. Women largely organized the event, making banners, cooking, and decorating for the picnic. During the rest of the year, they organized other entertainments—concerts, parties, teas, and picnics. Attendees "could not fail of noticing the striking difference [from] . . . those they attended before the temperance reform began. . . . Then intoxicating drinks met at every turn . . . consequently the female portion of the community were excluded from all part in those celebrations, while the other sex brutalized themselves."[33] Martha Washingtonians were thus significant in the construction of a sober, working-class masculinity. They also helped put a respectable face on a movement that middle- and upper-class Americans might otherwise have viewed with suspicion. As Sean Wilentz noted, Washingtonian experience meetings could be rowdy affairs, including "barroom boasting stood on its head, a recitation of past exploits transformed into a confession."[34] The sizable presence of women helped to protect the movement from the criticism of the members' social superiors.

Washingtonians' urgent need of female aid is clear in the sometimes harsh denunciations of women who did not give their full energies to the cause or those who actively harmed the cause, even if unintentionally. Although mainstream temperance literature at times admonished women for dereliction, it primarily portrayed women as victims or angelic moral guardians, both largely passive roles. Washingtonian literature more often included tales of women who endangered the sobriety of reformed drunkards. In fact, so harshly did Washingtonian papers deal with women, one female reader wrote into the *Michigan Washingtonian* to complain, saying that in all the stories published, "the lady is made to drive the gentleman into deeper drunkenness."[35] In one such story, a Washingtonian's wife reportedly told him he would never be anything but a drunk and taunted him with "what he had been, instead of hiding the past from his mind." Indeed, "he was almost driven to his cups by the unkindness of his wife," and it was only the sympathy of others that kept him sober. He did not stay that way, however. Another woman, a lady saloonkeeper, lured him to his demise with her hospitality, which stood in stark contrast to his wife's coldness.[36] A reformed man needed the personal support of his female relatives to stay sober, but more importantly, he needed the collective aid of the female community to redefine and resituate the arenas of leisure. A renewed life of alcoholism was as close as the nearest saloon, which stood at the center of working-class male sociability.[37]

The story of the lady saloonkeeper reveals the extent to which Washingtonians articulated a male culture of dependence that stood in contrast to the insistence on independence at the center of middle-class masculinity. The drunkard's fate in the above story was completely at the mercy of others, and more significantly, at the mercy of *female* others, a fact that underscored his dependence. The Washingtonians, having once been slaves to alcohol, exhibited far greater comfort with personal need than did middle-class reformers. Not surprisingly, then, Washingtonians also displayed much less ambivalence towards female activism. The temperance organization functioned in almost opposite ways for middle- and working-class men; for the former, it distanced them from female influence, while for the latter, it removed distance. Washingtonian papers urged readers to "shun the bar-room," the more familiar domain of a working-class man, and to "reverence the fireside. Admit no rival here."[38]

Although Washingtonian gender ideology subverted the idea of male independence and offered women a more prominent and active role in reform, it was still generally patriarchal, and Washingtonians would be dismayed when their efforts helped spawn temperance participation by women who championed the full individuality and equality of their sex. The Augusta, Maine *Washingtonian* expressed horror that "there are . . . schemes in contemplation to make the Washingtonian cause tributary to the advancement of matters having no connection with the reformation of the drunkard." Specifically mentioned were the "movements of female preachers of 'moral reform,' and other theories no less odious to well wishers of society," and "doctrines notoriously demoralizing and polluting to the mind of youth."[39] Although the Washingtonian movement's cultural challenge to the mainstream movement still affirmed patriarchy, its feminized masculinity and the access it afforded women suggested that alignments between temperance and gendered roles and identities were by no means at fixed points.

One woman with whom the Washingtonians would undoubtedly find fault, Amelia Bloomer, began her temperance career subsequent to her initial contact with the working-class reformers. When the movement arrived in Seneca Falls, New York in 1840, Bloomer reported that it "produced a great sensation, almost revolutionizing public sentiment on the subject," and not simply among those of lower station.[40] She found herself inspired, as she heard Washingtonian speakers depict "in burning words the sad lot of the drunkard and his family."[41] Bloomer's curiosity led her into a variety of activities—attending gatherings, serving on committees, and writing articles for the local temperance paper, *The Water Bucket*.

Her interest had been aroused, and she was not alone. By 1841, there were enough active women in her town to organize a Female Temperance Society with a membership of hundreds. In 1848, the society, reconstituted with new zeal, founded a newspaper edited by Bloomer that represented the unique perspective of women on temperance. After an inauspicious start (including a swindling by a male temperance lecturer who offered his aid), the *Lily* published its inaugural issue on January 1, 1849 as the nation's first and only newspaper owned and operated by a woman.[42] "It is *Woman* that speaks through the *Lily,*" Bloomer wrote in her first editorial, "It is an important subject, too, that she comes before the public to be heard. Intemperance is the great foe to her peace and happiness. . . . Surely she has the right to wield the pen for its suppression."[43]

Other prominent women duplicated Bloomer's path into temperance activism through the Washingtonian movement. Mary Livermore, who would become a leading temperance and women's rights advocate after the Civil War, began her temperance work in the wake of the Washingtonians' arrival in her town of Duxbury, Massachusetts.[44] She joined the editorial staff of a local temperance newspaper and began work with the children's Cold Water Army. Susan B. Anthony likewise began her illustrious career as an activist within the Daughters of Temperance, an offspring of the Washingtonian movement.[45] That organization blossomed in the early 1850's with a membership of twenty thousand. Bloomer, herself a member, called the organization "a salve to the wounded feelings of the women," who had felt excluded for much of the antebellum movement's run. It was "the first organized movement ever made by women to make themselves felt and heard on the great temperance question."[46] It seems the Washingtonians did not simply revolutionize female participation for working-class women; they also influenced the position of women within the larger temperance ranks. The example of working-class women seemingly ignited enthusiasm in women of higher stations by offering them alternative activities to the middle-class movement's increasingly political ones.

Bloomer's early temperance work makes clear that her initial concerns were of a decidedly domestic nature. She reserved most of her criticism for women themselves, those who continued to cook with alcohol or those who had yet to involve themselves against it. Of the former category, Bloomer wrote, "What examples these ladies are setting! Have they a husband, a brother, or a son, and have they no fear that the example they are not setting them may be the means of their filling a drunkard's grave? Have they a daughter? Their example teaches her to respect moderate-drinking young men."[47] Indeed, "a word, or a look from women, may and has had an influence to save many from drunkards' graves."[48] She confronted apathetic women with "the experience of thousands of their own sex," whose lives had degenerated from "every happiness that wealth and station can impart" to the "lowest depth of misery and degradation" as a result of alcohol's destructive power.[49] Woman's calling came from her "peculiar goodness," that "her gentle voice" could "persuade men's sterner souls to leave the path of sinful strife."[50] As a powerful moral figure, woman might lead the drunkard "back to the paths of sobriety and virtue, and to bind up the wounds of the afflicted and broken hearted." Bloomer expressed her belief that women's particular calling to temperance work grew out of alcohol's invasion of the home—woman's "empire"—and that they could fulfill that calling "in a manner becoming the retiring modesty of our sex."[51]

Over the next several years, however, Bloomer's newspaper and the work of other female temperance reformers gradually fed into a more direct and gendered critique of the larger movement. The apparent lethargy of the cause, the lack of real results in reducing alcoholism, and the continued suffering of women as the chief victims of drunkenness drew the ire of female reformers. "Men have too long dallied with the subject," Bloomer wrote in 1850, "while thirty thousand of their fellow beings are annually swept into the drunkard's grave. . . . We want something more than talk to convince us that men are sincere in their professions."[52] She declared she was "disgusted" with male reformers and the meager results of their efforts and called for women to take a greater role.[53] But women found that when they tried to expand their activities, they faced resistance and poor treatment from male reformers, who preferred to assign women merely trivial work. Susan B. Anthony railed against the "senseless, hopeless work that man points out for woman to do," while men heaped upon "angel woman" empty rhetorical praise for their moral superiority.[54]

Increasingly, temperance-minded women chastised men for what they perceived to be lackluster attempts to destroy drunkenness through political and legal channels. Anthony pleaded with the women in attendance at an 1853 temperance meeting in Walworth, New York to "agitate on this Temperance question, do all in your power to awaken the true temperance men of your town." The "secret of the defeat of temperance tickets," she claimed, was that temperance men put too much trust in "the old parties to nominate true men." If women could not participate in the legal and political fight against temperance, they could not ensure that "he who votes for you by proxy, be duly instructed, that he may not long misrepresent you at the Ballot Box."[55] She told another audience in Albion, New York that "to merely relieve the suffering of wives and children of drunkards, and vainly labor to reform the drunkard was no longer to be called temperance work," and argued that "woman's temperance sentiments were not truthfully represented by man at the Ballot Box."[56] Anthony's statements make clear that by the 1850's some women reformers rejected moral suasion, the traditional and acceptable tool of female reform, as an effective tactic. Bloomer, too, wrote in 1854, "People have gradually lost confidence in individual moral action, as a *measure* . . . to destroy drunkenness." Prohibitory legislation like the Maine Law was "the only cure—the last resort."[57]

As previously noted, the movement's shift to legal measures was motivated at least in part by the desire to strengthen male authority in the home. But this change in tactics ironically gave women in the movement an argument for suffrage.[58] Though women, "having no political rights available . . . *seem*[ed] to be excluded," they continued to believe they had an apposite claim to temperance work as moral authorities and victims of drunkenness.[59] In this, they simply reflected the sentiments long advanced by the larger movement. The conclusion drawn by many female activists was that legislative action was part of woman's domain as well. "In the name of all that is sacred *what is woman's business* if the law and customs which bring misery, crime, degradation and death to her home and hearthstone be no concern of hers?," Bloomer asked a New York audience in 1853.[60] By continuing to insist temperance was an issue that affected the domestic circle yet adopting prohibitory means, temperance reformers created a link between the imagined gendered spheres of society, a fact not lost on female reformers like Bloomer, and certainly not on their more radically feminist sisters.[61]

It was this latter group of women, most notably Elizabeth Cady Stanton, who channeled the frustrations felt by women within the temperance movement into outright feminist reform. Stanton's influence on Susan B. Anthony is well-documented, but Amelia Bloomer also credited Stanton with awakening her to the fact that "there was something wrong in the laws under which [women] lived" and ushering her into more radical reform work.[62] The three women joined forces in 1852 to begin the New York Women's State Temperance Society, which promoted a decidedly radical agenda while under Stanton's leadership.

The immediate impetuses for the society's formation were the repeal of an 1846 prohibitory statute and female reformers' continued frustration with the limitations male-led temperance groups placed on their activity. Stanton noted that when women acted as victims, as did some New York women who violently protested the repeal of the License Law, they were "applauded for these acts of heroism by the press and temperance leagues." But when women sought to engage the cause as men's equals, through associations and conventions, "then began the battle in the temperance ranks, vindictive and protracted for years."[63] The new women's temperance society angered many male reformers immediately. This was particularly the case when Stanton issued a circular to the women of New York that urged the wives of alcoholics to divorce their husbands. When delegates from the society attended the state's temperance convention in June 1852, the men present treated them cordially at first. But when Anthony tried to mount the platform, the proceedings erupted in angry debate over the right of women to participate fully.[64]

Other prominent women's rights advocates became heavily involved in the cause all around the country in the early 1850's. Francis Dana Gage assisted the Woman's State Temperance Society of Ohio, which had formed in the wake of the Maine Law debate at the state's constitutional convention. She attended two of the society's conventions in Cincinnati and Dayton in 1851 and 1853, respectively. Gage recollected that the Dayton community nearly shut out the convention; it finally secured a meeting hall from the local Sons of Temperance. Another women's rights reformer and the editor of the *Windham County Democrat* in Vermont, Clarina Howard Nichols, traveled around Wisconsin as an agent of the state's women's society. She argued that women's claim to being the "'greatest sufferers,' the helpless victims of the liquor traffic" was made possible only by man's "disabling laws" and the "legal and political disabilities" with which they left women vulnerable. Male community leaders and the state's male Temperance League vigorously protested her work wherever she traveled.[65]

Sometimes other women opposed the melding of temperance with women's rights. A group of Dayton, Ohio women interrupted the 1853 convention attended by Gage to express their disapproval of women calling temperance conventions. They also termed the conduct of Antoinette Brown, an ordained minister who attempted to mount the platform at the 1853 World's Temperance Convention in New York, "unseemly and unchristian."[66] Even within the New York State Women's Temperance Society, feminist agendas met with mixed reviews; the society garnered a diverse membership, and Stanton's views on divorce and suffrage did not match those of all her constituents. At the first annual meeting of the society, in June 1853, Stanton forcefully argued that temperance "carries us legitimately" into a call for women's full equality and characterized those who worked exclusively for temperance, "superficial reformers, mere surface workers." Many of those present disagreed, including one woman who said she hoped that the society "would not take in all the 'ites' and 'isms' and 'ologies' and then baptize the whole with the name of temperance." Stanton was not returned to the presidency.[67]

Unlike Bloomer and Anthony, Stanton never saw temperance agitation as an end in itself but as work that informed and enlightened women on their overall degradation and domination by a patriarchal society. She wrote to Anthony in 1853, "The right idea of marriage is at the foundation of all reforms. . . . I ask for no laws on marriage. . . . Remove law and false public sentiment and woman will no more live as wife with a cruel, beastly drunkard, than a servant in this free country will stay with a pettish, unjust mistress."[68] After Stanton's ouster from the presidency of their temperance organization, she instructed Anthony "to waste no powder" on the matter: "We have other and bigger fish to fry."[69]

In the 1850's, such female reformers did indeed make temperance a major weapon against the larger enemy of gender inequity. Temperance arguments gradually blended with agitation for divorce reform and women's suffrage and against the patriarchal notion of coverture. Nowhere was this more apparent than in the verbal attacks women reformers leveled at drunkards and even drunkards' wives, those sorrowful creatures who sacrificially stood by their husbands even unto death. The mainstream temperance movement portrayed the drunkard's wife as the embodiment of feminine virtue, a caricature that enraged feminist reformers. The *Lily* blasted an article in the *New York Organ* that instructed women to "cling to the besotted and rotten carcasses of their husbands, even if by doing so they suffered ten thousand deaths," and "spoke glowingly of the opportunity thus afforded the drunkard's wife for exhibiting the noblest and most heroic traits in her character." The *Lily* mused that "it almost made drunkenness itself a virtue" and suggested that the "rum suckers and beer swillers" deserved kicks, not kisses, from their wives.[70] Jane Grey Swisshelm, editor of the reform paper the *Pittsburgh Visitor*, saw a gendered motive in "the diagnosis of drunkenness . . . [as] a disease for which the patient was in no way responsible;" it made long-suffering women out to be "angels" called to re-make men through their own submissive endurance. "It may be very angelic for a pure-minded, virtuous woman to love and caress a great drunken beast," she wrote, "But for our share we have not the slightest pretensions to being an angel."[71] In expecting higher sacrifice and morality from women, men denied their equality and individuality. The drunkard's wife's own happiness, and even her life, was incidental compared to its sacrifice for the sake of her husband. For feminists, the families of alcoholics exhibited not the elevation of female virtue but the loss of female personhood. Just as bad, misguided conservative temperance reformers exalted this erasure as inspirational sacrifice.

Feminist temperance advocates went further to argue that such sacrificial living only enabled the drunkard's lifestyle and that a wife might do her husband (and herself) better service to simply "leave him, and take with her the property and the children."[72] The alcoholic's knowledge that "the gentle being whom the law and public sentiment declares to be his wife is his slave" gave him little real incentive to reform.[73] Jane Swisshelm put it more baldly; to require a wife to stay and minister to her drunken husband "is a violation of the laws of God, and the dictates of common sense and common decency. A woman who will persist in so living should be shut up in a lunatic asylum."[74]

Such talk raised red flags for many male reformers, who viewed the use of temperance by these women as subversive of not only one of the favorite devices of the movement—the drunkard's pathetic family—but of the institution of the family itself, as it rested on male authority and female dependence. The ATU commented that although the idea of a woman's temperance society was "very imposing," it could not approve of the activities of Stanton, Stone, Anthony, and their cohorts, as they instructed women "that the marriage covenant is only a matter of convenience." The argument that drunkenness was an acceptable cause for divorce was "at variance with the Bible and cutting off also the last hope of reform for the unfortunate inebriate."[75] Anthony called these suspicions "all wrong and calculated to produce much evil in society."[76] She insisted that she and her colleagues advocated legal separation, not divorce, in the case of intemperance. A woman should remove herself, her children, and the family's property out of the reach of the offending husband until he reformed.[77] But more radical feminists, including Elizabeth Cady Stanton and Lucy Stone, did employ temperance to argue for the relaxation of the nation's divorce laws. They believed that the "marriage question ... underlies the whole movement" and divorce was "a doctrine which is to strike the most effective blow at the sin of drunkenness."[78] At the June 1853 meeting of the New York Women's State Temperance Society, Stanton went so far as to argue that a marriage should be dissolved any time "the unity of soul" disintegrated, whether it be from intemperance or any other cause. In a bold assertion of individual rights, she declared, "Any law or public sentiment that forces two high born souls to live together as man and wife, unless held there by love, is false to God and to humanity."[79] Few other members of the society fully agreed with such a radical statement on marriage, most preferring Anthony's more moderate stance.

Less controversial among women's rights supporters was female suffrage. As with the issue of divorce, complaints about men's impotence or indolence in passing prohibitory legislation fed into a call for women's political participation. "The sad truth [is] that hitherto those who have claimed to be woman's rightful representatives and protectors have legislated against her interests and happiness and turned loose upon her a fearful foe to desolate her home and subject her to a life of poverty, shame and sorrow," Bloomer told a Council Bluffs, Iowa audience.[80] "It is quite time that their rights should be discussed, and that woman herself should enter the contest."[81] Consequently, instead of being woman's protector, the law became her enemy. Swisshelm wrote that "self-preservation" was a law higher than the Constitution, and women would obey it first. Woman "cannot preserve her home, her happiness, her life without setting your wily, wicked laws in defiance."[82] Feminists therefore supported women who took the law into their own hands and vandalized saloons in the 1850's. Although conservative temperance men praised such action by female "victims" of intemperance, feminists offered a different interpretation. "'Moral suasion'" deemed "useless," "the ballot-box . . . closed against her . . . the law-making power . . . denied her," and "men lack[ing] courage and efficiency to do what they have the power to do," women must "rely on the strength of her own right arm . . . meet the foe face to face."[83] By physically and often violently coming to their own defense, even "horse-whipping" rumsellers, as one praiseworthy Cincinnati woman did in 1852, women mounted a physical attack on the gendered order that they could not combat legally.[84] If the law would not protect them and men would not represent them under the law, women would subvert law and order themselves. And if the law did not acknowledge them as persons, if the law disembodied them, then they would physically employ their own bodies in a realm outside of it.[85]

The problem of intemperance and the inability of the movement to eradicate it gave feminist reformers an arsenal against the legal subjugation of women. "The law in its *magnanimity* presupposes every woman to have a *male* protector," Anthony told an audience in 1853. But the law as it stood failed to offer a woman the promised protection "when the husband and father becomes a besotted drunkard, and ceases to provide for his family." Far from protecting women, the law "makes [their] condition more hopeless" by confining them to brutal marriages, leaving them without a political voice (even on "domestic" matters like temperance), and making it virtually impossible to be financially independent from men. Bloomer asserted that coverture went against natural law by subjecting some humans to others. Patriarchy was an "unnatural assumption of power"—"Man has degraded woman from her high position in which she was placed as his companion and equal, and made of her a slave to be bought and sold at his pleasure."[86] According to Anthony, the purpose of law was "the weak protected against the strong. . . . The law should be his guardian, and those who make the law, the ones to be held responsible and suffer the penalties for crimes and misdemeanors he may perpetrate."[87] By refusing to acknowledge the individuality of each human being within its realm, American law seemed to do just the opposite.

In contrast to the Washingtonian movement, the feminist version of temperance overtly combated the mainstream movement's culture of the self-made man. Feminists employed temperance as a vehicle to achieve and as a venue to discuss the larger agenda of female equality and personhood. In the process, these women articulated a unique version of temperance itself, one that rejected female victimhood and morality and male responsibility and authority. Temperance was less a statement of mastery by self-made men than an admission of poor governance by male dictators and a call for female self-rule.

Of course, women were not the only antebellum Americans denied their individuality. A call for gender equality was inflammatory in itself because it would disrupt some of society's most basic institutions and assumptions. But the issue additionally informed and was informed by those of slavery and racial equality.[88] The subjugation of women and that of blacks bore obvious similarities: Both groups were excluded from citizenship and full legal and social equality. In the dominant temperance discourse, the supposed dependence of both women and blacks bolstered the idea of white male independence and authority. Not surprisingly, then, just as feminists found temperance could aid the cause of women's rights, African Americans and abolitionists saw connections between temperance and racial equality under the law and constructed their own temperance cultures based on this idea.

Frederick Douglass made this connection when he climbed a temperance stage in London on August 4, 1846. The famous black abolitionist had been invited to speak by British activists, and his address came after a sequence of American orators sang the praises of their nation for its leading role in the movement. Douglass's remarks, however, created quite a stir among the American delegation. This was especially true of his declaration that he could not "fully unite with . . . their patriotic eulogies of America, and American Temperance Societies" since there were "three millions of the American population, by slavery and prejudice, placed entirely beyond the pale of American Temperance Societies."[89] With these words, cries of "Shame! Shame!" and "Sit down!" arose from the American delegation. Nonetheless, Douglass persisted through the commotion and finished his speech.

After he took his seat, John Kirk of Boston mounted the platform and informed the audience that Douglass had "unintentionally misrepresented the Temperance Societies of America. I am afraid that his remarks have produced the impression on the public mind, that Temperance Societies support slavery."[90] Later, another attendee, Samuel Cox, wrote a letter complaining of Douglass's conduct to the New York *Evangelist*. In his mind, Douglass, "the colored abolition agitator and ultraist," had "lugged anti-slavery or abolition" to the podium with him, "ruin[ing] the influence, almost of all that preceded!"[91] The *Journal of the American Temperance Union* agreed that the incident was "greatly regretted by every friend of good order and true sobriety."[92]

Although Kirk and Cox believed "that the cause of Temperance was not at all responsible for slavery and had no connexion [sic] with it," Douglass clearly saw an intersection between the two reforms, as did other black advocates of temperance.[93] Slavery in the South and racial discrimination everywhere limited blacks' ability to participate in the movement. Southern laws prohibiting the assembly of slaves meant their participation in organizations of any kind, including temperance ones, was impossible. And in the North, whites habitually excluded blacks from their temperance societies. When northern blacks organized their own societies, they at times became the target of white violence.[94] Douglass indicated that he himself had faced discrimination while working for the cause when he contrasted his treatment within the American temperance movement with that during his association with the movement in Ireland, where he undertook a speaking tour in 1845. "How different here, from my treatment at home!" he wrote to William Lloyd Garrison, "In this country, I am welcomed to the temperance platform, side by side with white speakers, and am received as kindly and warmly as though my skin were white."[95]

Douglass saw the obstacles faced by blacks in temperance participation as indicative of "the impediments and absolute barriers thrown in the way of [blacks'] moral and social improvement . . . [holding] them in rags and wretchedness, in fetters and chains, left to be devoured by intemperance and kindred vices." Slavery was, of course, the ultimate degradation, as it stripped people of their humanity, individuality, and right to self-improvement and elevation. But racial discrimination could deny even a free black the tools needed to thrive in American society, which included a body of supporters to help him lead a sober life.[96] Douglass believed that racial prejudice originated in the unequal conditions in which blacks and whites lived. "The white man is superior to the black man only when he outstrips him in the race for improvement," he told the readers of the *North Star*, "And the black man is inferior only when he proves himself incapable of doing just what is done by his white brother." To end racial prejudice and discrimination, he concluded, "We must do what white men do," and surpass them in the realms of progress and self-improvement.[97] He left that task up to African Americans themselves. The American system might divest blacks of basic economic, political, and social equality, but it had "not yet been able to take from us the privilege of being honest, industrious, sober, and intelligent." The enemies of equality would love nothing more than to see blacks confirm their own inferiority through poor character and low morals. But if African Americans could exhibit exemplary character, including lives of abstinence from alcohol, prejudice would be "abashed, confused and mortified."[98]

Douglass saw temperance as an important part of an overall moral elevation, and other northern blacks similarly made the connection between total abstinence and black equality. They recognized that the virtue and morality of their own community called attention to the humanity of the slave. "On our conduct, in a great measure, [the slaves'] salvation depends," argued the *Colored American*. "Let us show that we are worthy to be freemen; it will be the strongest appeal to the judgment and conscience of the slave-holder and his abettors." In addition, measures of self-improvement, like temperance, proved that all blacks, slave and free, deserved full civil rights and economic opportunity, "as men and citizens."[99] After its June 1832 meeting in Philadelphia, the Second Annual Convention for the Improvement of the Free People of Color issued a circular that urged blacks to "be righteous, be honest, be just, be economical, be prudent.... Live in constant pursuit of that moral and intellectual strength which will invigorate your understanding, and render you illustrious in the eyes of a civilized nation." And above all, "beware of that bewitching evil, that bane of society, that curse of the world, that fell destroyer of the best prospects ... *Intemperance*."[100] A sober African American community would be the most upright and industrious and consequently the most effective argument for its own equality. Black leaders supported prohibitory legislation like the Maine Law in order to keep alcohol away from black users, particularly "the very class of our people to whom we are to look as warriors who are to fight ... for our liberty, and our rights." With the grog shop outlawed, the black community elevated, and a sober, black elite in position to lead, "we will see a marked difference in the Colored People of this country, in a political and social point of view."[101] On the other hand, if African Americans did not join the moral reform bandwagon of the antebellum years, "the contrast between our condition and that of our white brethren will be widened."[102]

Like feminists, African Americans viewed temperance as an avenue through which individual equality and identity might be claimed. Temperance was a mark of manhood, in both a human and gendered sense. But for blacks, temperance also became an arena of racial competition, and the stakes were very high. Through temperance, white men made themselves stronger, more virtuous, and more successful. If black men did not similarly fashion themselves, their claim to manhood—any sort of manhood—would become increasingly weak, as the differences between blacks and whites grew more numerous and more obvious. Intemperance acted much like slavery in the destruction of African American humanity and equality. But unlike slavery, intemperance might be defeated by the black community itself, despite white attempts to exclude blacks from the movement.

Temperance highlighted not only the general issue of black equality but the specific issue of slavery's abolition. On an organizational level, a temperance-abolition nexus was well-established from the origin of both movements through the participation of individual reformers. William Goodell, Gerrit Smith, Elizur Wright, Joshua Leavitt, George Cheever, and others chiefly known by the 1850's for anti-slavery work had been deeply, and even primarily, involved in temperance in the 1820's and 1830's. A letter from Henry B. Stanton to Elizur Wright in 1841 provides one example of the overlap between the two reforms. He complained that the "temperance and abolition folks continue to get two or three, and sometimes four or five long speeches a week out of me," and indicated that he supported a plan to "run a ticket in this country this fall—heading 'No slavery! No alcohol!'"[103] The son of an alcoholic, William Lloyd Garrison began his reform career as a temperance man when he took the American Temperance Society pledge in 1826, soon after the organization's founding. Before starting the *Liberator,* Garrison was the editor of the Boston-based *National Philanthropist,* whose motto was "Devotion to the suppression of intemperance and its kindred vices."[104] This latter category included slavery; reformers of Garrison's stripe viewed it and alcohol as twin evils.

The presence of abolitionists within the temperance movement was a constant obstacle for the ATS/ATU as it sought to build a national movement. Although temperance sentiment had always been stronger in the North, the movement showed potential in the South as well. In the 1830's and 1840's, the ATU's organ included many reports of the cause in the South, and national temperance conventions included delegations from southern states.[105] Still, the South generally lagged behind the North in temperance enthusiasm and activity. For example, though the South contained forty-four percent of the American population, it could claim less than nine percent of its temperance pledges in 1831.[106] Both southern and northern reformers believed that ties between temperance and abolition at least partly accounted for this disparity. At the founding convention of the ATU, there was much discussion over its predecessor's (the ATS) connections to various anti-slavery societies and the ATU's commitment to maintain temperance as its "sole object."[107]

The goal of building a southern movement meant that those members of the ATU who held abolitionist principles would have to make them secondary to those of temperance. The *Journal of the American Temperance Union*—though its editor, John Marsh, had at least moderate anti-slavery leanings—included features that acknowledged the interests of southerners and refrained from criticism of southern slavery. In 1837, the paper printed a letter from a Kentucky hemp farmer who reported great success and productivity after hiring a teetotaling overseer and enforcing strict abstinence among his slaves. He claimed that the effect of his temperance management practices "has been evidently good on their health, cheerfulness and obedience, and no accident whatever occurred." No editorial comment accompanied the letter, and the same issue of the paper included a notice from a temperance society in Natchez, Mississippi asking northerners to subscribe to its newspaper. Here, Marsh added his own plug and reminded the readers that temperance was "a question that should bind together in one solid phalanx every friend of humanity throughout our common country and the world. Let us show our southern brethren that we love them and sympathize with them."[108]

Edward Delavan, an officer of the ATU and the dominant force behind the New York State Temperance Society, took the same negotiated path. Though Delavan was an active member of the Albany Anti-Slavery Society, he kept his reform works segregated. He wrote to his friend Gerrit Smith (a radical abolitionist) in 1837 that he was "not yet convinced that in urging Temperance we should introduce abolition—or that in urging abolition we should introduce Temperance."[109] And given a choice between them, Delavan put temperance first. When the ATU selected a southerner, John Cocke of Virginia, as its president in 1836, Delavan defended the decision: "We want our Southern brethren to like us better than they have lately . . . to have their full share in this great work."[110] In 1840, when Smith asked Delavan to consider running for New York Governor on the Liberty Party's ticket, Delavan insisted he had neither the ability nor the inclination to engage in such an endeavor. He sternly replied to Smith, "I have a *decided* objection to anything of the kind; my desires being . . . to devote what remains of my life to the best of my ability to persuade my countrymen and the world . . . of the duty of abstaining from the use of intoxicating drinks . . . in order that intemperance with its long train of evils may cease everywhere."[111] Clearly, for Delavan alcohol was the greater threat to the nation's virtue. By 1851, he was urging Smith to "let the Niggers alone for a little time" and devote himself to other causes.[112]

Gerrit Smith also held both temperance and abolition dear but took the opposite course when he felt compelled to choose between them. By the 1840's, he had resigned his membership in the ATU, though he still supported the Washingtonian movement. Many other radical abolitionists made similar decisions. William Lloyd Garrison, for example, hardly bothered at all with temperance by the 1840's. George Cheever's pet cause by the 1840's and 1850's was definitely abolition, particularly within American churches. The same was true for Lewis and Arthur Tappan, even though the latter had once been on the executive committee of the ATU.[113] But many of these reformers, instead of abandoning temperance altogether, persisted in an attempt to amalgamate it with other, more troublesome reforms like abolition. As the larger political debate over slavery reached a crescendo and the nation stood on the verge of civil war, the intrusion of abolition became exceedingly risky to the temperance movement.[114] If temperance bound northern and southern men together in a common pursuit of authority, abolition ripped through that bond by attacking the basis of southern men's masterhood and threatened not just the movement but the nation.

While moderates struggled to hold their cause together through its isolation, more radical reformers increasingly argued that temperance should be one part of a wholesale eradication of human degradation, whether it came in the form of alcoholism, slavery, gender inequality, or even class exploitation. The career of William Goodell illustrates well how temperance might be configured into such a program. Goodell, an orthodox evangelical Christian and pastor from New York, began his long reform career as editor of a series of temperance newspapers in the late 1820's and 1830's.[115] He was a member of the New York State Temperance Society and an early agitator within the movement for total abstinence; his opposition to communion wine and medical usages of alcohol distinguished him from more moderate temperance men.[116]

A letter to his father-in-law, Josiah Cady, in 1831 demonstrated that even early in his reform work, Goodell departed from the mainstream of the temperance movement. He complained of the moderation of many in the ATS, their refusal to espouse true total abstinence, and their often elitist attitude. His ideal temperance organization—which he called "The People's Temperance Union"—would welcome "*all who will pledge* to abstain from *all* intoxicating drinks, including malt liquors and mixed wines, and traffic in them, whether medicinally or otherwise." All members would share equal access to leadership, which would be based on high character, not social standing. "This would terminate the farce of a luxurious nobility," he wrote. "It would equally secure the work from the blighting influence of those clergy who claim to mould it so as to suit such parishioners and church members as those just described. . . . It would be a rallying point for the *real and thorough* friends of the cause." It would be streamlined, both politically and financially, by avoiding alliances with political parties and having no permanent funds.[117]

In his newspaper work, Goodell demonstrated a penchant for branching out from temperance as well. Upon taking over the editorship of the *National Philanthropist* in 1829, he declared his intention to include information on a variety of subjects pertaining to politics and morality, including abolition; in his mind, "a paper exclusively devoted to the cause of temperance is deemed tedious by many readers." And though the paper, and others on which Goodell worked, included the standard temperance fare, it also exhibited links between it and abolition. One article shocked readers with the title, "Slavery in New England," then made an extended analogy between southern slavery and intemperance, ending with a plea to the young men of New England to "rise nobly up and throw off his shackles.... His name is Rum."[118] He used the same tactic as editor of the *Genius of Temperance* by arguing that "Man is Free" and not meant for slavery or drunkenness.[119]

By the 1840's, Goodell had become increasingly radical, uncompromising, and ever more interested in the cause of equal rights, and he gained prominence as one of the leading figures of the anti-Garrisonian wing of the abolitionist movement.[120] He became a pre-eminent agitator for abolitionism and general reform within American churches and a leader in the "come outer" movement.[121] In 1843, he accepted the pastorate of a church in Honeoye, New York founded on immediate emancipation, prohibition, and greater democracy within churches (including lay ordination and equal participation by all members). So firmly did he believe in anti-clericism that he refused ordination upon assuming the pastorate of the Honeoye church; as a result, other clergymen questioned the legitimacy of the marriages he performed.[122]

Later in the decade, as a co-founder of the Liberty Party with other anti-Garrisonians, including Gerrit Smith, he would apply similar principles to politics.[123] Goodell told Josiah Cady that he and Smith wanted it to be a party of real and total democracy, standing for "*all* the rights of *all* men, as well as for the freedom of the *colored* man." He then related a wish-list of reforms, including the replacement of the tariff system with direct taxation (he called free trade an "inalienable right" and believed the current tax system oppressed the poor), the reduction of government salaries, and an end to executive patronage. The overall aim of the party was "in a word, the conforming of Civil government to its *original business of 'doing justice between a man and his neighbor.'*"[124] He believed government's purpose—as ordained by God—was to protect human rights, which were the basis for morality. All individuals, regardless of race, sex, or class, had a right to "self-ownership," the right to freely pursue industry, improvement, a livelihood and property, and to participate in government.[125] The American government violated these human rights through the protection of slavery, through privileged "class legislation" such as tariffs and the sale of public lands, through the subjugation of women, and through the licensing of the liquor traffic, which ravaged people's self-possession. All of these issues were interrelated, and Goodell abhorred "one idea" organizations, like temperance societies, that picked and chose from reforms that Goodell believed came together in the single goal of human equality. "Such societies," he argued, "not only become opponents of other good objects, but fail of fidelity to their own special trusts." Single-minded reformers failed to see society and its problems as they really were, intricately linked and connected, impossible to alter in part. Goodell thought reform should seek "but the simple restoration and protection of human rights."[126]

As Goodell's vision grew in breadth, temperance remained very much a part of his work. For Goodell, scripture and republican government demanded "a genuine and radical Temperance," total abstinence in one's personal habits and complete dedication in one's political obligations. Intemperance was a "national calamity," and "all public calamities of this sort arise from individual calamities or improvements—there is no way to have a prosperous and solvent community . . . without private, individual, family thrift, industry, economy, and prudence." Instead of viewing prohibitory legislation as a restriction of personal freedom, Goodell saw it as a protection of human dignity, much like the abolition of slavery; the alcohol trade produced only "poverty and pauperism and crime."[127] He always put the problem of intemperance within the larger framework of injustice, human degradation, and bad government. The inability or refusal of mainstream temperance reformers to do this frustrated him. He believed this was a major flaw in the movement and the culprit that slowed its momentum by the 1850's. In an 1847 address, he repeatedly attributed the shortcomings of the temperance movement to its myopia, "from the attempt to limit attention and effort within narrower bounds than the case demanded." In fact, Goodell argued, any time reformers worked exclusively for one cause, the effect was to "[divide] ourselves against ourselves . . . nullifying our own votes."[128]

Goodell made a significant contribution to radical reformism by incorporating the popular cause of temperance into an all-encompassing vision for the reform of American society that rested, at bottom, on a democratic interpretation of law.[129] In his ideal America, each individual stood equally in all respects, regardless of race, sex, or class. Goodell was unique in his equal pursuit of a variety of reforms, but he joined with the other reformers discussed in making temperance a point of origin for larger purposes. While mainstream reformers continued to view temperance as an emblem of respectable, white, middle-class manhood, reformers like Goodell employed temperance to magnify the weaknesses and failings of a system built around it.

Washingtonian, feminist, African American, and abolitionist temperance cultures revealed the vivacity and complexity of the antebellum temperance movement. These reformers shaped the language and ideas of the popular cause into their own discourses, whether of self-assertion or societal reform. Temperance became a common tongue for multiple cultures and ideas. By the 1850's, however, the dialogue of temperance grew increasingly contentious and momentous as the issues of war and slavery loomed large. The debate within temperance surrounding racial and gender equality entangled it in the mounting conflict between North and South. In 1853, this reality dramatically manifested itself in the events surrounding the World's Temperance Convention in New York City.[130] What was supposed to be a display of the movement's strength and solidarity around the world degenerated into a bitter confrontation over the immediate issue of women delegates and the more general issue of the movement's larger ideological grounding.

The trouble began in May 1853, when temperance reformers met in New York to plan the convention. They included reformers of all kinds—men and women, northerners and southerners, those in the mainstream of the movement and those on its fringes, including abolitionists and feminists. Their differences quickly consumed their common support for temperance. An attempt by the abolitionist Theodore Wentworth Higginson to have the feminist Lucy Stone appointed to a committee threw the meeting into chaos over the issue of female delegates. Having anticipated controversy, Rev. Nathaniel Hewitt, a Congregational minister from Connecticut, rose to deliver a prepared speech, in which he argued that it was "contrary to established usage to have Women take part in Temperance Meetings." Higginson replied that if the reformers present meant to have a World's Convention, "Woman should be represented, otherwise it would be only a Semi-World's Convention." More debate ensued, including both support for the ladies' faithfulness to the cause and criticism for their intention to harm it by blending it with the troublesome issue of women's rights. In the discussion, Susan B. Anthony, Abby Kelley Foster, Emily Clark, and Lucy Stone each tried to speak, but the majority shouted them down. With that, Higginson requested his name be struck from the roll and invited those who resented women's exclusion from the convention to meet that afternoon at Dr. Trall's water-cure establishment. Around a dozen reformers, many of them women, followed him from the gathering.[131]

The exodus resulted in the staging of two temperance conventions the following September and a vigorous, rancorous debate between the two camps in the interim. The *Whole* World's Temperance Convention, which included delegates from the New York State Women's Temperance Society, commenced on September 1, 1853, while the World's Temperance Convention began as originally scheduled on September 6. In their presentations of the immediate and practical issues of temperance, the two conventions differed little. Both advocated the Maine Law, condemned rumsellers and distillers, and portrayed alcohol as a great enemy of the nation. But as the two conventions' names reflected, they offered different versions of temperance, one that related to the authority of white men and one that challenged that authority by asserting the inclusion and equality of women and African Americans.

Most of the dialogue centered on the issue of women's rights, since the question of women's participation in the convention had been the most immediate cause of the division. The Whole World's delegates asserted that male reformers' empty flattery of women's moral authority and the movement's claim to act on behalf of female victimhood merely distracted from gender inequality and the men's failure in their sworn duty to protect dependent women. The Whole World's delegates found it absurd that male reformers called a World's Convention and then "voted [women] as not of the world" by refusing their active participation. "What does this mean?" asked the *Anti-Slavery Bugle*, "Do they consider women appendages to persons? In this latter capacity we suppose they would be glad to have them attend their convention."[132] The convention's speakers boldly argued that woman, the chief victim of intemperance, had been made so by "the laws of this country [which] bound her hand and foot and given her up to the protection of her husband."[133] The evidence clearly showed that protection to be insufficient. Clarina Howard Nichols, one of the numerous women who addressed the convention, claimed she "would not stand here," if "intemperance did not invade our homes and tear them from over our heads ... take from us our clothing, our bread, the means for our own self-development and for the training of our children in respectability and usefulness."[134] For the delegates at the Whole World's Convention, temperance clearly demonstrated that female victims of alcohol needed the removal of male authority, not its strengthening.

In presenting this argument, the Whole World's Convention challenged one of the central tenets of the movement's mainstream and stoked the ire of its members. Delegates to the World's Convention argued that while women's assistance to the cause was important, these particular women had not come to aid the temperance movement but to "subvert the whole order of things" by "undertaking to manage and control in company with mankind, to whom God has given the headship, the great governmental affairs of this world."[135] The movement welcomed the participation of women, "but let them come as *Women* and not as *Men,* just as they come into families, and into Christian assemblies and Christian churches."[136] A woman's usefulness to the movement lay in her "meek and quiet spirit," not in her militant self-assertion. A New York temperance journal echoed this sentiment; woman was powerful because she was "frail, delicate, dependent, limited to a defined and retired sphere.... From this glorious height the new set would drag woman down and despoil her of all that mighty influence."[137]

The most dramatic confrontation between the two camps was an attempt by Rev. Antoinette Brown to mount the platform of the World's Convention. Her comrade George Clark of Rochester prepared her way by reading a resolution: "That this Convention invite *all* the friends of humanity without respect to age, sex, color or condition, to participate in the deliberations and aid in its glorious work." When delegates responded with angry shouts and hisses, Clark defended himself "as a friend to the cause of Temperance, having been a worker for many years" and insisted he was motivated only by the desire for "the powerful aid of angel woman." He held the floor through "a general hurricane of words," until Brown mounted the platform, inaugurating a firestorm that consumed the remainder of the afternoon session.[138] Brown recalled hearing both virulent attacks, "hissed through the teeth as though coming out of the heart boiling hot," and encouraging words from supporters.[139] One delegate growled that a convention "where *both women and niggers had had their say*" had been held the week prior, and now they should "leave decent white men alone."[140]

This telling comment revealed that the gendered challenge brought by the Whole World's convention had its context in the mounting conflict over slavery and race and in the temperance movement's attempt to maintain national unity. Equally telling was the more surreptitious exclusion of James McCune Smith, a black doctor and reformer. According to Smith, a man stopped him for his credentials at the door, then turned him away "on the ground of informality." An avid temperance supporter for two decades, Smith expressed his dismay that he had been unable to bring information before the delegates regarding the progress of the movement in Africa. His barring proved the convention's sympathies were with only "three quarters of the globe, while the fourth was left to grope in outer darkness of the *Rum Trade* and its twin brother the *Slave Trade*."[141]

Smith's exclusion, like the response to Antoinette Brown, was for the purpose of keeping the World's convention "on message" and promoting temperance as the moderate cause of white men, North and South. In 1853, the temperance movement still had a sizable southern following, but the convention's minutes made clear that maintaining the southern presence was a delicate matter. When George Clark offered his initial resolution, that the convention should be open to all reformers regardless of sex, age, and race, a Virginia delegate complained that southern delegates had come "with the belief that they would . . . [be] spared these disgusting embarrassments."[142]

But northern delegates had an interest beyond the comfort of their southern brethren in keeping temperance free of reforms that sought its use for upsetting the racial or gendered status quo. For the majority of male reformers in the temperance movement, their cause was not intended to be a radical reform but one that bolstered white male authority. As one abolitionist paper put it, the actions and words of the majority of the World's delegates revealed their central aim: "They wished to retain supremacy over the people."[143] The convention's supporters described the cause in similarly conservative terms. "Its very name of Temperance is a rebuke to all fanaticism," the *Times* editor wrote. "It . . . is wholly alien to that spirit of excitement, of lawlessness, of public and private turbulence." The "prudent" delegates of the World's Convention should be hailed for having "uniformly kept their movements free from the fanatical ultraisms by which other worthy causes have often been so deeply divided."[144] Reformers like Brown or the abolitionist Wendell Phillips, who was also ejected from the World's Convention, were devotees of a greater "fanatical infidelity" that threatened to upset the convention, the movement, and society at large. Dr. Smith also pursued a subversive agenda, his presence "for the purpose, confessedly, of introducing an African element into the . . . deliberations."[145]

Ultimately, the temperance debates of 1853 concerned the larger basis of the movement, whether the self-made man, the symbol of male authority and identity, would continue to be the visible image of the movement or whether other reformers who did not fit that mould would employ temperance to assert themselves, both within the reform and in society. In other words, would temperance remain the domain of "decent white men" or would it be a vehicle for people who did not fit that description? The conventions showed that the icon of the self-made man, rather than serving as a unifying symbol of the movement, proved to be a divisive hazard

Temperance Counter-Cultures and the Coming of the Civil War

Figure 5. *The Great Republican Reform Party, Calling on their Candidate* (Currier and Ives, 1856). This political cartoon skewering the Republican Party's association with reformers of various stripes also illustrates moderate temperance reformers' worst fear, that temperance (depicted by the character on the far left, who is asking that alcohol use be made a "capital crime") would be associated with radical feminists (seen here clad in bloomers and smoking a cigar), socialists, free love advocates, abolitionists, and other radical reformers. Library of Congress, Prints and Photographs Division, LC-USZ62-10370.

to its health. This was particularly true given its political context by the 1850's: A vigorous debate over southern slavery and a looming civil war. The World's Temperance Convention controversy displayed how temperance reformers, in discussing the ideological grounding of the movement, entangled it in this broader conflict, as well as how the national crisis informed and provoked a vigorous struggle within temperance. Twelve years after the two-convention show-down, and after the Civil War had come and gone, this debate was largely irrelevant, as was the icon of the self-made man itself.

Chapter Three
"Let Patriots Join Hands:"
The Civil War and the War on Alcohol

"Let us not, however, lose sight of the great and glorious cause of Temperance. Whisky, after all, is of greater consequence to us than even the slavery question . . . more important to-day than ever before. . . . I trust we shall not allow any other question to overshadow it."

—Myron Holley Clark to John Marsh, 1866[1]

In August of 1865, temperance reformers met in Saratoga Springs, New York to regroup after the tumult of war had left the movement in confusion. Three hundred and twenty-six delegates (including six women) from twenty states voted to dissolve the American Temperance Union and start fresh with the new National Temperance Society and Publication House, its primary objective to print and disseminate temperance literature in order to revive interest in the cause. Many prominent antebellum reformers of various persuasions were in attendance. Samuel Fenton Cary and John Marsh attended alongside Gerrit Smith and other more radical reformers. There would be no upheavals at this convention, however, only a discussion of how the movement might recover from the blows dealt it by the war and whether or not prohibition should continue to be its primary focus. The latter discussion arose from the fact that most of the legislation passed before the war now lay dead or defunct. The NTS challenged the nation to refuse to regard the war as the conclusion of the work of moral reform: "The war has ended; but another begins. . . . Let patriots join hands to overthrow the monster that to-day threatens the nation's life. *A land of tipplers can never be a land of self-governing freemen.*"[2]

E.C. Delavan, who had disagreed with his friend Gerrit Smith in the 1850's over the prioritization of temperance and abolition, wrote to him in 1865 with words of encouragement, urging him, "Don't give up the ship." He believed the August convention would be "a great affair," but he feared the total abstinence position stood to be moderated and appealed to Smith, "Your voice and eloquence must be ready."[3] But the convention must not have eased Smith's mind, for the next year Delavan reprimanded him, "I can't get over your calling the Temperance reformation a 'failure.' . . . This *failure* will in time I doubt not be remedied." Delavan considered the retention of total abstinence as the official stance of the movement one example that it was still "a wonderful success."[4] Two years later, he continued to maintain the work had not failed but did admit "*great weakness in the joints.*" He consoled Smith, "I think you and I can depart in peace as to our Temperance efforts as having done all that we could do."[5]

The demoralization expressed by reformers at the close of the war reflected discouraging realities. The Civil War disrupted normal American life, as all things assumed secondary importance to the rescue of the federal union's very existence. With regard to temperance, the question of the nation's moral character moved to the battlefields and assumed much larger proportions than whether or not its citizens consumed alcohol, and American manhood was tested in martial courage and physical strength rather than in total abstinence. For the movement, the war ushered in a period of transition, not only in organization but in scope and ideology. Most notably, the war dimmed the spotlight on the antebellum image of the self-made man in temperance discourse, particularly with regard to its gendered implications. The self-made man represented a temperance movement concerned with self-mastery and authority; it was chiefly a personal cause, about strengthening the individual man, his place in his home and society by extension. But the Civil War, and new cultural and political realities in the period after, inspired a temperance movement that was almost wholly political, collectivist, and national in scale. Temperance became an outwardly focused war for American society; temperance men became an army of warriors engaged in a political battle against alcohol. But just when the political function of manhood became increasingly important for temperance, reformers employed temperance to express new doubts about that function—as the alcohol industry grew in political and economic might, as big business gained a stronghold in American government, and as the racial and ethnic composition of the electorate changed. As alignments between temperance and masculinity shifted, so did those between temperance and femininity, setting the stage for new roles and functions for women in the movement and for a new gendered icon in the Gilded Age.

Temperance remained as vital a cause as ever after the Civil War, and reformers renewed their efforts wholeheartedly. They had much ground to make up. The war had not ended the problem of alcohol; in fact, according to temperance reformers, it had produced a degeneration of American drinking habits. For millions of young men serving in the army—an entire generation of them, in fact—alcohol was an accepted part of camp life. The stress of battle, the treatment of disease, and the shortage of anesthetics justified and encouraged the resort to the bottle.[6] Official policy on alcohol was inconsistent and checkered. In 1863, the War Department did finally prohibit alcohol as part of the enlisted men's rations but continued to allow officers their private supplies, a fact that outraged reformers.[7]

But soldiers were not the only ones drinking during the Civil War. Among the general population, though consumption levels for hard liquor remained constant, consumption of lager beer in 1865 was double what it had been fifteen years before, and these numbers continued to climb through the end of the century. The war only partially accounted for this trend; increased immigration and the improved organization and clout of the alcohol industry provided a better explanation. Most disturbing to the temperance ranks was the formation in 1862 of the United States Brewers' Association as a lobbying group for the industry.[8]

Even decent, native-born Americans seemed to abandon total abstinence. Besides the liquor industry, the new enemy to the cause in the years after the war was "fashionable drinking," particularly the partaking of wine by the upper classes. They made drink look respectable, even glamorous, thereby setting a poor example for society at large. One temperance newspaper placed even heavier blame on the fashionable drinker than on the rum-seller himself, since the latter depended on his trade for his livelihood. "The man of influence in society, who has wealth, a good name and perhaps occupying a high position in church and state" did not need to associate with alcohol, and when he did, he became "the greatest obstacle which the Temperance cause has to encounter."[9] "It is astonishing how many conscientious drinkers there are," remarked the *National Temperance Advocate* in 1866, adding, "They are found in the circles of respectability and fashion."[10]

Moderate drinking gained respectability even among those who, in the antebellum years, generally supported total abstinence. Clergymen had always been a key constituency for the movement.[11] Though this generally held true in the postbellum years as well, a coterie of Presbyterian ministers led by Rev. Howard Crosby began to attack the total abstinence position in the late 1860's. Crosby agreed that alcohol remained a problem in American society and that total abstinence was necessary for alcoholics. But he vigorously attacked reformers who insisted that such a lifestyle was compulsory for everyone and insinuated that those who employed the Bible to support total abstinence "mutilated, perverted" the scripture, since it nowhere decried moderate drinking and revealed Christ himself as a wine-drinker.[12]

In addition, it seemed to many reformers that drinking among women, widely regarded as the creators and keepers of social mores, was on the rise. "Drinking is again becoming fashionable," the National Temperance Society declared, "and the ladies are responsible for this retrogression." Reformers indicted women for increasingly serving alcoholic beverages at parties and dinners, blamed them for drunkenness within their families, and assigned them responsibility for changing social customs. The organization also claimed that the incidence of female alcoholism among all classes of society was on the rise. The NTS purported to have "the best authority for stating that some of the most elegant ladies of our leading cities will pass the summer not at Saratoga or Newport, as usual, but at an asylum for inebriates."[13] One temperance paper, while admitting that purely anecdotal evidence could "hardly settle the question of whether or not intemperance is on the increase," argued that women's growing approval of drinking was a disturbing trend in that direction.[14]

The loss of cultural dominance and the expanding influence of the alcohol industry translated into major political disabilities. When war broke out in 1861, the movement had already suffered a string of political defeats that ironically came on the heels of some of its most impressive victories. In the late 1850's, courts in several states reversed some of the legislative gains made by the movement by declaring prohibitory laws unconstitutional. For example, judges revoked New York's prohibitory laws of 1846 and 1855, and the legislature replaced them with a licensing system that omitted beer from the list of beverages subject to excise.[15] During the war, the movement suffered more legislative setbacks, culminating in the passage of the Internal Revenue Act of 1862 by the United States Congress. The law, designed to help fund the North's war effort, licensed and taxed the alcohol industry; for reformers, it represented an endorsement by the United States government of alcoholic manufacture, sale, and consumption.[16] By the 1870's, though the movement had begun to retake some political ground, the defeats still mounted. In 1873, the Republican governor of New York horrified reformers by vetoing a bill allowing local option.[17]

Not only did the movement suffer concrete defeats during the war era, the war also challenged the movement on the level of ideology and identity. One new uncertainty concerned the confluence of temperance and masculinity. For millions of American men, the military camp became their chief environment, their workplace, and their home. It proved to be a construction site for a new male culture in the ranks, one that challenged the domesticated, middle-class manhood idealized by the antebellum temperance movement and incorporated drinking into the definition of manhood. Whereas good, middle-class gentlemen were somewhat feminized, the army demanded brute force, raw masculinity. Robert Paterson of the Christian Commission, an organization that attempted to fight the moral degeneration of camp life, did not wonder that many young men succumbed to alcohol and other immoralities. Military life confused "the ignoble vices of the camp and the noble patriotism of the army," secluded men from "the influences of public opinion and from the refining influences of female society," and subjected them to "wearisome and monotonous drill" and "equally monotonous indolence."[18] Even young men from good families might be corrupted under the circumstances.[19]

The temperance movement responded first by trying to keep soldiers focused on life after the war and urging them to recall their families at home. An army chaplain wrote to John Marsh, the secretary of the ATU, that the solution to the problem was "home influence . . . the more of it which can be infused into our tracts the better."[20] So the ATU, the Christian Commission, and like-minded organizations filled the pages of their papers and tracts with reminders of how choices made in camp had long-term ramifications. A soldier might return home a drunkard, devastating his family and his postwar success, or he might be "welcomed home a sober, useful man—honorable wounds perchance on your limbs, but not a scar on your character."[21]

Reformers tried to maintain the argument that alcohol bred failure, in war now rather than in the marketplace and in life-and-death terms rather than in pecuniary ones. Reformers vigorously argued for a link between victory in battle and sobriety, both on a moral and on a practical level. If the North compromised its own morality, it weakened its cause. "No nation can successfully contend for that which is morally right, while itself is morally wrong. . . . A drunken government, a besotted Congress, an army led by drunken generals to fight for liberty and law, would be an anomaly and an absurdity too great for earth to bear."[22] Among the troops, immorality could weaken even a physically strong army: "Physical power is but the handmaid to moral. If there is no moral, the physical is of little worth."[23] But on a more concrete level, alcohol could cloud the judgment and fighting abilities of Union officers and enlisted men, risking success and the lives of the men. The ATU's paper during the war years included parables such as "Easy to Kill and Why," the story of an intemperate soldier who received a flesh wound in battle, only to die of gangrene due to his overall poor health. At times temperance reformers directly confronted the new confluence of drink and manhood emerging in army camps. The ATU organ declared that "if soldiers are drunken, they no longer are men," and the Union army might as well "depend upon a herd of swine for victory."[24]

But in many cases, reformers worked without the cooperation of the men who likely had the most influence on ordinary soldiers—their officers. Though there were many examples of abstemious officers, there were as many instances of whisky-swilling ones, and even claims of officers drunk on the field of battle.[25] A unit's officers made the difference between a bibulous and a temperate camp, for an officer was a role model not only of valor in battle but of manhood itself. "If the officers are men of the right stamp," argued the ATU's journal, "the soldier can bear up under all temptation, and grow stronger in manhood as he wins repeated victories over himself."[26] And a drunken officer had dire consequences not just for the morality of his men; such an officer represented "a public evil of the most heinous character" because of the risk he posed to the war effort.[27] One of the North's chronic military ailments was poor leadership, and the ATU cited this as proof of the problem of alcohol. Reformers suspected, for instance, that General Joseph Hooker's disastrous defeat at Chancellorsville and his subsequent dismissal actually resulted from his intemperance.[28]

A general like Hooker effectively reinforced temperance reformers' point about the relationship of alcohol to failure, whether on or off the battlefield. This very argument had been instrumental to the movement's success among antebellum Americans, scrambling to compete in a new social and economic order; it was also an essential intersection between temperance and middle-class masculinity before the war. As the war progressed, however, Americans obtained a new martial hero, the man credited with winning the war, Ulysses S. Grant. As Grant racked up victories and then when President Lincoln made him commander of all northern armies, he became one of the most celebrated figures in the North. All of the adulation was in spite of the fact that Grant was no pristine paragon of middle-class virtue. Rather, he was a visibly flawed, late-blooming man with a rumored drinking problem.[29] The weary nation who lauded him and the over-burdened president who promoted him concerned themselves only with the positive results he achieved. As Lincoln dismissively remarked when questioned about the general's habits, "I can't spare this man. He fights."[30]

Grant represented a real problem for the temperance movement because he seemed to disprove the link between abstinence and success, alcohol and failure. If Grant was indeed a drunkard, temperance reformers risked losing one of their most compelling arguments for total abstinence as a mark of true manhood. The effort expended by the ATU to defend Grant's reputation is instructive of this concern. Reformers sang his praises when, in 1863, Grant ended the whisky ration to his troops, and they made no mention of his reported personal habits. They focused instead on his reputation as a family man and depicted him, even on the field of battle, as a thoroughly domesticated gentleman. The ATU published a letter from a major in his army who claimed that if Americans "could see the General . . . with his wife and two children, looking more like a chaplain than a general," they "would not ask me if he drinks."[31] The ATU's paper continually maintained that he did not and portrayed him as "absolutely abstemious, modest, gentlemanly and in every way worthy of the fame which his splendid military successes have given him."[32] Reformer John Kirk addressed the specific rumor that Grant had been drunk at Shiloh and claimed that his victory there would have been impossible if Grant had allowed even "a drop of liquor to pass his lips on that occasion."[33] Surprisingly, the ATU continued to defend Grant even after he lifted the ban on the whisky ration in his armies after the difficult spring campaign of 1864, including the costly debacle at Cold Harbor. Because of his overall good character, the ATU's paper explained, the organization deferred to his judgment. "There are good uses for things that are ordinarily exceedingly injurious," and Grant's decision should give opponents of temperance no cause for celebration. The following month, the *Journal of the American Temperance Union* once again claimed that the general neither drank nor swore.[34]

By denying Grant's drinking habits, reformers attempted to secure a connection between their cause and the model of manhood produced by the war. Another way reformers confronted the war's concept of masculinity was through a more general reconfiguration of the total abstinence lifestyle and participation in the temperance cause in the image of the warrior. Martial language and symbolism flooded temperance literature in the 1860's, as temperance reformers "waved the bloody shirt" in an attempt to establish a link between their cause and the war, their men and soldiers.[35] Reformers portrayed the war for the Union and the war against alcohol as two engagements of equal importance in a greater conflict for a more moral society. "Which is worse," asked a Michigan temperance journal, "*Rebellion*, or the floodgates of intemperance lifted up, and 'liquid death' rolling over the nation, North and South alike!"[36] The *National Temperance Advocate* declared in 1866 that "from 'Headquarters' comes now the 'marching-orders' to fall into line and assault the stupendous popular sin of *Drunkenness*."[37] A Good Templar paper called for "volunteers" for the "temperance army," and, in an explicit appeal to the manhood of reformers, added, "Cowards need not apply as the brave ladies in our ranks do not want association with them."[38] In an attempt to portray the temperance fight as perilous and sacrificial as the war itself, temperance literature contained violent imagery. Rumsellers were "infernal venders, who thirst for blood," and the victory against drink was likely to arrive "by violence and blood."[39]

For the individual, reformers reconceived the central tenet of the movement, the total abstinence lifestyle, in warrior terms as well. This served two functions: It addressed the argument that one could drink moderately and still be capable and successful, while it cloaked abstinence from alcohol in more heroic and martial terms. One temperance article allowed its readers to "admit that you are safe [as a moderate drinker] ... your head is so strong that you are not easily overcome," but went on to plead total abstinence as "self-denial for the good of others ... for the welfare of men."[40] Notable reformer George Burleigh distinguished between abstinence out of "simple self-preservation" by one in danger of becoming an alcoholic and abstinence out of "heroic self-sacrifice." The latter could "[draw] the gentleman and the scholar from the lap of ease to wrestle with the frost-giants in the hyperbolean darkness!" Burleigh contended that denying oneself for others' sake, which was what the soldier did in battle, was a higher form of morality that encompassed "true manhood."[41] Sometimes the literature used explicit comparisons between the total abstainer and the soldier in war, as did one article on "self-denial" that compared the voluntary abstainer to maimed veterans who "gave up precious limbs for the sake of country and liberty."[42] "The Cold Water Battle Hymn" contrasted total abstainers with respectable, middle-to-upper class defenders of moderate drinking, like Howard Crosby (whom the author specifically mentioned), with their "miserable pleading for wine!" and concluded with the refrain, "Fling out the old flag to the sky, While the temperance legions march by!"[43] In other words, true temperance men were manly, valiant soldiers at war who made sacrifices for the welfare of others, while their detractors were pathetic, effeminate men living leisurely lives. They might get away with their drinking, they might not destroy their lives and success with alcohol, but they were not "true men," soldiers for a cause.

For the cause as a whole, the war provided not simply metaphorical inspiration but tactical direction as well.[44] Reformers noted that the war represented the triumph of the anti-slavery cause through military and political action, not through persuasion, and urged their fellow reformers to "emulate the example of those who fought to destroy African slavery.... Let *all* the machinery be brought into play."[45] Prohibition fit better than moral suasion into the military trope reformers adopted in the 1860's.

Reformers referred to the ballot as "a weapon . . . better than the bayonet," in that it "executes a freeman's will . . . as lightning does the will of God."[46] The *National Temperance Advocate* called prohibition a "war, aggressive and defensive," and contrasted the current phase of the movement with the antebellum emphasis on moral suasion, when the ideal reformer was "bound to exhibit a degree of patience, forbearance, docility and courtesy." Now, the author declared, temperance reformers would return blow for blow, attacking any enemy of the cause "with whatever of energy and ability we can command. . . . We shall wage a sturdy and perpetual war."[47] In the years after the war, then, temperance reformers shifted to ever more militant and nationally-focused prohibition, culminating in the formation of a third party in 1869, and the use of the state to achieve their ends.[48]

Postwar America faced enormous changes and new realities that provided ample justification for these actions. Not only had the movement lost political and cultural ground during the war itself, the alcohol industry's grasp on American government stood to benefit from the growing power and wealth of business in general and the greater pluralism and inclusiveness of the political system. Temperance reformers associated the alcohol industry with wealthy capitalists who unfairly used their economic might for political gain and curtailed ordinary Americans' access to government. In addition, with the increasing influx of immigrants and the emancipation and enfranchisement of the former slaves, the army of alcohol potentially stood to gain allies among new voters who were either culturally predisposed to side with it or could be easily manipulated into doing so. Temperance reformers' response to this situation, particularly with regard to the former slaves, demonstrated a racial and gendered fear over the health of the body politic and a lack of confidence that even white, native-born men could and would employ their political might to safeguard the country's future.[49]

The class dimensions of the political conflict with alcohol translated into a coalition between middle-class and working-class reformers and the portrayal of the rich in increasingly villainous terms.[50] During and after the Civil War, fraternal societies like the Good Templars and the Sons of Temperance, which attracted a sizable working-class constituency, emerged as the strongest and largest temperance organizations.[51] The more middle-class NTS worked closely with these groups, and reformers from both camps joined together in 1869 to form the Prohibition Party. However, the cooperation between these reformers did not completely negate the potential for class tensions within the temperance ranks. Although there was significant overlap between the membership of fraternal orders and the NTS and plenty of middle-class reformers who belonged to fraternal societies, the Good Templars and Sons of Temperance had their detractors among middle-class reformers. John Marsh, an officer in the NTS and in its predecessor, the ATU, complained that these "secret societies" seemed to exist more for the enjoyment and self-importance of their members than for the benefit of the community. He also argued that such societies, with their "childish" system of ceremony and regalia, repelled "serious-minded men," particularly clergy and other professionals.[52] Nor did the middle-class aversion to poverty disappear after the Civil War. The Connecticut State Temperance Union used the familiar argument that alcohol, not flaws in the economic system, caused poverty: "The reason why thousands of laborers do not become capitalists is that they deposit at the wrong bank—the grog-seller's till, instead of the savings bank."[53] Rev. George Hepworth called the middle-class "the only noble class in the entire community" and credited it with any success the movement enjoyed.[54]

But it is apparent that all agreed the wealthy were the far bigger problem. As we have already seen, the wealthy became frequent antagonists in temperance literature because of their use of wine. One reformer thought it lamentable that the cause was "confined . . . to the middle and lower classes" because "there is greater need of reform among the higher than the lower classes."[55] Temperance stories often bore titles such as "Wealth and Wine," the story of an upper-class family torn apart by wine-drinking, or "Wouldn't Marry a Mechanic," which told the tale of a woman who turned down a good, sober working-man to wed a rich, intemperate one, who, in the end, made her life a misery.[56] Both these tales also alluded to a link between wealth and femininity and the collusion between the upper-classes and women in negatively influencing the nation's drinking habits. That the partaking of wine was considered fashionable was a sign the nation "yield[ed] to luxury and effeminacy."[57] Rev. H.C. Fish claimed, "Nearly two thousand of the applicants for admission to the Inebriate Asylum at Binghamton have been *rich men's daughters!*"[58] The "drawing room alcoholism" of upper-class women demonstrated "a distinct moral relaxation . . . a new sort of womanly recklessness."[59] This discursive link made a couple of points on behalf of temperance followers. First, it hinted at the effeminacy of the rich and of drink in general, which contrasted nicely with the masculinity of working- and middle-class total abstinence proponents. Second, it cast doubt upon the overall morality of the wealthy. If even their women were a bunch of drunkards, there could be no help for them. George Burleigh came close to calling rich women prostitutes when he claimed that "my lady, in her carpeted *boudoir*, is only the silk-clad and jeweled copy of the blowzy Bridget in the basement."[60]

The immorality of the rich had wider political implications, given the larger class battle in which temperance reformers viewed their cause. Reformers saw temperance and prohibition as part and parcel of the emerging class conflict between labor and capital and of capitalists' corruption of government. They portrayed the alcohol industry as a "monopoly" that influenced government with its "money power," thereby endangering democracy.[61] "In the liquor traffic they make money easily," claimed the NTS, "and [they] do not scruple or hesitate to spend it freely in order to promote . . . their cause."[62] The Prohibition Party's 1870 and 1872 platforms reflected these concerns and included planks advocating silver currency and the reduction of railroad rates and opposing "any discrimination in favor of capital against labor, as well as . . . all monopoly and class legislation." The platform also declared that prohibition would "emancipate labor and practically promote labor reform."[63] In addition, reformers viewed the sale of alcohol to those who really could not afford it as a form of class exploitation. "The people have two enemies, wealth and rum," explained Wendell Phillips, who renewed his temperance career with vigor after the war. "The first grinds them into dividends. The second delivers them shorn to their enemies."[64]

In addition to the confrontation between labor and capital, reformers observed another clear political battle line in the war with alcohol between "American" culture and immigrant cultures. They saw their country being invaded by immigrants with different religious and social customs. This nativist fear existed before the war, but it grew enormously after, with the political organization of the liquor industry and the political exploitation of immigrant communities, particularly in cities.[65] When a convention of brewers, many of whom the NTS claimed were German, met in Chicago in 1867 to discuss their political goals, the NTS cried, "Every man to his post!" and argued the alcohol industry gave reformers no choice but to wade into the political fray with full force.[66] By the 1870's, temperance reformers asserted that the liquor industry controlled the caucus and convention processes of both parties and that both parties contained opportunists willing to "push everything else aside for expediency" and bend to the will of the alcohol industry's political and monetary might. Reformers believed collusion between immigrant voters, the alcohol industry, and corrupt politicians threatened to subvert the political process and the government itself. This had already occurred in cities like New York, which temperance noteworthy Neal Dow described as "the cesspool into which the off scouring of Europe is poured;" another reformer claimed the entire city had been taken over by "ruffians."[67] The face-off with immigrants had religious elements as well. Temperance reformers viewed themselves as Christians and immigrants as "heathens." In 1870, when the Massachusetts legislature passed a law favorable to beer brewers, one temperance speaker declared the lawmakers had "counted out God, and had counted in the German and Irish."[68] Reformers also made much of German American opposition to Sunday Laws in the cities of New York and Chicago, which sought the closure of saloons on Sunday. Two engravings in the *Advocate* contrasted "the Sabbath they propose to take from us" and "the Sabbath they propose to give us." The former featured a family seated in their parlor in a quiet, domestic scene, while the former depicted a chaotic beer hall filled with men, women, and children.[69]

In addition to immigrants, there was another demographic that seemed well within the reach of alcohol's clutches and with equally grave political consequences: Black men. While temperance reformers generally celebrated the Civil War Amendments as a great moral victory that lent hope to their own cause, they also expressed concern about the fitness of African Americans to employ their new political rights in the best interest of the nation. Reformers viewed the former slaves as a weak link that might be exploited by the alcohol industry in its cultural and political onslaught. Disturbing reports came in from the South that drinking among the former slaves was on the increase because the freedmen believed that alcohol represented a "free heart, noble nature and independence of spirit."[70] In other words, as black men constructed their gender identity as free men, they viewed alcohol consumption as congruent with masculinity. The fact that the former slaves, and blacks everywhere after the ratification of the Fifteenth Amendment, could vote meant their weakness and ignorance might make them political pawns. Reports that corrupt politicians bribed the freedmen with liquor in order to get their votes sent shudders down the spines of temperance folk.[71]

Reformers believed, however, that unlike immigrants, who bore heavy cultural baggage, black men might be transformed into temperance voters. Because they deeply feared that the enemies of temperance could exploit the former slaves and influence their concept of masculinity, reformers made the freedmen a major target of their work. Temperance reformers tried to counter the association of drink and freedom by convincing the former slaves that alcohol was simply another form of slavery.[72] Agents and lecturers journeyed South to start societies among the freedmen, and the NTS published tracts aimed at them, such as one entitled, "Freemen or Slaves?"[73] When the cause made progress among the freedmen, temperance newspapers reported it eagerly, even flatteringly. In 1869, the *National Temperance Advocate* included a letter from a reformer working in Georgia. She detailed a speech given by a sixteen-year-old mulatto boy, who said he feared drink would never be eradicated "unless they get someone like me for President. I'd sweep it all off the face of the earth."[74] The NTS reported in 1874 that black and white Good Templars had gone en masse to the polls in Raleigh, North Carolina to defeat a license law. The article singled out "the exertions of our colored brethren . . . [who] amid denunciations and threats, stood squarely and *manfully* [mine] up to their principles as temperance men."[75] The message of such reports to black men was clear: If you want to achieve the status of true manhood, temperance is the path to follow.

The solicitation of black support represented a spirit of greater racial inclusion in the movement that was purely pragmatic and had little to do with a belief in racial equality. In the minds of most reformers (and indeed most Americans), this latter question had been settled once and for all with the passage of the Civil War Amendments.[76] "The black man has risen to the dignity and to the immunities of manhood," claimed one speaker at the NTS annual meeting in 1872, "Whatever rights yet remain for him to enjoy, he will soon receive." Intemperance not only was worse than slavery, it was presently the "greatest enemy" of African Americans. These statements are stunning when one considers the extent to which race relations degenerated at the time of their utterance. But to temperance folk, any disruptions the nation faced pointed back to the problem of alcohol and its supporters. When Gerrit Smith withdrew his support from the Prohibition Party in 1872 because it benefited the Democratic Party—which he called "the murderer of the colored race"—the NTS paper responded, "Which is worse, to murder one colored man or a hundred white men?"[77] It was critical that all Americans, black and white, put other matters aside and join together against alcohol in "one solid phalanx," "the blood of different races on the same battlefield," as it had been during the late war.[78]

In building "one solid phalanx," temperance reformers had to balance the need to gain black support with that of soliciting southern white support. White southern men would also figure in a political fight with alcohol, as the nation reunified and southerners once again enjoyed full political participation. Nothing better illustrates the careful balancing act on race within the movement than the controversy over black membership in fraternal organizations. The Good Templars and Sons of Temperance were undoubtedly the most democratic temperance organizations, more open to people of varying races and to both genders.[79] But in the 1870's, the Good Templars were nearly rent in two over segregated black lodges. The issue might not have come up at all, except that these orders included a large British membership that pressed for fuller racial equality. White southerners were outraged, and many southern divisions seceded from the national organization.[80] The position of northern temperance reformers on the whole was one of appeasement; pushing integration threatened temperance support among both blacks and whites. Reformers maintained that segregated lodges were the "prayer" of southern blacks themselves.[81] They further argued that the entire matter was "not a question of 'civil rights' or 'equality'," but one of how best to further the cause of temperance as a collective enterprise for America, North and South, black and white.[82]

Neither was it a statement of "equality" when reformers complimented the "manful" actions of African American voters. The statements surrounding black participation in the movement revealed as much about reformers' fears for white manhood, and the male body politic in general, as they did about their views of black manhood.[83] What did it mean, for instance, when ignorant former slaves behaved as better citizens—as better men—than did their white counterparts? With the forces of alcohol everywhere assaulting American government—as an organized lobby, as a wealthy monopoly, as the wielder of immigrant votes and the manipulator of black ones—it fell to the white, native-born men of America to defend democracy as voters and citizens. Instead, many thousands of them capitulated through their own weakness to drink or their sycophantic devotion to party above principle. Such men threatened the polity's destruction. "Rum makes its victims blind to the obligations of manhood," the NTS instructed. Reformers viewed the political process as controlled by "noisy, rowdy, rum-drinking partisans," "coarse, vulgar and ignorant men ... [who] have elected men who have brutalized their bodies and demonized their souls." The appeal, "Defend the ballot-box!," went out to "decent men, and men of honor and nerve, to step forward and utter their protest against a power which threatens to destroy the privileges and advantages of civil liberty."[84] Such discourse was tinged with both gendered and racial implications. "When our fathers decided upon manhood suffrage, they meant the ballot for men, not for imbruted, not for ignorant men, not for savages, but for *Men*. And we must take care in the future that this dreadful power for good or for evil be kept only in the hands of men."[85] As this statement reveals, the increased monetary and political power of the alcohol industry, the greater racial inclusiveness of politics, the broader definition of political manhood, and the increasingly political war with the alcohol industry represented a crisis of citizenship that had deep repercussions for prohibition's success. And prohibition's success had deep repercussions for the future of American society.

The temperance dialogue on Native Americans further illustrates this point. As the West degenerated into violence between whites and Indians after the Civil War, temperance reformers viewed events through the lens of alcohol's corruption of government and the failure of American men to safeguard their society. They blamed whites for supplying Indians with alcohol and the government for dereliction in keeping it from Indians. "The State is bound to protect the Indian from the devastating effects of the white man's 'firewater,'" argued the *Advocate*. Instead, government agents looked the other way, as did the "beer-bloated politicians and wine-drinking representatives" in Washington.[86] It is interesting that reformers did not censure Native Americans for western violence; quite the opposite, they employed the temperance of chiefs like Red Cloud to shame white American men for their toleration of alcohol. Temperance discourse portrayed Indians as helpless children begging for aid from "the great father." Red Cloud, who spoke at the Capitol against alcohol, was a "dusky child of nature," and yet he favorably contrasted with so many white men in his belief in total abstinence. One temperance article pointed out that Native Americans had been completely temperate until whites introduced alcohol and claimed that the Cherokee had actually passed the first prohibitory law in the United States. The main purpose of such assertions was to say that if these primitive, child-like people were advocating total abstinence and prohibition, white men who did not shirked their responsibility and produced the denigration of white society to a position beneath that of even the Indians. "The idea of white man's territory being desecrated by rum is a shame to our advancing civilization," one temperance article on the issue read. It concluded with the question: "Must we return to the barbarism of savage life to secure territory uncursed by rum traffic?"[87]

As the temperance movement redefined the cause as a grand political struggle and faced the unprecedented political and economic might of the alcohol industry, racial realignments and gendered redefinitions cast serious doubt on the health of the male body politic and on the capabilities of American manhood in general. Indeed, prohibition itself, even as it represented a heroic, manly battle, also contained the fear that men did not have the capacity for self-mastery. "Men who are able to govern themselves have been persuaded to practice total abstinence," explained reformer J. R. Sypher, who went on to ask, "What now shall be done with the men who are not able to govern themselves?"[88] The answer was for the state to protect such men from alcohol by eradicating it altogether. Complete prohibition was necessary because men were not manly enough to resist alcohol on their own.[89] Of course, the question then became, were American men manly enough to win the political battle for prohibition? The answer to that was not at all certain, particularly as it hinged on the changing composition of the male body politic.

In the years during and after the Civil War, the temperance movement's discourse and its tactical direction explored and tried to address the concern that changing notions of masculinity—both personal and political—could bring great harm to the movement and the nation. Not surprisingly, the movement discussed the future of femininity as well. The concern over female drinking raised the concern that women as well as men endangered American civilization. If more and more women drank, as reformers seemed to believe, it meant the morality of American women, and American society by extension, stood on the brink of collapse. Young, upper-class women in particular seemingly redefined acceptable female behavior to include social drinking, and reformers were horrified. They spoke distastefully of women "who can sit down unblushingly and guzzle wine in a promiscuous company of gentlemen," and of "the belle of the ball-room, whirling half-naked in an immodest dance, her face unnaturally red, and the smell of liquor on her breath."[90] Medical doctors enlisted in the cause expressed the opinion that alcohol had a much more degenerative effect on women than on men; it more readily destroyed them physically, mentally, and morally. The latter onslaught was most distressing, because alcohol "destroys [woman's] innate love of truth, justice and purity of thought." It "denaturalized" women in a way that could be passed on biologically, and "thus leads to the degeneracy of the race."[91] Indeed, there was no limit to the depth to which even respectable women might fall once they encountered drink; one temperance story juxtaposed a lady drunk with a "respectable" black man, from whom she begs money. She asks him, "Now, who will dare say that I am better than you? Though you are black and I am white."[92] Just as complimentary statements about black voters revealed concerns about white manhood, this account employed race to express fears for white womanhood. In both cases, reformers explored racial and gendered concerns about the future of American society through the trope of alcohol.

At the same time that they worried alcohol would redefine femininity, temperance reformers forwarded an updated notion of "true womanhood" that was more public and activist than the antebellum version had been.[93] The war itself served as one inspiration and explanation for this, as it did for new alignments between temperance and masculinity. The preoccupation of men during the war years and the war metaphor adopted by the movement provided women with new opportunities for work and leadership. Just as the war had been a national, collective enterprise that required women's aid, so too did the temperance "war" necessitate women fight alongside men to save the nation from alcoholic peril. In addition, amidst doubts about men's abilities and the fitness of the male body politic, women's more aggressive aid seemed doubly vital.

Although the warrior image upon first glance seemed even more exclusively male than the self-made man of the antebellum years, in the context of a wartime culture of necessity, collectivism, and service, it could be conceived as a female image, too. War time rhetoric solicited and celebrated women's work as nurses, philanthropists, and patriots as of equal importance to the work of soldiering, at times employing martial language. For example, when asked about the nursing services of Mary "Mother" Bickerdyke to his army, General Sherman replied, "She outranks me."[94] As Barbara Cutter has demonstrated, women's war time work—even their actual presence on the battlefield—was not that controversial. It easily meshed with the nineteenth-century image of women as morally superior and self-sacrificial. They acted in the context of national emergency, on behalf of their country, not for selfish gain.[95]

Women's roles in the temperance movement, in both reality and rhetoric, followed this logic as well. With men distracted during the war, women assumed a large role in the work, even positions of leadership. One of the chief explanations for the growth of groups such as the Good Templars and the Sons of Temperance during the war, when the rest of the movement languished, was these groups' history of openness to women and the unprecedented opportunities for leadership they offered women during the war.[96] These groups grew out of the Washingtonian movement of the 1840's and reflected its heritage of expanded female activism. In the 1850's, the Sons of Temperance admitted women to non-voting membership, and the Good Templars allowed female membership "on terms of perfect and entire equality."[97] During the Civil War, women assumed leadership positions within these orders, and their postwar activism continued to be encouraged. In addition, the orders explicitly endorsed women's political, social, and economic equality. Secret society newspapers featured articles that argued for woman suffrage based on men's failure to prohibit alcohol.[98] One Templar tract boasted that the order had "first of all other moral reform associations . . . taken the advanced position of perfect female social and civil equality—woman is man's . . . equal."[99] The NTS also allowed for greater female activism; six female delegates attended the NTS's opening convention in 1865, and by 1868 the organization included a female vice-president. The NTS even showed signs of a softened position regarding women on the platform. One article acknowledged that a "few" women might be accomplished enough to speak publicly for temperance; another claimed "the platform is only dangerous to those who seek it for selfish and unholy purposes" and "woman naturally shrinks from notoriety."[100]

In addition, the supposed rise in female drinking gave women reformers a field of endeavor entirely their own. This mirrored the Washingtonian movement's admission of female alcoholism and its concomitant allowance for women's activism; after the Civil War, these trends were dominant ones. In New York City, women created the largest ladies' temperance society prior to the WCTU. The basis of their efforts was getting women, many of them former alcoholics, to sign a pledge. Its membership climbed with each report; by late 1870, it reached fifteen hundred. Though women assumed full leadership of the society, male reformers in the city also contributed to its meetings with speeches and prayers. But as one temperance publication put it, though men might offer assistance, "the labor is for our wives and mothers." "This is a field of reform where only women, and these married women of unimpeached and unimpeachable character, self-sacrifice and Christian courage—can labor with any fair hope of success."[101]

Not only did the movement hail a more public role for women, it seemed to revise the meaning of female privacy. Ironically, the "separate spheres" rhetoric that figured so prominently in the antebellum movement became suspect in the new context of the Gilded Age. A female reformer described a woman who confined herself to private undertakings "at the risk of becoming unladylike" and as shallow and useless. "We do not need ladies who dream away life in easy chairs, or who . . . spend whole nights shedding crocodile tears over love-sick novels," explained one female orator in 1868. She went on to say that although woman's "proper place . . . may be the domestic circle," when duty called, as it did with temperance, she was obligated to answer.[102] Male reformers echoed such beliefs. At times, they even associated the notion of separate spheres with the problem of alcohol. One reformer argued that women's privacy, instead of keeping them secure from immorality, might actually contribute to their moral demise. Woman's "retired life favors the fostering of secret indulgences. . . . She may confine herself to her own house," he warned. He believed that, especially in an age where household chores were not as time-consuming, there was a positive correlation between women's domestic confinement and the rise in female drinking.[103]

Instead of encouraging women's support in the symbolic and passive roles of the antebellum era, postwar temperance literature cast women in the "warrior" role and as part of a larger temperance "army" and their work as sacrifice for the cause. The NTS organ printed an article by Mrs. M.B. Dickinson in 1872 that spoke of the "moral courage" women must possess to enter the work, the "false modesty" that led many women to a "shrinking from duty," and the potential need for a woman to "take her life in her hand" to fulfill her obligation.[104] Another article spoke of woman as a "'recruiting agent'" in "the conflict that rages;" while she was not on the front lines, she was no less a warrior, as her support "will turn the tide of battle for or against the right."[105] The Good Templar paper *The Rescue* gave an account of women in New Paris, Ohio taking "possession" of a saloon in 1868. It painted quite a martial portrait, with the women "armed with knitting needles," their "siege" lasting an entire day, and the "enemy"

76 · Gender and the American Temperance Movement

Figure 6. *Woman's Holy War* (Currier and Ives, 1874). Here is an explicit depiction of women as warriors against temperance after the Civil War. Library of Congress, Prints and Photographs Division, LC-USZ62-683.

refusing to "surrender."[106] The NTS put out a "bugle call" to all reformers: "Organize!!. . . . If men loiter, let women advance."[107]

The juxtaposition here of women's work with men's is instructive. As temperance took on new meaning for men, women's roles within the movement changed. In the antebellum period, when temperance was a vehicle for male identity and authority, women's place in temperance discourse was a corresponding display of female sanction and dependence. In the new context of the Gilded Age, as the alignments between temperance and masculinity shifted, so too did women's roles. The advancement of women in the temperance cause had its context in the "loitering" of American men, or at least in the fear that they would loiter.

Since the loitering of American men had political ramifications, reformers began to reassess the idea of woman suffrage. In American society at large, the issue had been raised anew by the passage of the Fifteenth Amendment. In temperance ranks, opinions varied but on the whole showed greater receptivity. The Good Templars and Sons of Temperance unequivocally supported woman suffrage. The Prohibition Party platform likewise endorsed the vote for women as a means of bolstering the fight against alcohol. Only twenty-two delegates out of five hundred at the party's founding convention voted against the suffrage plank. Where opinions divided, the issue did not provoke bitter infighting; those in the temperance ranks who opposed woman suffrage did so somewhat reservedly, usually by deflecting attention back to the issue of alcohol. Rev. Newman told temperance women that whether they got the vote or not, their main concern should be using their "influence in favor of total abstinence."[108] Another reformer lamented that the "great hue-and-cry . . . raised about woman suffrage" overshadowed the more important issue of "the wrongs attached to the liquor interest. . . . Does any sane woman doubt that women are suffering one thousand times more from rum than from any political [disadvantage]?"[109]

Those who did support woman suffrage made their case in terms of the political fight with alcohol and hinted at the doubts surrounding the male body politic. If women were the "'better half' of humanity, so would their votes be the *better* half of those cast at the elections . . . The policy that excludes them, does but invite dangers to the public."[110] In addition, supporters argued that woman suffrage would not bring a gendered revolution. Prohibition Party member Albert Williams argued that although woman suffrage might "open the door for one depraved woman to vote, it would open the door for twenty-five pure ones to vote also," women who would vote "nearly or quite as generally as the men."[111] In his speech justifying the inclusion of woman suffrage in the Prohibition Party's 1872 platform, James Black expressed his belief that "God's appointed 'help-meet' . . . will find a fitting sphere in the civil as well as the domestic relations of life."[112] In other words, these reformers supported women as voters as a way to strengthen morally the body politic and to redeem it from its current crisis.

The greater gendered inclusiveness of the movement after the Civil War, like the outreach to African Americans, was more pragmatic than ideological. The meaning, strategy, and context of the temperance movement had changed; women's full participation seemed necessary, even vital, for the grand struggle in which reformers now engaged. In addition, in the larger intellectual climate after the Civil War, an expansion of women's public role no longer necessitated a dialogue on individual equality as it had in the antebellum period. The passage of the Fourteenth and Fifteenth Amendments, which failed to grant women civil equality, dealt the women's rights movement a harsh blow and separated gender and racial equality in American law and thought.[113] The pairing of race and gender within a broad argument for individual rights in the antebellum years had been an explosive combination that threatened not only sectional conflict but the foundation of society on white male authority. The potential for social change was enormous. By legally disentangling race from gender, the Civil War Amendments proved that greater racial equality did not have to lead to massive social upheaval or the unraveling of society's gendered fabric. Instead of potently mixing with the idea of racial equality to promote a revolutionary concept of individual rights, women's roles now became the "stable reference point" for the changes brought by war and emancipation. The expansion of women's public, political function—even suffrage itself—could be reconceived in less ominous tones.[114]

Furthermore, the antebellum concept of female moral authority might be fully mined of its political resources. The employment of female morality in an overtly political fashion would not only bathe the cause in righteousness but in nostalgia. Historians have demonstrated the violence done by the Civil War to the antebellum belief in individual perfectibility, moral suasion, and utopian optimism; this helps explain the shift to increasing state activism by the temperance movement and other reforms.[115] But historians have also demonstrated that this intellectual shift was not a complete paradigm change and that Americans were not altogether comfortable with the wholesale adoption of new values.[116] The temperance movement's retention and elevation of the concept of female morality after the Civil War speaks to this point. The crusading woman, which would become the image the temperance movement projected in the Gilded Age, represented the realization of women's political potential in context of this nostalgia, as well as that of the political war with alcohol, doubts about the efficacy of male citizenship, and the conclusion of a dialogue on individual rights.[117]

Chapter Four
Crusading Women
The Creation of a New Temperance Icon

"I grew up with an exalted conception of the power of a woman's prayer."

—Dio Lewis[1]

In December 1873, Dio Lewis, a noted reformer and physician, gave a speech in Washington Courthouse, Ohio entitled "The Power of Woman's Prayer in Grog Shops." He urged women to take the initiative in the war against saloons by employing their moral authority and shutting down the establishments with their prayers. It was not a new speech—he had in fact been delivering it for some twenty years—but this time, the women in his audience took his message to heart and carried out his suggestions in their town with great success. By New Year's, all the saloons in the town had closed, their owners' consciences heavily burdened by the meek pleas of their female visitors. Rumsellers there reportedly trembled in fear "that unless they conformed to the wishes of these praying women, the avenging wrath of God would be thundered upon them."[2] This was an early episode in the great Woman's Crusade, in which thousands of American women took to the streets on behalf of temperance and through which a new, revitalized period of activity against alcohol began in the United States.[3] Dio Lewis's movement spread quickly throughout Ohio and beyond in the winter and spring of 1874. By the end of January, over thirty towns in Ohio, Indiana, Iowa, and Tennessee reported Crusades; by the end of February, one hundred and fifty communities in twelve more states joined the movement.[4]

Historians have usually seen the Crusade as a feminine outpouring of frustration with men's failure to dispose of the alcohol problem that ravaged many of the Crusaders' own homes.[5] While this explanation certainly held true in many cases, it is also true that the image of the Crusader was as much a male construction as a female one and as important to men as to women. The Crusader image employed antebellum nostalgia to lend new vitality and definition to the postbellum temperance movement. As we have seen, the Civil War's disruption of temperance produced significant ideological shifts, particularly with regard to its use of gender. The antebellum icon of the self-made man lost much of its power, as reformers re-imagined temperance as a political and cultural war. In the face of doubts about men's political abilities and in the absence of any real political victories, the movement constructed the Crusader as a new icon to revitalize its base. The icon performed a few functions for the movement. It resurrected the movement's antebellum heritage, which many feared was lost. It dramatically and spectacularly reaffirmed the rightness of the cause, thereby reinforcing male reformers' political work. And it employed female publicity and women's large presence in the movement in a context other than political feminism.

The most immediate context of the Crusade was the fallout from the formation of the Prohibition Party. In 1869, a number of temperance reformers took a major, and much-debated, risk when they formed a third party, primarily to put pressure on the two major parties to adopt prohibition planks. Those in favor of creating the party believed the transitional nature of postwar politics made it an ideal time for a third party movement, and they were disillusioned with the Republican Party's lack of initiative on temperance issues. James Black, one of the party's founding members, argued that both parties "have turned against us;" another member argued "the mission of the Republican Party has ended" and the Prohibition Party might be the next great reform party.[6] But other reformers believed abandoning established parties was not the best means to achieve prohibitory measures. The climate of political transition might mean reformers had an opportunity to influence the parties from within.[7] There were also those critics who faulted the Prohibition Party for its broad platform that combined temperance with woman suffrage, free trade, labor reform, and other issues that potentially distracted from prohibition. "We trust [the party] will not be strangled before it is fairly born," an editorial in the *Advocate* remarked.[8] Still others thought the party was too narrow and doubted temperance men would abandon all other political loyalties and concern for other issues to make prohibition paramount. Horace Greeley, though he supported prohibitory measures, declined to support the party because he believed "that other issues should and must dominate over prohibition."[9]

The issue provoked at times bitter conflict. The organ of the NTS deeply regretted the "unkind feelings and harsh words among those who have long labored for a common end" and worried the controversy could bring "disaster" to the cause.[10] Federal Dana wrote to Gerrit Smith in November 1869, "There must be something radically wrong, when three-quarters of our energies are worse than wasted in combating each other."[11] As for Smith, he was involved in one of the most vigorous debates over the party. When the NTS as an organization refrained from endorsing the party, preferring to allow each member to decide for himself, Smith called the NTS a "sham" temperance society and claimed the incident had "[exposed] its bad character."[12] An editorial in the NTS organ in December 1869 begged for unity, amity, and "*full, free discussion,* but with *fair treatment* of honest dissent." "We have got a tremendous fight on our hands," it concluded, "We have quite enough to do without wasting our strength in assailing each other."[13]

Not only did the Prohibition Party divide temperance supporters, it failed in its major objective of inducing support for prohibition within the two major parties. Those reformers who opposed the Prohibition Party put their faith in the Republican Party, which was, historically, the party of reform and included many notable teetotalers. Temperance men, for instance, earnestly defended President Grant, as they had General Grant, now for the political stakes they placed on him. During Grant's 1868 candidacy and in the early days of his first term, reformers repeatedly defended against the charges that Grant was "a common drunk." William Dodge, the president of the NTS, claimed to have "had a long talk with him" and concluded that, not only was Grant not a drunk, he was an abstainer.[14] In addition, the pages of the *Advocate* and other temperance publications contained numerous anecdotes of Grant's refusal of wine at official dinners.[15] But both Grant and the Republican Party soon disappointed temperance folk. By Grant's second term, the Republican Party still had no temperance plank, and rumors of Grant's drinking abounded. The *Advocate* admitted now that Grant did drink, though not heavily, and added almost apologetically, "We wish the president and all other public officials . . . were total abstainers."[16] Grant's drinking habits became a minor concern, however, when in 1873, the Republican governor of New York and war hero, John Dix, outraged temperance supporters with a surprise veto of the state's local option bill. The *Advocate* called him "the official ally of murderers" and declared his action "the death-knell of the Republican Party." The disillusionment was deep for those reformers who had shunned the Prohibition Party in favor of the Republicans. "We have been among those who believed it was the true policy of temperance men to seek accomplishment of our political purposes through the Republican Party," the *Advocate* lamented.[17] But political options remained few, and at its annual convention in September 1873, the National Temperance Society voted against separate political action.[18]

In the wake of this debate and disillusionment, many reformers began to question the movement's exclusive use of prohibition in achieving victory over alcohol. In the immediate aftermath of the Prohibition Party's creation, the *Advocate* wondered, "Is the moral phase of the movement to be abandoned?" and declared its support for "both moral and legal suasion."[19] The following month, the paper reported that the question "has brought forth strong articles in several papers declaring continued adherence to the doctrine of 'moral suasion.'" The paper again called for "moral and legal suasion combined. . . . We will vote as we pray . . . so that we can pray as we vote."[20] Indeed, prohibition without some moral/religious underpinning left many in the movement uninspired. One reformer declared his belief that the frenzy for political action damaged the cause by stripping it of "emotional feeling, the true heart-force." He claimed temperance forces should "*out-feel*" its enemies.[21] NTS officer Theodore Cuyler agreed that the third party movement had more than failed; not only was it unsuccessful in achieving any real victories, it had led to the abandonment of "old fashion meetings to promote total abstinence." He argued that, as a result, the cause was "*weaker than before*" and urged reformers to return to "the old work."[22]

Some reformers called for the disbanding of prohibition efforts altogether and the wholesale return to the movement's heritage of moral suasion. The most noteworthy of these was Dio Lewis. Lewis virulently opposed prohibition because he believed it "meddled" with personal freedom and violated the idea that "each and every individual [deserved] the free and full enjoyment of all his natural rights of person and property."[23] The saloon owner's right to sell alcohol was as valid as the consumer's right to refrain from its purchase or use. Lewis also emphatically believed that the shift toward prohibition had devastated the temperance movement's success. The dusting off of moral suasion, which sought to convince people to voluntarily shun alcohol, was the democratic solution and the movement's only hope.[24]

His stalwart opposition to prohibition and his placement of temperance within a framework of individualism made Lewis a bit of an anachronism in the 1870's, but the starring role women played in his vision proved to be quite timely indeed. His gender philosophy combined the antebellum notion of female moral superiority with more modern ones of female empowerment. Lewis extolled woman as the ruler of the "social sphere," "the fountain-head of social, moral, and religious influence." Women were entirely pure, their "pivotal passion . . . the maternal [while] . . . man's . . .

is in the sexual." It was women's "slavery to man's passions," both on an individual and cultural level, that compromised their strength and equality. If woman ceased her concern for man's pleasure or approval, if woman could release herself from constrictive clothing, the frivolity of fashion, "the shilly-shally, lace, ribbon and feather life," she might take her place as an equal in society and "be strong enough in soul to take us men in her arms and carry us to heaven."[25] Lewis's own mother largely inspired these ideas, as well as his deep commitment to issues affecting women, including temperance. His father had been an alcoholic who abused his mother and failed to provide for his family. "She was father, mother, general provider, cook, housekeeper, and nurse," he recalled. Witnessing his mother's strength and hearing her pious prayers in the midst of suffering left a lasting impression. His mother became almost deified in his imagination, and through his reform career, he assumed the role of her champion. And he became forever a believer in the power of moral suasion wielded by good Christian women to defeat any social evil.[26]

The experience of one such good Christian woman demonstrates several trends in the Crusade as a whole. Eliza Jane Thompson was a member of a prominent Ohio family, the wife of renowned attorney Henry James Thompson and the daughter of a former Ohio governor, Allen Trimble. Her hometown of Hillsboro, Ohio, though it was actually the third that inaugurated the Crusade, became known as the "cradle" of the movement, and Thompson herself achieved emblematic status.[27] Other Crusaders called her "Mother Thompson" and credited her with being one of the founders of the movement. Thompson's temperance activity, though intermittent, reached back to 1836, when she attended the first national convention in Saratoga Springs, New York as a young woman with her father. She was the only woman in attendance.[28]

Thompson's Crusade involvement stemmed from her long-time temperance leanings, but it had a more immediate and personal appeal as well. Both her son, Allen, and her husband, James, had drinking problems that may have contributed to the family's poor financial condition by the 1860's and certainly brought Eliza much heartache. It seems Allen's alcoholism was more severe, eventually contributing to his death in 1867.[29] James may have been a more moderate drinker, but this was concern enough for Eliza and her father, particularly in the face of Allen's struggles and the family's financial difficulties. Allen Trimble wrote James Thompson a stern letter in 1861, in response to a request for money and at Eliza's apparent urging, in which he told him any financial assistance would be "with the understanding, that the unfortunate *habit* you had fallen into, would be abandoned, and that . . . your family, should be relieved from the painful thought that the indulgence referred to was *increasing.*" Eliza's father further warned his son-in-law that financial difficulty was only the start of the potential damage his drinking incurred; his reputation and "the most *cherished* elements of the household," priceless in their worth, could be the next casualties. He concluded that "there is *no* safety for you but . . . that you will abstain from the use of intoxicating drink—and that you owe it to your family . . . and to your character and manhood to take the pledge of total abstinence."[30]

Three years later, the problem had not abated. Allen Trimble had allowed James and Eliza to move into his house, in part so Eliza could care for her ailing father but also to alleviate the couple's "financial difficulties," under the condition that James "would quit the use of intoxicating drinks." Instead, James had continued drinking, which left his father-in-law to doubt "whether our acts of kindness . . . will be of any avail, in adding to the happiness of your family." He wondered how "*the grief and agony of a wife and children such as few men have,* will not move the heart of him who cause their suffering," and found it "astonishing . . . that a man of your sagacity, and kind feeling, seeing . . . that you are murdering . . . your wife and inflicting deepest mortification upon your children, continues to drink." He specifically mentioned Allen Thompson's own dire struggle with alcoholism and conveyed Eliza's worry that "your example, upon this subject of using liquor, will have an unhappy effect upon him."[31] Allen's death in 1867 may have converted his father to teetotalism once and for all; by the time of the Crusade, James appears to have become a temperance supporter.[32]

Although Eliza Thompson never mentioned her family's own woes, they likely played some role in her involvement in the Hillsboro Crusade.[33] She did not attend Lewis's lecture in Hillsboro, but her daughter did and urged her mother to accompany her to the organizational meeting the next day. After much soul-searching, in which she contemplated "the awful responsibility of the step," she went to the meeting, family Bible in hand. Her husband, though by this time a temperance activist, initially belittled the idea of women praying saloons out of business as "tomfoolery." But Thompson chided back that "the men had been in the 'tomfoolery' business a long time . . . and it might be God's will that the women should now take their part."[34]

To her surprise, those present at the meeting elected her president of the Crusade. Her family's prestigious position in the town and in state politics may have been the deciding factor in this selection. In fact, the Crusade included many such "respectable" women, a major reason behind the movement's success. Another leader explained that in confrontations with critics, "It was worth everything . . . that ladies of the highest station, as also of deep piety and respectability, were leaders and constant, earnest workers."[35] Whatever the reasons behind her selection, Thompson accepted leadership apprehensively and reluctantly. She recalled that at the subsequent meeting, when a male pastor, who had been serving as chair, invited her to the podium, "her limbs refused to bear her." Her brother, who was also in attendance, suggested to the chair that all the men in attendance depart the meeting and "leave this work with God and the women." It was only then that Eliza Thompson mounted the platform as the leader of the Hillsboro Crusade.[36]

She was less retiring, though no less modest, as she led the visiting bands of women to the town's saloons. Eliza and the other women acted as bereaved and pious wives and mothers. Eliza often led the prayers as the women knelt on the streets and sidewalks outside the establishments. A journalist reported that "passers-by uncovered their heads, for the place whereon they trod was 'holy ground.' The eyes of hardened men filled with tears, and many turned away, saying they could not bear to look upon such a sight." The women followed their prayers with the singing of hymns, "such as our mothers sang to us in childhood days. We thought, can mortal man resist such efforts?"[37]

The saloonkeepers realized the potency of such female appeals, but they also sensed that male involvement lay behind the feminine face of the Crusade. One such individual, Robert Ward, preferred "to have a talk with Dio Lewis." Thompson replied that Lewis had nothing to do with the women's work and urged him instead to "look upon some of the faces before you, and observe the marks of sorrow, caused by the unholy business that you ply."[38] Male involvement in the Hillsboro Crusade mostly went on behind the scenes, but sometimes it became quite visible, as when men accompanied the women on their visits. On one such occasion, in March 1874, a mixed group of Crusaders closed the saloon of a Mr. Uhrig. Rev. S.D. Clayton offered the closing prayer and then set Uhrig's entire stock of alcohol on fire.[39]

One saloon owner, W.H.H. Dunn, demonstrated his awareness of male participation in the Crusade in the notice he issued to the women of Hillsboro informing them of the legal action he was taking against them. Citing the "great pecuniary damage" he had suffered as a result of their "riotous and unlawful" actions, he instructed them that "each of you, *together with your husbands* [emphasis mine] . . . and the persons who are thus aiding you with their money, encouragement and advice in your unlawful proceedings, are hereby notified that I can not, nor will not, longer submit to your daily trespasses on my property and injury to my business."[40] A court subsequently issued an injunction against further picketing by Crusaders. The women of Hillsboro honored the injunction in the short-run but declared that "if judgment is finally against them they will disobey it," since "the rum-sellers have been for years disobeying the law.... The ladies' transgression is in the interest of law, order and morality."[41] The men involved in the Crusade, meanwhile, had Dunn brought up on eight counts of violating liquor laws already on the books but largely unenforced.[42] The court battle with Dunn lasted for over a year, until May 1875, when a jury found the Crusaders guilty of trespass and fined them five dollars.[43]

Several features of Thompson's story are borne out in the larger record of the Crusade. First, the Crusade spectacularly resurrected moral suasion through the employment of female victimization and morality. The overall message of the Crusade was that it represented a spontaneous and divinely inspired outpouring of the burdens and righteousness of American women. Their power lay in their meekness, gentility, and femininity. They acted sacrificially, leaving the comfortable sphere of the home and subjecting themselves to all sorts of mean, crude, and violent treatment in order to rescue the victims of alcohol—some of them members of their own families—and the nation's morality. At this point in the movement, only women had such power.

The Crusade vividly demonstrated this in its methodology. Women went out in bands of a few to several dozen and quietly entered a saloon or knelt on the street outside it. There they prayed, sang, and conversed with the owner and patrons of the establishment. The scene of a Crusade seemed to affect its spectators deeply. When he went to Ohio to observe the movement, John Gough, an old Washingtonian reformer, expected to witness an odd, circus-like spectacle. Instead, what he saw moved him beyond words. "They stand by the curb-stones, not hindering the passing. I noticed some lifted their hats respectfully as they passed them. They would sing ... so sweetly. Then they would read a scripture, and all kneel while one prayed." Watching them, he said, "My heart was so full."[44]

The Crusaders articulated the view that God had elected to use their meek, pious femininity as a potent weapon on behalf of temperance. The women felt they had particular attributes and gifts—"moral courage," "keen perception," "earnest sympathies," respect only for "justice and right" and not "expediencies"—that made them well-suited as moral warriors.[45] Annie Wittenmyer, later the first president of the WCTU, called the movement "God's method of arousing public sentiment and consolidating the moral forces of the land" and the Crusaders "His chosen instruments for this important and unusual work."[46] Eliza Stewart, another Crusade "mother," explained that God's calling alone could have prompted women "to yield up their preconceived ideas of what was a lady's place" and

Figure 7. *The Ohio whisky war, the ladies of Logan singing hymns in front of barrooms in aid of the temperance movement* (sketch by S.B. Morton, 1874). A group of clearly respectable, middle-class women visit a saloon. Library of Congress, Prints and Photographs Division, LC-USZ62-90543.

venture into such unfeminine work. "Not a few carried the subject to their closets, and there on their knees fought the battle with self and pride before the Lord, till He gave them the strength and they came forth anointed for the war."[47] The *New York Times* reported that Crusaders claimed to be "endowed with the 'power of the Holy Spirit,' and fight zealously not only against intemperance but against sin of every description."[48]

The portrayal of the work's results in fantastic and even supernatural terms reinforced this claim. Accounts of the Crusade contained numerous stories of saloonkeepers or patrons tearfully submitting to the ladies' meek entreaties and prayers. One bar owner in Mother Stewart's hometown of Springfield, Ohio told a reporter he knew if the women targeted his establishment, he would have to quit the business because "they have the advantage on us."[49] Another man met crusading women in Jacksonville, Illinois with a gun at the door to his saloon. Unswerving, the women began singing, which so affected the man, he lay down his weapon and started sobbing uncontrollably. The successes of the movement at Washington Courthouse led an observer to surmise that the town's liquor dealers must be "tormented" day and night by thoughts of "committees of . . . [women] flitting in and out of their stores."[50] "Men may say what they please about the weakness of being moved by such demonstrations," reporter J.H. Beadle wrote, "But when one . . . sees old gray-haired mothers and middle-aged matrons pleading with rum-sellers . . . it has a telling effect." He concluded that only those rumsellers "endowed with a great deal of brute-nerve" could withstand the women's appeals.[51] In Cleveland, a Crusader reportedly even subdued rabid dogs set upon her with a "laying on of hands" reminiscent of Christ's casting out of demons.[52] Crusaders' accounts also claimed divine retribution when saloonkeepers refused to submit. In Cleveland, one German saloon owner, who mocked his female visitors by holding his own satirical prayer meeting, was mysteriously killed by his horse the next day.[53] A female saloon owner in Washington, D.C., who told Crusaders that even "God cannot shut me up," died in a carriage accident just weeks later. The account of her demise concluded that it was a "token of *God's visitation*."[54]

The ultimate symbol of the Crusaders' moral strength was John Calvin Van Pelt, the owner of a saloon in New Vienna, Ohio. The women of that community visited his establishment every day for three weeks and endured verbal abuse and showers of dirty water and beer. His treatment of the women was so severe that the town's authorities jailed him. Upon his release, rumor had it he was ready to relinquish the fight, and the entire town turned out to see what would transpire the next time the women paid him a visit. Not only did Van Pelt hand over his axe to the Crusaders and allow them to destroy his stock of alcohol, he became a temperance lecturer who traveled around the country in support of the work. Recalling these events in subsequent speeches, Van Pelt credited the "prayers and suffering" of the women in converting him. Over the years, many reformers had attempted the same feat but had failed, he said, "because there was no heart in them. Men . . . failed because they were not sufficiently interested." The women were "the injured parties. . . . They alone can succeed."[55]

Male temperance reformers agreed wholeheartedly. Many within the temperance ranks hailed the Crusade as a new dawn for the movement, a return to its roots in moral suasion and Christianity through women, the best representatives of both. Despite their "instinctive modesty from public place," women had acted "with weapons of prayer and love, and gentle persuasion . . . to rid our homes, to save our children, from the abominations of the dram-shop. She has entered upon the work with womanly delicacy and tenderness."[56] One journalist similarly concluded, "The success of the women was due to love. They conducted warfare on the gospel method of moral persuasion instead of force."[57] Indeed, many

Figure 8. *The Temperance Crusade, or Four Hours in a Bar Room* (A.J. Fisher, 1874). Here is a comical illustration of Crusaders' uncanny ability to wear down saloon keepers. Library of Congress, Prints and Photographs Division, LC-USZ62-2446.

male reformers deduced that God himself had ordained the women's activism. When the National Temperance Society met in June 1874, its president, William Dodge, declared the Crusade could only be explained "on the ground that it is from above;" after long years of praying and suffering quietly, women had "at last received a baptism from on high, and they have gone forth banded together."[58] Another NTS member agreed that "Woman has become the instrument in God's hands, prayer and love, the lever which moves the heart and wins the victory.... Out of weakness, God has perfected strength. The greatest sufferers have become avengers."[59] Rev. W.C. Steel of New York City wrote that the Crusade bore "the unmistakable signs of its divine origin.... The whole course of the movement has been that of a genuine and thorough religious revival.... In hundreds of instances, woman's gentleness has overcome man's obstinacy."[60]

Whether or not the Crusade had its origin in God and in woman, there is ample evidence that man had a hand in it as well. The outpouring of male support and approval, the rush to imbue the Crusade with divine authority, and the willingness of male reformers to step aside and allow Crusaders a starring role is not at all surprising when one considers the degree to which men themselves were involved and how the Crusade served their own purposes. While there is no doubt that Crusaders acted on their own accord and often for personal reasons (as was the case with Eliza Thompson), men as well as women orchestrated and directed the temperance Crusade.[61] This began with Dio Lewis himself, who remained deeply involved in the movement. After he helped inaugurate the demonstrations at Washington Courthouse and Hillsboro, he was in great demand as an organizer elsewhere around the state. In several cases, those wanting to start the movement in their towns seemed to believe his presence was absolutely necessary. In Xenia, Lewis chaired the planning committee for the demonstrations there.[62] The town of Dayton relied on him to kick off its Crusade in February. When the town of Toledo appointed a committee to organize a movement, it concluded the town should "get Dr. Dio Lewis, if possible, to inaugurate it here."[63] Lewis went to Columbus twice to attempt to start a movement; the first time, his efforts were met with "little enthusiasm, which was a clear indication that the ladies of this city did not care about taking hold of the movement to any great extent." The women did meet after his departure but elected to wait for his return before taking any action.[64] By the end of February, Lewis had been deluged with so many invitations to organize Crusades around the state of Ohio and elsewhere, he had trouble replying to them all. Instead of continuing his work in Ohio, he elected to go to New England to attempt to lead a movement there.[65]

When he could not be present to assist with a Crusade, Lewis offered guidelines on how best to organize one. He suggested a town hold a meeting for those interested, at which women willing to participate, the town's clergy, and any other interested persons should be present. Attendees were to appoint several committees: one organizing committee consisting of three women and two men; an Advisory Business Committee of men only, including representatives from all churches, temperance organizations as well as other "prominent citizens"; and of course the committees of women, who would actually go out visiting saloons. A reporter and organizer, J.H. Beadle, added, "The women should do all the street work, but . . . the men . . . should neglect no opportunity" to support them, and "the ministers should be outspoken."[66]

Lewis's own involvement, these guidelines, and the countless accounts of Crusades, including Eliza Thompson's, reveal the deep involvement of men in the organization of these temperance demonstrations. This was especially true of clergy, who assumed leadership positions in many cases. In Cincinnati, the movement began with a meeting of the town's Methodist ministers, then all the ministers in the town. Although when they called a general meeting, twice as many women as men showed up, the city's clergy clearly led the proceedings and directed the women in their work.[67] The same held true in Philadelphia, where ministers, as well as prominent members of the Sons of Temperance and the YMCA, actively worked to mobilize the city's women.[68] New York's clergy did not believe the visitation method could succeed in such a large city, but they did organize women into other kinds of temperance work.[69] The report of activity in Columbus, where Lewis had tried with only mild success to rally female support, seemed to indicate that the organizational muscle was male, not female: "It was with great difficulty that enough ladies could be found who were ready to fill the official positions to which it was necessary to assign them."[70] Finally, there is Matilda Carpenter's account of her work in Washington Courthouse, Ohio, in which she stated that "from the beginning of the crusade the Temperance Association had been officered by men. 'The Women's Temperance League' was often spoken of, but, in point of fact, there was no woman's league. There was simply a Visitation Committee." She went on to say that all the mass meetings and prayer meetings surrounding the "women's movement" had been "directed . . . conducted by men."[71]

In addition to organizational work, men assisted women in their visitation in various ways. Sometimes they remained in prayer meetings while the women marched against the saloons, but often they took on a more active role, actually accompanying the women on their visits.

Mother Stewart reported that male supporters tried to provide for the women's comfort by bringing them extra shawls or coats to shield them from the cold, holding umbrellas over them, and in one case, even putting a stove on the street to help keep the women warm. At the conversion of Van Pelt, a company of men actively marched with the women and helped them pour his supply of alcohol into the street, that is until Van Pelt requested that "as this was a women's meeting, and their work, he wished the men to cross the street, with the exception of the ministers."[72] As did Dunn, the Hillsboro saloon owner who sued Mother Thompson's band of Crusaders along with their husbands, Van Pelt clearly noticed a male presence in the Crusade.

Indeed, Crusade leaders like Eliza Stewart of Springfield, Ohio welcomed and encouraged male participation. Stewart explained that the sight of men supporting the Crusaders was "a very convincing argument to the average rum-seller's mind" and maintained that "the movement was not woman's, nor man's, but God's."[73] She worked very closely with Springfield's clergy and continually urged them to solicit male assistance for the movement. "This is a hard siege work," she told them at one meeting, "We must have more help." Stewart urged the ministers to tell men "their wives would be killed in this work if they did not come to their help."[74]

Male reformers actively supported and organized the Crusade because it aided their own political work and furthered the cause as a whole. They understood the Crusade as an antidote for disillusionment with political work and as a salve for their guilt over the lack of results that work had achieved. One reformer remarked that the Crusade could be seen as "a violent reaction from the too general disuse of moral power in the past."[75] Another reformer explained that, though he had initially been critical of the Crusade, he reversed his position because of his "complete disappointment with the temperance men in the country." Specifically, he mentioned many temperance men's support in 1872 for President Grant and the Republicans.[76]

Despite the disenchantment expressed by these men and others, they had no intention of abandoning political warfare themselves. Alongside the women's marches, male temperance activists persisted in their legal and political work, petitioning state and local government for the enforcement of laws already in existence and promoting the election of prohibition candidates.[77] It is clear that the National Temperance Society continued to place emphasis on this sort of work, though the society hailed the Crusade; "through the medium of prayers and persuasive efforts of consecrated, Christian women," the movement had brought "a mighty power quickening unto life, a renewed assurance of the divine presence and strength in the temperance cause."[78] In fact, the Crusade displayed, on the surface at least, a kind of duality within the temperance movement, with women very visibly engaging in moral suasion-type activity and men continuing political pursuits behind the scenes. The NTS explained the distribution of labor: "Crusading belongs to the women, but they cannot register their vote. Thus men must try to supplement the work of the women."[79] The reason given for this division arose from the differing realms and natures of men and women. As one shopkeeper in Washington Courthouse saw things, women could "exert their moral power without hindrance" because they were "free from political entanglements." He concluded, "A hundred women can do more for a moral reform than ten thousand voters. We can only make laws, but they can touch the heart."[80] Thus, the Crusade's ideological function was to make women's work the preserve of an older, antebellum style of reform that relied on moral suasion, while men's work continued to move forward into increasingly sophisticated and aggressive political pursuits.[81]

In reality, though, women's work was not quarantined away from politics but was an integral part of the political battle over temperance. The Crusade, though it appeared to be a religious and moral movement, had a definite political function. The women's activity dramatically demonstrated who was right in the political battle against alcohol. The meek, praying women who entered saloon after saloon served as a powerful foil to those who supported those saloons.

This was especially true when saloonkeepers and their patrons mistreated the Crusaders, as they frequently did. The women suffered all sorts of indignities, from taunts to bombardments of food and drink to arrests by the police. At times, the women's treatment became violent, as it did during a Cleveland march, when a mob "rushed upon the kneeling women, kicking one badly in the side, another in the back and striking others with their fists."[82] One of the largest mob scenes connected with Crusade work was in Chicago, where several thousand people gathered to harass a group of women who had petitioned the city government there to reverse its decision to repeal the Sunday liquor law. Mrs. Moses Smith, a Crusader, listed the mob's numerous abuses toward the women: "jostling them . . . ; spitting tobacco juice on their dresses; pulling at their chignons; in some cases tripping them up; knocking the hats off their escorts—brothers, husbands, or sons—giving the latter kicks, cuffs, and digs in the ribs. . . . The most obscene phrases were bandied about; the foulest epithets were applied." The women responded with a mixture of courage and feminine recoil and frailty (at one point, several women were said to have fainted with fright). Due to the flagrant violations of gendered etiquette by the mob, Smith assessed it as "the most outrageous proceeding ever witnessed in a civilized community." "It must now be counted among the other delusions dispelled in this age, that men, no matter in what position in life, entertain a natural regard for the fair sex," she said. "The mob on last evening completely refuted this flattering unction. Savages would have shown more respect to captive Amazons. . . . It is safe to say that never before, in this country, did an equally respectable body of ladies receive such brutal treatment."[83]

In these cases, the saloon crowd played right into their opponents' hands. The Crusaders' passive resistance in the face of such behavior only heightened their moral authority and vividly contrasted them with their attackers. It also diverted attention from the argument that the women's own activity flaunted the rules of gendered propriety by placing them in the role of weak victim. Eliza Stewart claimed all such attacks on women only insulted "manhood" and made their perpetrators look like barbarians. The crusading women explicitly ordered their husbands not to retaliate on their behalf because it would elevate the position of their attackers by providing them with male opponents. In addition, the mobs would likely be less restrained if their victims were male. This was certainly true in the Cleveland incident; a man present who rushed in to defend the women was beaten to the point of permanent injury. Mother Stewart recalled men telling her "they stood with clenched fists and grinding teeth, looking on, exerting the utmost self-control to restrain themselves from rushing into that drunken mob and protecting their defenseless wives."[84] But even when and if temperance men got involved in these confrontations, the effect was no less dramatic; in those cases, temperance men appeared as heroes defending damsels in distress.

More savvy supporters of alcohol demonstrated an acute awareness of the Crusaders' political function. This was true of the saloonkeeper in Thompson's town who commented on the participation of the women's husbands and then fought back in court instead of on the street, where nothing at all could be gained. The friends of the liquor industry in Watkins, New York certainly understood the Crusade's political function; when a vote went in their favor in the summer of 1874, they celebrated by *"burn[ing] a woman in effigy"* in a very overt association of women and politics. The NTS, in an explicit revelation of the Crusade's political capital, reported the incident as proof that the Crusade gave the cause a political boost.[85]

On a grander political scale, the Crusade not only visibly contrasted "rummies" with temperance folk, it juxtaposed a native-born, Protestant culture with an immigrant, Catholic one. Historians have demonstrated that most Crusaders and their supporters were native-born and Protestant, while many, if not most, of the saloon owners and patrons they faced were immigrant and/or Catholic.[86] Those involved with the Crusade recognized this conflict as well. Annie Wittenmyer closed her history of the movement with statistics on the ethnicity of those involved in the liquor traffic. She claimed that "more than two-thirds of the entire liquor business is in the hands of a low class of foreigners, although the entire foreign population of the country constitutes less than one-sixth." She cited a study done by the Philadelphia Reform Club that found the vast majority of saloon owners to be of foreign, particularly of German or Irish, descent. Of over eight thousand liquor dealers in the city, only 205 were native-born. Wittenmyer also saw a clear connection between immigration, alcohol, and larger social problems like poverty and prostitution. She concluded, "We are slowly learning the fact that we are building jails and almshouses that ought to have been built in Germany and Ireland, and that America is rapidly becoming a sewer for the moral filth of Europe."[87]

Jack Blocker, who has written the most comprehensive study of the Crusade, argues the ethno-cultural differences between Crusaders and their opponents was accidental, pointing out instances in which Crusaders made a special effort to reach out to immigrant communities and include them in the work.[88] While these examples tend to demonstrate an absence of ethnic hatred, there is no doubt cultural conflict and prejudice played a role in the movement. Those involved in the Crusade spoke of their cultural claim on the customs and laws of the United States. Wittenmyer believed "some of the best people in our land are foreigners" but went on to describe such immigrants as "Americanized citizens who came . . . to find a home with us, and who respect our institutions and obey our laws."[89] Mother Stewart's opinions also reflected the belief that native-born culture should have pre-eminence; she even stated that if the immigrant "is not satisfied with our institutions, as he finds them, let him by all means return whence he came. . . . What right has he to claim special consideration above the native?" Stewart particularly resented the political influence immigrants had achieved on the city level and claimed, "If not arrested, this continual thrusting of the foreign element forward and above the natives in every political contest will bear its fruit not very far hence."[90] A Presbyterian minister involved with the Crusade in Hillsboro saw the battle over temperance as merging into a larger ethno-political war between "American ideas of liberty and right" and those of a "German infidel" origin. He concluded these remarks with gratitude for American women in their fight for the former.[91]

The cultural tension recognized by many Crusaders worked in tandem with the issue of gender. Proponents and opponents of the movement portrayed each other as being in violation of gendered propriety. From within the German community, which was most threatened by an attack on alcohol, emerged some of the most vocal critics of the women's behavior. While male temperance supporters hailed the crusading women as the brave defenders of morality and the pitiful victims of alcohol's ravages, German men, like Pastor Kroell of Cincinnati, "condemned the women in unmeasured terms" at a meeting of anti-temperance people in the city, attended by mostly Germans. He argued "woman's place was in the home, not on the streets." Another speaker saw the movement as an explicit attack on German culture, calling it a revival of Know-Nothingism.[92] For their part, temperance forces called attention to the immigrant character of many of the outrageous mobs that confronted female demonstrators. Wittenmyer went so far as to claim that "all the mobs that insulted the women . . . were made up largely of a criminal class of foreigners." The impropriety of these mobs' assaults on respectable Christian women was readily apparent. The fact that some of these mobs included immigrant *women* only underscored the low nature of a culture that sold and drank alcohol. An account of the Dayton, Ohio Crusade estimated that "the worst elements in these noisy mobs was the women, mostly of foreign nationalities, who joined their screaming to the shouting and swearing of their male relatives."[93]

Not only did Crusaders play an important symbolic role in a larger political conflict, they actively assisted the political aspect of the work on numerous occasions.[94] Dr. D.H. Mann's account of a Crusade in Delhi, New York demonstrates how closely women participated in political efforts. In fact, the women's work there was almost entirely of a political nature, though Mann claims it as part of the Crusade. In concert with a drive to elect anti-license officials to local government, the women canvassed door-to-door, handed out ballots, and stood outside polling places on election day. Mann credited the women with the victorious results for temperance.[95] Elsewhere, Crusaders frequently petitioned city and state governments. At a February 1874 statewide meeting of Ohio's temperance ranks, including Crusaders and their supporters, a Mrs. Coggeshall offered a resolution requesting the body appoint a committee to ask the state legislature if Crusaders could hold a meeting in the rotunda.[96] At a subsequent meeting of Ohio's temperance forces in June, female Crusaders actively supported a resolution "to fight intemperance by all means including 'political influence.'"[97] In Indiana, Crusaders began petitioning state and local governments for better enforcement of the Baxter Law, which put numerous restrictions on the sale of alcohol and allowed an alcoholic's family to sue a dealer for damages. After relaying this information to his readers, reporter and temperance supporter T.A.H. Brown provided this assurance: "Though the movement took a somewhat legal turn, it never for a moment lost its eminently religious character."[98]

Such assurance was necessary because the idea that the women's Crusade could become so overtly connected with the political movement seemed to cause deep distress in many temperance men, most notably Dio Lewis, who ardently opposed political work in general and believed female moral suasion should be the exclusive method of reform. At both the above mentioned Ohio conventions, conflict over this issue disrupted the proceedings. After the first meeting, which took place in Columbus, the presence of both Lewis and a noted prohibitionist lecturer, John Russell, left the temperance ranks in "a divided and disorganized condition." Many who had been active in the Crusade "expressed themselves as feeling very much discouraged by the way things have changed, and that a few more such meetings would be instrumental in disbanding the army of good women now engaged in the cause." The result in Columbus was that men and women conducted separate meetings. The *New York Times* surmised this would put the movement "once more . . . on a solid and permanent basis."[99] At the June convention in Springfield, Mother Stewart reported that the resolution to use political means to fight alcohol "caused a stir. . . . There was a strong fight on the resolution, or rather that one very alarming word 'political.'" She said the opposition came from the men, not the women, in attendance. A group of men even approached her to use her influence as a Crusade leader to get the word "political" removed. Believing such men put the cause at risk, she adamantly refused.[100]

The political purpose of the Crusade, as much as the sensibilities of the temperance men involved, necessitated Crusaders behave as victims or moral authorities, that their work at least *appear* apolitical, and certainly that it not be connected with anything controversial like women's rights. Crusaders themselves seemed intent on maintaining gendered propriety, as was Eliza Thompson, who not only balked at the prospect of leading the Hillsboro Crusade but refused an even more prominent role at the first statewide meeting of Crusaders in June 1874. That convention elected her to the chair, but "she very modestly requested that. . . . Bishop Walden be made Chairman in her stead."[101] Thompson's actions seemed a genuine expression of her personal style, but at times Crusaders more intentionally assured their audience that they acted strictly out of moral obligation and had no intention of revolutionizing gender roles. M.E. Winslow, the female author of a book of short stories based on the Crusade, included such assurances repeatedly. In one story, a judge involved in a case brought by a rumseller against Crusaders is inclined to rule in favor of the former, because he believes the Crusaders should be "minding their domestic concerns." His daughter takes him to a Crusade meeting, where he is at first offended by the women speakers featured. But his attitude quickly changes when a reformed drunkard who tells of the Crusaders' sympathy toward him is revealed to be the judge's long-lost son. The judge concludes, "Where men, with all their wisdom and multiplied organizations have failed, God has given the victory into women's hands, simply because they have used his weapons and trusted him." In another story, a husband and wife argue about the legality of the saloon; the wife challenged her spouse, "timidly, as accustomed to defer to the masculine head of affairs." Another tale featured a young girl who tells a male schoolmate she will not join the Crusade because she "would not presume to counsel a gentleman on any subject." Both of the characters end up overcoming their feminine recoil and timidity to join the Crusade out of a sense of divine calling.[102]

Assurances that Crusaders acted reluctantly and were wholly apolitical in their motivations belied not only the Crusaders' political function but also the complexity of the women's identities and aims. In the sea of mothers, wives, and victims marched politically-conscious women. While the best-known and most radical feminists vehemently criticized the Crusade (Elizabeth Cady Stanton said it was "little more dignified than mob law"),[103] other, more moderate women's rights supporters saw the Crusade's potential for opening up more public and political roles for women. Eliza Stewart, "Mother" though she may have been called, was one such woman. Her views and experience demonstrated the complexity of the Crusader image and how that image provided a façade for more controversial positions.

Eliza Stewart had aggressively engaged in temperance activism in the years immediately preceding the Crusade. She recalled in her memoir that she first began work on behalf of the cause as early as the 1850's, when she and her family lived in Athens, Ohio. Disturbed by the bibulous habits of University of Ohio students, she presented to several professors and ministers a paper urging the university and town to take action. Nothing came of her initial efforts, she believed, because she was a woman. At one meeting with a Presbyterian minister, she said she "realized my insignificance as I entered his presence. Why, I was nothing but a woman, and I had the temerity to approach a minister with the seeming, at least, of dictating his duty to him, and [as] he scanned my paper, I could see that something of the same thought was in his own mind."[104] Frustrated, she next attended a district meeting of clergymen and convinced one of them to read a temperance resolution for her, "very kindly concealing the fact that it emanated from a woman."[105]

But it was two decades later that her activism commenced in earnest. In January 1872, she gave a temperance address in her new home of Springfield, Ohio. It was, to her knowledge, the first temperance lecture by a woman in the town. At the time, some male temperance workers had begun a campaign to help drunkards' wives sue saloonkeepers under the 1870 Adair Law, which allowed a woman to pursue legal action against anyone who sold alcohol to a son or husband. One man in Stewart's audience, Clifton Nichols, approached her after the conclusion of her lecture and requested that she gather a group of women to attend an Adair Law trial the next day. She instead opted to go alone, for fear that most women would be offended by the trial's revelations about the unsavory world of the saloon.[106]

In court, she was surprised and a bit chagrined to be directly involved in the trial by the prosecutor, who was a friend of her family. He made the unusual request of the judge to allow Stewart to make the opening plea to the jury. The judge consented, as did Stewart, reluctantly, but "because I knew I could speak for [the plaintiff] as no man could." Her speech angered the defense attorney, most likely for its effect as much for its impropriety. He bitterly instructed the jury that it was "infamous to bring a female in to influence the court and jury," and he felt Stewart should "be ashamed to thus come into court" rather than remain at home "attending to her legitimate duties." The jury found in favor of the plaintiff, awarding her one hundred dollars. Stewart's appearance caused "a sensation" and much grief for the defense attorney, who was teased mercilessly by the city's male contingent "for letting an old lady beat him."[107] The defense repealed the ruling in a higher court, where Stewart was barred from participation, but she nonetheless continued to assist the legal war against saloon owners whenever she could. The wives and mothers of alcoholics deluged her with requests for her advice and aid, and she became a fixture at Adair Law trials in the county. One defense attorney remarked that he would rather see "ten lawyers at the table than Mother Stewart."[108]

Her activism expanded beyond the courtroom as well, in ways that anticipated the Crusade. After carefully observing one saloon in Springfield violate moribund liquor laws, she decided to gather definite proof in an attempt to convince the men of Springfield to prosecute the owner. Stewart disguised herself as an old Irish woman, entered the saloon, and purchased a glass of whisky. In selling it to her, the owner violated two Ohio statutes, one prohibiting the sale of alcohol by the glass and another banning its sale on Sunday. She immediately took the glass to a nearby temperance meeting and made a rousing speech urging legal action against the saloon.[109]

By the time Dio Lewis arrived in Springfield in February 1874, Stewart had already helped organize the town's women as Crusaders and was the natural choice for their leader. But as in Hillsboro, Stewart and the other women had much male help behind the scenes. At an initial meeting in January 1874, Rev. J.W. Spring presided and organized the women of the town in preparation for saloon visitation. Next, a committee of three men submitted recommendations, which urged the men of Springfield to continue political and organizational work while the women demonstrated at saloons. Of the actual crusading, his recommendations concluded, "We deem it important to keep this work in the hands of the women of our city." When Lewis arrived, he encouraged the reorganization of the Crusade efforts into a committee of three women and three men, who would cooperate on planning strategies and the mobilization of the town's women.[110]

Unlike many other Crusaders, Thompson for instance, Stewart's views on gender matched her actions. By the time of the Crusade, she "had long since learned that woman was not man's equal before the law" and believed women deserved full political equality. But these were not principles that she, nor others involved who were like-minded, declared loudly for fear it would disrupt their work by splitting the movement. She explained that women with conservative notions of their place "were sufficiently numerous in the beginning of our work to make a great deal of trouble." Those with more progressive views "were reticent about it."[111] Therefore, she kept her progressive views to herself and instead projected another public image—that of a pious, Christian mother. This was not mere calculation; a sincere and dedicated faith fueled her work as strongly as any views on women's rights. She considered her temperance activism "working for Jesus," the flowering of a divinely imparted "sympathetic nature, a heart easily affected by the sufferings even of the lowliest brute of creation." It was this aspect of Stewart's motivation that seemed to surround her, as reflected in her nickname of "Mother." She seemed an angelic figure to those who witnessed her work, and the response to her, even among "the worst rummies and saloonists," amounted "almost to love or hero worship."[112]

It is unclear how "Mother" Stewart acquired her nickname, whether it was given to her or whether she created it for herself. But it was undoubtedly equal measures of sincere expression and pleasing veneer, just as Stewart's work was both personal and political, and the Crusader image itself both spontaneous outpouring and tactical concoction. On either side of the equation, the image performed a valuable function, as it allowed thousands of women a public outlet for their personal convictions and the movement an emotional, nostalgic spectacle for its political struggle. Indeed, the Crusader could be seen as redeeming that struggle from a mire of failure, confusion, and doubt. The image—the icon—of the Crusader would continue to perform a valuable function, as the movement became organization, as the Crusade became the Woman's Christian Temperance Union. The Crusader would serve as a device to build a broad, political coalition for prohibition. Temperance reformers of various stripes could embrace it and agree upon it in the Gilded Age, just as they had contested and warred over the self-made man in antebellum America.

Chapter Five
A "Knitting Together of Hearts:"
The Crusader, the WCTU, and the Building of a Temperance Coalition

> "What a sequel is this to your Romance of the Crusade! Was there ever such knitting together of hearts as this temperance work has accomplished? 'In essentials unity; in non-essentials liberty; in all things charity.' ... O! may the crusade fire be newly lighted on the altar of each heart."
>
> —Frances Willard, 1878[1]

In August 1874, a national Sunday School convention met on Lake Chautauqua in New York. A group of Crusaders were among the attendees, and as they exchanged tales of saloon visitation, "'their hearts burned within them,' and new thoughts took possession of their minds"—thoughts of transmitting the spirit of the Crusade into a national organization. They immediately went to work brainstorming and planning. As with the Crusade, male support aided their efforts. The women enlisted John Heyl Vincent, the Methodist minister who had organized the Chautauqua convention, to help them plan and publicize a national women's temperance convention to be held in Cleveland that November.[2]

The meeting that subsequently convened, however, was a "woman's convention;" although scores of men attended as guests and curious onlookers, they were excluded from voting and membership. The women managed the proceedings with a self-conscious femininity, surprising themselves with their professionalism and priding themselves in the "rare sweetness ... blessed communion ... and great social enjoyment" they exhibited. Eliza Thompson represented her district almost blushingly and maintained that were it not for the undeniable propriety—the "gentle, sweet, cultured womanhood"—of the Ohio state president, she would not have attended, "for Conventions had always been associated in my mind with men of business, of Church or State, and especially with political nominations." Her inner conviction that the cause urgently needed women's assistance prompted her to step outside the conventional, just as it had led her to visit the saloons of Hillsboro.[3]

As the women present explored the relative novelty of female organization and administration, they made clear that their work was simply the next phase of the Crusade. The Committee on the Plan of Work expressed its belief in women's special moral power, that they had been "set apart as the apostles of the Temperance Gospel." The delegates agreed that their work would be primarily in the vein of moral suasion, through visitation, "gospel temperance" meetings, publication (women were by 1875 writing the majority of temperance tracts), and children's programs in public schools and Sunday Schools. Resolutions appealing to voters, lawmakers, churches, clergymen, and physicians to honor the principles of total abstinence were, in their final form, polite, gentle, and moderate. There was little talk of politics and none of woman suffrage. The nearest the convention approached to such issues was a resolution stating that since most legislators were either drinkers themselves or controlled by the forces of drink, "the women of the United States in this convention represented do hereby express their unqualified disapprobation of . . . placing intemperance men in office."[4] The choice of Annie Turner Wittenmyer as the Woman's Christian Temperance Union's first president also demonstrated the new organization's Crusader origins. Famed for her Civil War philanthropy, Wittenmyer, a middle-aged widow and pious Christian, was reluctant to take the organization into political work and maintained that woman suffrage would "strike a fatal blow at the home." She believed society could still be reformed through women working in antebellum fashion, winning one individual at a time.[5]

The ideological basis for the WCTU likewise traded on the Crusade's roots in antebellum "true womanhood." Women were specially suited to this work because they were morally superior, physically weak, and highly religious. WCTU speakers and writers made much of their feminine constraints. Wittenmyer told the national convention in 1875, "We are so weak that we are forced to trust God and to lean upon his almighty arm, from whence cometh our strength."[6] Women were like empty vessels waiting to be filled with divine power. So important was the spiritual nature of women's work, the 1876 national convention adopted two resolutions urging that any increase in the level and variety of the organization's activities should never come at the expense of "the spiritual aspect of our work."[7]

When it came to the issue of women's social constraints, any challenge was pained and reluctant, as it had been during the Crusade. Writers and speakers seemingly had to plead with the mass of retiring, respectable women to "leave your cherished sphere" and respond to the urgent, extraordinary calling to save the nation's soul.[8]

Though the organization began as an extension of the Crusade, by the end of the 1870's the WCTU clearly contained reformers and asserted positions that seemed decidedly at odds with that heritage. Whereas the image of the Crusader rested upon the use of moral suasion, the WCTU almost immediately and forcefully began to delve into political work. In addition, the organization openly promoted woman suffrage and women's social and economic equality; the Crusader embodied female domesticity, morality, and victimhood. But the careful maintenance of the Crusader façade—by the WCTU's second president, Frances Willard, by the organization's overall culture, and by the male temperance movement—allowed the WCTU not only to mask and contain potential conflict directly pertaining to these issues, it allowed the organization to serve a vital political function for the movement as a whole. In the late nineteenth century, the WCTU would partner closely with the male movement for prohibition, continually imbuing its work with the aura of Christian morality. The organization would help build a national coalition for prohibition and forward the cause of sectional reconciliation. It would also provide a vehicle for establishing a racial and ethnic consensus at a time when American society faced deep divisions and anxieties surrounding new cultural realities.

The Crusade itself took place amidst a growing dispute over the temperance movement's increasing reliance on prohibition and its abandonment of moral suasion. The Crusade helped contain this conflict by showcasing moral suasion and delegating it to female reformers. But the debate over prohibition heated up again as the WCTU began delving into politics. At the WCTU's opening convention in 1874, its chair, Jennie Willing, told the audience she felt they had "no need to be reminded that this is simply and only a religious movement.... Many are praying for us."[9] But in fact there was already discussion of the organization's support for prohibition. As one delegate from Indiana explained, it was "not for us to say, 'Keep out of politics.' The other side forces it there if we do not."[10] By the following year, Annie Wittenmyer had backed away from her initial opposition to political work and approved a petition drive to Congress urging opposition to license laws.[11] When a delegation of male and female reformers presented the petition to Congress, Wittenmyer herself testified before a Senate Committee.[12] Under Willard, the WCTU increased its political work enormously, and by the early 1880's she attempted to marshal prohibitionists and the remnants of the Prohibition Party into a new Home Protection Party.[13]

The WCTU's prohibition work, as well as prohibition in general, was controversial and at times provoked open conflict. Many southerners shied away from supporting legal measures, especially on the federal level, and believed women in particular should stay clear of political work.[14] In 1889, a small group of WCTU women, many of them southerners, walked out of the annual convention and established an alternative, non-political temperance organization.[15] Within the temperance movement as a whole, prohibition continued to have opponents. Howard Crosby persisted in his opposition to both prohibition and the NTS's insistence on total abstinence as the only standard for temperance.[16] Reformers like Dio Lewis, who openly broke with the WCTU in 1883, believed prohibition violated personal liberty and polluted women's moral influence.[17]

The prohibition issue informed the even more controversial issue of woman suffrage. From its inception, the WCTU's membership included advocates of woman suffrage, some of them quite prominent, like Mary Livermore, who served as the president of the Massachusetts WCTU from its creation and was well-known as an orator and reformer by the mid-1870's.[18] Others, like Mother Stewart, more subtly supported suffrage and only occasionally made it an issue, since the majority of the women involved in the organization were not yet comfortable with that position.[19] But at times suffrage supporters explicitly aired their beliefs. At the WCTU's second annual convention in 1875, Zerelda Wallace introduced a resolution urging that prohibition be "submitted to all adult citizens, irrespective of race, color or sex." Although the resolution couched this appeal in the context of women's suffering due to the traffic and confined the call for women's political participation to the issue of alcohol, it nonetheless demonstrated a possible confluence between the WCTU and a call for women's rights.[20]

Frances Willard's own suffragist beliefs predated her temperance activism and put her at odds with Annie Wittenmyer and others who opposed woman suffrage during the WCTU's early years. At first, Willard deferred to Wittenmyer's authority as president and agreed with Wittenmyer about "keeping suffrage out." But so strong was Willard's belief that temperance required woman suffrage that she wrote to Wittenmyer in 1876, "I don't know how long I can 'stand it' to withhold the very best word I have to offer."[21] That same year, Willard professed her beliefs to the national organization against the wishes of the WCTU president. Feminists hailed her stance; Susan B. Anthony wrote Willard with congratulations that she had "at last ... obliged the 'inner light'" instead of heeding "timid, conservative *human* counsels."[22] Within the WCTU, the response was not quite so warm. Her speech ignited a three-year tug-of-war between Willard's and Wittenmyer's supporters that ended when the organization elected Willard president in 1879.[23]

Willard's triumph hardly disposed of the woman suffrage issue; it would require her careful management for the duration of her presidency, particularly as she sought to build coalitions between divergent reformers. At the same time she maintained ties with Susan B. Anthony, Elizabeth Cady Stanton, Mary Livermore, and other prominent and outspoken feminists, she worked tirelessly to build support for the WCTU in the South, where she was constantly reminded that "the prejudices of the Southern people are all against women doing anything in public."[24] When a woman like Anna Dickinson, who was not only a feminist but an actress and a Unitarian, wrote to Willard in 1875 with interest in joining the cause, Willard told Wittenmyer, "I want the temperance women to rally around her. She may yet be all we wish as a Christian and a philanthropist."[25]

As with the prohibition issue, the suffrage issue at times threatened divides both within the organization and in the temperance movement as a whole. In 1881, a group of anti-suffragists bolted the WCTU's national convention and founded the Evangelical Temperance Association. The group maintained it did not wish to harm the cause in any way but did want to provide more opportunities to aid temperance to women who were "discouraged under the embarrassments to their work by the suffrage question."[26] At times male reformers attacked Willard for her stance on suffrage. One reformer requested a meeting with her in 1880, only to assail her for speaking to audiences that included men and to question whether she was "*a member of the church*." Anna Gordon, who reported the incident to Willard's mother, said his accusations deeply affected Willard: "The tears rushed to her eyes and her lips quivered and for a moment she could not speak."[27]

Two years later, she defended herself once again, on the pages of the *National Temperance Advocate*, after the alcohol industry claimed the WCTU was "captured by woman suffragists." In her article, Willard explained that she had always supported "equal franchise, where the vote of woman joined to that of man can alone give stability to temperance legislation." She also argued that the WCTU's Committee of Franchise only functioned in states "*that so desire*" and that the WCTU recognized "the individuality of the states." Addressing the presence of Susan B. Anthony at a recent convention, Willard assured readers it signified no "new departure" for the organization. She concluded the article with the very deliberate reminder of the WCTU's "divine origin as the organized and systematic outgrowth of the great Crusade of 1874."[28]

Willard's essay demonstrated how she and the WCTU negotiated potential conflict over suffrage and other issues. First, she put the position in question in the context of furthering the goals of the temperance movement. Second, she stated the organization's tolerance for ideological heterogeneity and local autonomy. Finally, and underlying the first two devices, Willard wielded the Crusader image to legitimize the organization. These tactics meant that the disturbances surrounding the WCTU's forays into politics and calls for woman suffrage remained relatively minor. The organization under Willard's leadership became a truly mass-movement of women and garnered the continued support and adulation of the male movement.[29]

In constructing an innocuous, consensual context for all of the WCTU's activities, Willard devised the "Home Protection" program.[30] A blending of feminism and domesticity, it envisioned a social, gendered revolution that would take place as good Christian women reformed all parts of their society to "make the whole world homelike."[31] Home Protection couched arguments for women's political and social equality in the language of female moral authority and victimhood—ideas that had deep, antebellum roots in the temperance movement and ones the Crusade dramatized. The celebration of female moral authority incorporated a more explicit Christian appeal than had the antebellum movement. Women held "the balance of moral power" in society because they were the most Christlike; "there was much womanliness in Christ and the woman side of human nature welcomed him." Willard maintained that over the centuries, Christ's "truest friends in largest numbers have been women."[32] The WCTU also accepted the idea that women were "the weaker vessels," at the mercy of "the brutality of men." This justified desperate action for self-protection, like demonstrating against saloons or petitioning the government for help. In an 1884 petition, for example, the WCTU petitioners referred to themselves as "the physically weaker sex" and begged the government to use the power women did not possess.[33]

But the rhetoric of Home Protection blended these notions with the claim of real gender equality. The WCTU took women's victim status into paths that transformed it into female empowerment. In the hands of Willard, feminine weakness underscored women's spiritual strength and men's spiritual failings, which, in the modern era, was the realm of more consequence. Applying Darwin's theories to the gendered competition for society, Willard explained that "spiritual force" had replaced physical strength in determining the survival of the fittest.[34] Likewise, Home Protection employed women's supposed moral authority to critique male dominance and urge an expanded role for women. A *Union Signal* article claimed that "men are but children of a larger growth, and a child needs a mother to tell him what and what not to eat."[35] The male-dominated society of the late nineteenth century had "long been fathered, but . . . not . . . mothered enough to make [it] normal."[36]

Woman suffrage flowed most logically from these ideals; if women were going to reform their society, they had to have some access to political power. As Willard put it, "The mother-heart must be enthroned in all places of power before its edicts will be heeded."[37] As had antebellum feminists, WCTU women, under the banner of Home Protection, argued they needed the ballot because men improperly wielded it for them and misrepresented their views and interests. Unlike antebellum feminists, however, the WCTU couched this argument in terms of the guardianship of the traditional home, social order, morality, and Protestant Christianity rather than an elevation of individual rights.[38] Willard claimed the WCTU supported suffrage for "practical reasons," to better serve its paramount goal of temperance and prohibition.[39] A representative of the WCTU to the National Temperance Convention in 1881 explicitly differentiated WCTU suffragists from feminists like Elizabeth Cady Stanton when she explained that "in no sense is the opinion held or advocated as that wedge driven into the best interests of society technically known as 'woman's rights.' Our commission is to 'tell the brethren,' not as enemies, not as belligerents, but as sisters, children of one God."[40]

Despite the careful distinction, Willard and other WCTU activists supported numerous feminist causes—like dress reform, better access to education, and expanded occupations for women—using moral arguments. In *How to Win: A Book for Girls,* Willard condemned corsets and "unnatural" means of attaining beauty, saying they subverted God's laws for the body, restricted the freedom of women and prevented their efficacy in society.[41] She encouraged girls to set high goals for themselves, to educate themselves and cultivate their gifts, and to aim as high as they could occupationally. Again, Willard put women's advancement in moral terms. In Willard's estimation, if middle- and upper-class women could achieve eminent positions, it left more jobs open to working-class women, "who, but for the vacancy thus afforded [them] in the world's close, crowded ranks, might be tempted into paths of sin."[42] In addition, as women entered more fields of life and more occupations, they would reform them with "refinement, compassion and conscience." She felt it was particularly important that women make inroads in the field of journalism, which she considered second only to philanthropy as the "natural calling" of women. Female journalists might use the media as woman's "pulpit . . . from which she can comfort humanity's heart" and lead it onto higher paths.[43]

With regard to women's social and economic equality, the issue that held the most danger for Willard and the WCTU was that of divorce. Willard posited an egalitarian view of marriage; she contended that women should establish themselves as individuals before marrying, that marriage should be based purely on affection, and that within marriage "natural law" dictated a balance of power.[44] By the 1890's, she had gone further, arguing women should at least have some input as various states considered the alteration of divorce laws. She also advocated women's sexual rights within marriage and for the equal custody of children. But neither she, nor the organization as a whole, ever reached the point of supporting no-contest divorce.[45]

This position was of great importance for the viability of the WCTU, and the issue illuminates Home Protection, and the Crusader image it embodied, as a consensus-building device. While suffrage and other feminist reforms could be couched in the language of domesticity and morality, there was no way to do this with divorce. If the WCTU claimed "Home Protection" as its overall mission, it could not endorse measures that might endanger the family by fundamentally redefining it. WCTU activist Mary Livermore did attempt to link divorce reform to the millennial vision of "Home Protection." When marriage could be based solely on the "irresistible magnetism of pure affection," it would be the blessing God intended it to be and become the basis for an "Eden come again to man."[46] But even Livermore maintained marriage was indeed the "everlasting granite on which the whole world rests" and did not endorse no-contest divorce; only in extreme violations—which included a husband's habitual drunkenness—did it become the "lesser evil."[47]

The WCTU's position on divorce must also be seen in the context of the general social climate relative to this issue. The postbellum years saw an upsurge in the number of divorces and renewed efforts by conservative reformers to shore up the American family.[48] Samuel Dike was one such reformer. A Congregationalist minister, he served as the corresponding secretary for the New England Divorce Reform League and later the National Divorce Reform League, both of which petitioned lawmakers for more stringent divorce laws. He served alongside such temperance notables as William Dodge and Leonard Bacon, both officers in the antebellum American Temperance Union and in its successor, the National Temperance Society, and Dike himself actively engaged in the temperance cause. Dike believed the family was "*the* unitary form of society," that on marriage rested "the whole order of civil life." He was disturbed that the "evil of Divorce" grew commonplace in the United States, particularly in the socially progressive states of New England. On these points, he would not find any disagreement with the women of the WCTU, neither would he find opposition to his belief that intemperance was a major enemy to marriage and the family and caused a great number of divorces. His conviction that the solution to the problem was not the moderation of divorce laws, but the prohibition of alcohol would find much support among WCTU women as well.[49]

But Dike was a gender conservative. Rather than viewing an expanded role for women as a mechanism to strengthen the home, he blamed the "new woman" of the Gilded Age for its destruction. He believed that "civil society ... is an aggregation of families" and that women's new status asserted too much "individuality" and threatened the family as a communal institution.[50] He included in this women's new position in the temperance movement and feared it would bleed into a greater gendered revolution. For instance, if society allowed women to vote on temperance, "why not let her vote to protect rights in labor? Does not the logic of the case push you to that position?" He argued women had "their rights to a well supplied home in the *wages* of their husband . . . and to a temperate home by the *vote* of the husband. . . . Let *his vote and his labor* be adequate to the necessities of the family."[51]

Despite the gulf between their views on women's roles, Willard was able to make common cause with Dike and his organization. She twice invited him to speak at WCTU conventions in the 1880's and promised him she would introduce any resolutions he submitted "on your specialty" to the convention, which, she reminded him, would be a large and influential assembly of three hundred women from forty states. But she added the proviso that she would introduce only those resolutions that "do not conflict with our settled opinion on woman's ballot as a 'Home Protection' weapon." She concluded her second letter by congratulating him "on your most beneficent work for the Home."[52] This correspondence reveals how Home Protection served as an ideological glue that melded various sorts of reformers together under the Crusader image.

Another way Willard and the WCTU accomplished the semblance of unity was by conversely promoting ideological diversity. While the national organization expanded in size and scope, it continued to emphasize local autonomy and individual initiative. Local chapters raised and spent most of the WCTU's money. Beyond paying dues and championing temperance, a local union had the liberty to pursue any work it chose, whether it be "helping the poor, or smoothing the path of wage-workers, or in any wise co-operating with other groups of good people who are trying to make the community happier, healthier and better."[53] Giving each union the freedom to construct its own agenda was one way the WCTU cultivated participation across regional lines, particularly in the more conservative South.[54] Local unions also approved their own membership, elected their own officers, and settled their own disputes. Willard stated that the national officers had "no authority whatever over local unions. All our methods are suggestive, not authoritative; they are meant to be a help, leaving each local group free to develop its own individuality."[55]

The WCTU fostered individuality in each member as well. No matter how large the organization became, it remained reliant on individual volunteers. Organization existed to provide an effective outlet for each woman's talents, not to stifle or rule over them. Writing in 1891, Willard expressed the WCTU's desire for "a simplicity and unity of organization . . . freedom from red tape," the preservation of individual responsibility and activity, and the use of each individual's special gifts.[56] In this spirit, the organization replaced committees with one-woman superintendences, which Willard felt maximized individual initiative. Using each woman's particular talents increased "beyond all computation the aggregate of the work accomplished" and provided the basis for an ever expanding program of reform.[57]

This program—called by Willard "Do Everything" reform—involved the organization in a flurry of new enterprises. This demonstrated the hope for a broad reform of society, but it perhaps insured, too, that there was a reform for each member, no matter where they resided on the ideological spectrum. A list of WCTU departments in Willard's 1895 "Do Everything" handbook might easily exhaust the reviewer: "Evangelism, . . . Juvenile work, Temperance instruction, Sunday School work, Literature, Fairs, Penal, . . . Purity, Peace and International Arbitration, Legislation and Petitions, Franchise, Systematic Giving, Anti-Opium, Work with Sailors, Work with Police, Savings Banks, . . . Relationship of Temperance to Labor and Capital aims, and others."[58] As this enumeration makes clear, the WCTU offered women a variety of ways to contribute to the cause, no matter their personal beliefs or persuasions or how much they conformed to or diverged from the Crusader image.

WCTU officers noticed and sometimes complained about the organization's lack of uniformity. In 1880, Esther Pugh, the editor of the WCTU publication *Our Union,* voiced her dissatisfaction to Willard's secretary Anna Gordon. "Every man or woman has done that which is good in his own eyes long enough," she wrote. She believed that unless the organization insisted on "a more systematic, concentrated, crystallized pronunciation or enunciation," the temperance cause as a whole might be damaged. In particular, she thought that the WCTU should insist that all members support the "temperance ballot," that is, allowing women to vote on matters pertaining to alcohol's sale and manufacture. Nonetheless, Willard continued to allow individual chapters a great deal of autonomy as a way of securing as much support as possible.[59]

Besides her creation of Home Protection and her pursuit of ideological heterogeneity, Willard intentionally paraded the Crusader image as a means of harmonizing the WCTU's, and the temperance movement's, various cultures. Willard vigorously preserved the memory of the Crusade at the center of her organization's life and bathed all the WCTU did in the nostalgic glow of its legacy. Nowhere was this more clearly seen than in Willard's relationship with Eliza Thompson. With Willard's dogged encouragement, Thompson made a career out of her status as a "Mother of the Crusade." Willard fostered a close relationship with Thompson, vigorously urged her presence at conventions, and solicited articles and Crusade items from her. At times, Willard's invitations sounded more like urgent pleas, as when she wrote to Thompson in September 1889, begging her attendance at the National Convention: "You *must* be with us . . . whatever the cost to us. . . . You shall be taken good care of and I guess we can make it without expense to you."[60] The next year, she again wanted her at the convention and asked her to bring the Bible from which she had been reading when inspired to join the Crusade ("the Crusade Bible") and to wear the shawl she had worn on her first visits to the saloons in 1874 ("the Crusade Shawl").[61] The next several years brought numerous appeals from Willard. In 1892, she requested that Thompson record her story "in your best and clearest voice" on phonograph for duplication and distribution "far and wide."[62] At times, Willard enlisted Thompson's daughter in attaining her services. Commenting in a March 1890 letter to Marie Thompson Rives on a recent article Thompson had written for the *Union Signal,* Willard urged Marie to "keep her at it from time to time; whatever *she* writes is read with so much interest by our dear white ribboners."[63]

Thompson's importance to Willard became most obvious when the WCTU faced controversy. When the organization experienced the 1889 schism over its political work, Mother Thompson reaffirmed her support for Willard's leadership and the continuity between the WCTU and the Crusade by symbolically draping the "Crusade Shawl" around Willard's shoulders.[64] After this incident and at Willard's request, Thompson wrote a defense of the organization that was published in the *Union Signal* and as a pamphlet entitled, "Mother Thompson on the Situation." She first reminded her readers of her domestic credentials and that her

Crusade work had been a significant departure for her. Although it might be expected that she should be against anything but "real, old style Crusade work," she supported the direction Willard had moved the organization, as the times demanded an increasingly aggressive role for women on behalf of the cause. "I declare myself in hearty sympathy with our National Union and its leader, as I was the morning when (against all my human tastes) I yielded to the divine call and led out the little praying band of seventy earnest women."[65] Similarly, as Willard set her sights on organization in the South, she enlisted Thompson's aid. In preparation for a large WCTU convention in Nashville, Tennessee in 1887, Willard sent Mother Thompson a rather demanding invitation that read, "*Don't fail us* at Nashville—we must have you on *southern soil.*"[66] She clearly felt it was important to have a visible reminder of the Crusade heritage as she brought the WCTU to the South. Additionally, Willard also sent another Crusade heroine, Mother Stewart, on a southern tour in 1882, ahead of her own visit the following year.[67]

But Thompson was Willard's most willing accomplice, as Willard did all in her power to sustain the memory of the Crusade within the WCTU and to keep it ever associated with the organization it spawned. Thompson's cooperation served her own needs as much as it did Willard's; the financial difficulties Thompson's family experienced in the 1860's apparently persisted into her old age, and the WCTU usually compensated her for her work.[68] She admitted to her daughter in 1893 that she felt as if she had already exhausted her Crusade work in her writings and would not think of continuing on in this endeavor "were it not for the constant need of money."[69] This need induced Thompson to maintain a grueling schedule of WCTU duties even after her age and health became an impediment. When all other "celebrities"—as Willard tellingly called the old Crusaders—failed to come through for an event, Thompson, it seemed, could be relied upon. Willard's secretary, Alice Briggs, remarked in an 1892 letter that included yet another invitation to a WCTU event, "It seems to be that it will require no further urging since you always seem ready and willing to grant whatever [Willard] asks."[70]

If Thompson was her star, Willard made sure she shone as brightly as possible. When a dispute over where the Crusade had begun threatened to topple Eliza's hometown of Hillsboro from pre-eminence, Willard weighed in on the side of Hillsboro as the "cradle" of the movement. "The record is made and nothing can change it," she assured Thompson and promised the incident was the end of the disruption over the "distribution of honors."[71] By the time old age and infirmity limited Thompson's work, she had achieved, with Willard's assistance, near mythic status. One of her last engagements came in December of 1893, when a delegation of five hundred temperance workers visited the now homebound Thompson at her residence in Hillsboro. She reminded them that "the woman's crusade against whisky came not by might or by power, but by my work, saith the Lord of Hosts." Her visitors then greeted her in a long procession. To the ladies present, she blew kisses, and once she accidentally offered the gesture to a man. Ever the retiring Crusader, Thompson caught herself. "I suppose I shouldn't kiss my hands to the men," she admitted, "But I do love to see them in this cause, and besides, I am so near to heaven it won't matter."[72] She died in 1905, hailed as "an example of what a good woman can do."[73]

Thanks to the iconic position the Crusader image continued to hold within the WCTU, the male temperance movement equally hailed the organization. In fact, in their praise, male reformers contributed to the Crusader's preservation. Men agreed that the very existence of an all-woman, mass-based organization like the WCTU was "one of the supreme fruits of the Gospel of our Lord Jesus Christ."[74] The adulation came despite the widely varying opinions among male reformers on women's rights and the WCTU's forays into that field of endeavor. Temperance noteworthy Joseph Cook wrote to Willard in 1879 that although his position on woman suffrage was "not as advanced" as some, he did support allowing women to vote on matters pertaining to temperance. "God speed the cause of Home Protection by woman's temperance ballot!" he enthusiastically concluded.[75] When Bishop Andrews of Washington, D.C. addressed the 1881 WCTU convention, he made clear that he did not support woman suffrage but nonetheless believed "there can be no such gathering of true and loyal women as are here gathered ... but out of it shall come good for us and for the nation."[76] Others in the NTS supported woman suffrage without equivocation and commended Willard for employing the WCTU to that end.[77] When Willard wrote the article for the *National Temperance Advocate* almost apologizing for Susan B. Anthony's presence at a recent WCTU convention, the paper's editor wondered why she would feel the need to do so, given Anthony's loyal support for the cause.[78]

Male reformers of various stripes overlooked any objectionable content of the WCTU and instead affirmed its Crusader image because that image, and the organization as a whole, greatly benefited their own position. With that image in tact, women brought moral authority to bear on any battle the movement encountered. For example, when Howard Crosby attacked the NTS's total abstinence stance and claimed the organization misused the Bible, the NTS called on WCTU activist J. Ellen Foster to reply. Employing her Crusader credentials (though she was in fact an attorney, not a housewife), she claimed Crosby's attack was "the latest marshalling of forces against the home." She specifically addressed Crosby's claim that total abstinence was an "unmanly" admission of weakness. She told a story of a mother who asks her son to sign the pledge, and he replies, "'Tis unmanly, mother, a strait-jacket and beneath my self-respect."[79] In this case, Foster defended both the temperance credentials of the NTS as well as the masculinity of its reformers by employing the moral authority and femininity of the WCTU and its claim to act on behalf of the home. Foster was not the only woman to do so in the case of Crosby; the *National Temperance Advocate* included articles by other WCTU members answering Crosby's attack.[80]

In addition to the moral support the male movement garnered from the WCTU, the organization actively cooperated with its male counterparts on a regular basis. Ohio's WCTU, for instance, often worked closely with male temperance forces in the state. When the WCTU proposed to assist the men's drive for a local option law by furnishing free lunches on election day, the men gladly accepted. In 1883, all Ohio's temperance organizations banded together to form a State Central Committee to coordinate efforts toward a prohibitory amendment to the state constitution and the destruction of the license system.[81] On the national level, virtually every temperance delegation to Congress included WCTU women, every petition drive was a joint venture of the NTS and WCTU, and every temperance convention, whether conducted by the WCTU or the NTS, included representatives of both, as well as of other male organizations, like the Sons of Temperance and the Good Templars.[82]

In addition, the WCTU aided the temperance movement's creation of a broad political coalition of people from different racial, ethnic, class, and sectional backgrounds through the use of its feminine, domesticated image. The organization strengthened the bonds between the temperance movement and labor through programs aimed at helping the poor and formed an alliance with the Knights of Labor.[83] Willard referred to temperance, woman suffrage, and the labor movement as the "sacred trinity of reform."[84] Just as she did the former two, Willard put the labor movement in the context of home protection. With workers' wages so abysmal, their wives and children often had to work, which endangered their health and weakened the home.[85] By 1890, Willard's ideas had evolved into Christian Socialism, a perspective enhanced by her reading of Edward Bellamy's *Looking Backward*. Capitalism violated Christianity in her estimation, as it rewarded the oppression of others for selfish gain. The nation's growing wealth should be something shared by all, "a national flower that shall glorify the common roadside of the common people's life."[86] While Willard's opinions were probably in advance of most in the temperance movement, she was able to gain support for labor among temperance folk through her use of Christianity, morality, and domesticity in forwarding her views.[87] Conversely, the WCTU gained support among labor for temperance and moral reforms by placing them in the context of worker's rights. For example, the organization argued that Sabbath Laws, which included prohibitions on alcohol's sale on Sunday, were needed in order to ensure workers one day a week for "home rest."[88] In building bridges between labor and temperance using domesticity, the WCTU provided political might for prohibition forces, as they confronted the "unholy monopoly" of the alcohol industry.[89]

More significantly, the WCTU's Crusader image helped the movement build bridges between the North and the South. This reconciliation was vital to the movement's goal of achieving national prohibition; as the report on "Southern Work" at the 1879 WCTU convention stated, "There will be little hope of securing Congressional legislation until the South united with us in such a demand."[90] All the major temperance organizations at the time—the Good Templars, the Sons of Temperance, the NTS, and the WCTU—made the South a major arena of activity, with notable success. WCTU annual reports consistently told of new chapters, new publications, and the fading of "prejudice" against women's work.[91] The NTS, too, reported the "incredible" growth of work in the South and some successes, such South Carolina's 1881 ban on the sale of alcohol within city limits.[92] Though practical considerations played a major role in the temperance movement's southern outreach, these efforts can also be seen in the context of a larger cultural yearning for national reconciliation. David Blight, Heather Richardson, and Nina Silber have demonstrated the pervasive influence of "romantic reunion" in American culture during the postwar years. The temperance movement, as it employed the language of reunion for its own political ends, served the function of reunion as well.[93]

The WCTU became a construction site for a discourse of reunion, and the Crusader image facilitated this process, as it masked the organization's feminist elements and emphasized a common sisterhood of morality, Christianity, and suffering.[94] At WCTU conventions, northern speakers repeatedly informed their southern sisters that alcohol was the "scourge of North and South," that "all over our beautiful land the blight has fallen," and that "it is women who suffer and weep; it is for them to work in faith and prayer."[95] Though the men of the North and South had once opposed each other on a military battlefield, the women of the nation, "the gentle, soft-voiced creatures who are afraid of guns and gunpowder," could "march side by side" on a "moral battle-ground."[96] The new battle facing the nation was one for "American civilization," that "North and South [might] rejoice in the downfall of this last great slavery and this last great National curse."[97] As good Christian women, northern and southern, came together to fight alcohol, they also stood to destroy another curse: "That sectionalism which is so dangerous to the welfare of our country."[98] As Mother Stewart declared at the WCTU's 1880 convention, the organization's southern temperance work might be "our new national peace policy."[99] Frances Willard agreed, speculating that "what statesmen have notably failed to achieve in uniting the two sections, will be slowly wrought out of the prayers and work of Christian womanhood North and South in defense of their tempted loved ones and imperiled homes."[100]

Southern women joined the call for unity through temperance, too. Sallie Chapin of South Carolina gave an emotional address at the WCTU's 1882 convention, a gathering that prominently featured the issue of national unity and symbolically took place in the nation's capital. Chapin told the audience she came "to ask for a place and to speak for my people." She almost pled with audience for their hospitality and reception: "I wanted to come inside. I want you to know us. We do not know one another. . . . We have come for this place inside of your hearts. We want you inside ours. . . . If you knew us better you would love us more." She wished for the restoration of peace between North and South and believed it would come "through the women." She concluded with a poem that spoke of the tragedy of the war and the hope that women's work "for our cause, for home, for God" might bridge "the cruel gulf by carnage made."[101]

A major theme of Chapin's address, and of the push for reunion by the movement as a whole, was that of race. She painted a sad picture of the freedmen's demise since emancipation. While under slavery they had been "naturally religious," they were now "demoralized" by their pursuit of freedom, drinking being one of its manifestations. She erroneously asserted that "you never saw a slave drunk," but "now the best of them get drunk." "Taught by barroom teachings they speak flippantly of sacred things, and they say they want whiskey and more of it," she lamented. She questioned their so-called "freedom," asserting the former slaves were "in far more abject slavery than we ever held them in." While "Christian owners" treated their slaves as "a responsibility greater than children," the federal government had ended the guardianship of masters without replacing that authority. "Who is responsible for them now?" Chapin asked. She urged prohibition as "the duty of the nation" in part to rein in the behavior of the former slaves. North and South "could work together" in this endeavor.[102] With her speech, Chapin used the language of temperance to present the southern view of slavery, freedom, and race—that slavery was a benevolent system of caring for those who could not care for themselves, that freedom was destroying the former slaves, and that the poor choices they made as free men threatened the nation.

By presenting this view, Chapin tacitly requested her audience's agreement and made southern participation in the cause conditional upon it. The WCTU faced the challenge of balancing race and section, a problem with which the movement as a whole had been wrestling since the 1860's. By the 1880's, a major theme of men's prohibition work continued to be the obstacle posed by southern blacks. But unlike in the 1860's, temperance reformers included few positive portrayals of blacks in their reports and seemed to acquiesce to the white southern view of the former slaves. The NTS claimed that "all the colored people drink nearly," that even black church members and clergy drank, and that black voters were responsible for defeating prohibitory legislation in many southern states.[103] Regarding local option laws pending in Virginia and North Carolina, NTS Secretary J.N. Stearnes predicted, "The majority of whites will probably support the law, but the colored people are against it."[104] Another reformer argued that southern blacks had been "alarmed and misled by unscrupulous and designing demagogues . . . to vote almost solidly with their whiskey enemies." He concluded that black voters would be a "dangerous obstruction" as the movement set their sights on national legislation.[105] Rev. Theodore Cuyler argued that political setbacks for temperance in the South were due to both parties "taking off their hats and bowing to their brother Sambo and Pompey for his vote."[106] Of course, by the time reformers offered these interpretations, southern blacks had virtually lost the free exercise of their political rights, and therefore it was unlikely their votes were responsible for any defeats prohibition suffered in southern states.[107] But temperance reformers more than ignored these facts, they forwarded the opposite interpretation, that blacks enjoyed their fair share of political power but lacked the good morals to use it properly. Cuyler asked his audience what the "real danger of the freedmen" truly was: "Social oppression? No; that day has gone by. Political wrong? No; thank God that day has gone by." He concluded that the forces of alcohol were in fact their worst enemy and that of the nation by the depravity produced in the former slaves.[108]

Echoing southern whites in voicing fears of black freedom, blaming prohibition's failures on blacks, and ignoring abuses to black civil rights stood to increase support for prohibition in the white South. However, this rhetoric represented not simply a political strategy of making common cause with white southerners but a genuine concern for the problem of alcohol in the newly freed black community. And acquiescing too much to white southerners might completely alienate blacks from the temperance movement and worsen what temperance reformers believed to be a real drinking problem among African Americans. For this reason, the NTS made overtures to black ministers and other black reformers during this same period. When the organization held a series of meetings on drinking among the freedmen, African American reformers addressed the gatherings and agreed that "the whole Christian culture and the progress of this race is in danger from this drink demon."[109] One black reformer argued alcohol was "the greatest curse to our people and the most determined enemy to our progress. Worse than poverty, worse than ignorance." Indeed, it was a "*second slavery.*"[110]

However, though all—black and white reformers, northern and southern—could agree that drinking among the former slaves posed a major danger to society and a potential political pitfall for prohibition, for African American community leaders, temperance continued to inform the problem of racism and the principle of equality as it had during the antebellum years. Temperance would help the black community "[keep] pace with all other people" and generate "social equality."[111] The point at which white reformers ignored the issue of "social equality" was where any kind of racial consensus the movement tried to achieve exploded. For instance, the NTS's support for segregated lodges in the Good Templars enraged black reformers. The African Methodist Episcopal Church's paper, *The Christian Recorder,* called the North American Grand Lodge "The Negro Driving Right Worthy Grand Lodge" and blasted white reformers for denying that "prejudice against the colored man is *the* great sin of the United States." "Colored people do not enjoy the rights guaranteed them by the amendments to the Constitution," wrote one black minister, "They are kept down, and even ku-kluxed and hunted to death like beasts. . . . And there is no redress."[112] For the white movement, bent on building a broad political coalition that might produce victories for prohibition, any such redress would completely alienate southern whites and defeat the cause on the national level. Any outreach to the black community had to be purely pragmatic and void of inflammatory language concerning racial equality.

As the temperance movement sought to build a racial consensus that would benefit its political work, the WCTU played an important role. The organization's Crusader image added domesticity and femininity to the cohesive power of temperance. The organization forwarded two contradictory racial discourses bound together by a common gendered thread. On the one hand, the WCTU promoted the idea of a broad, inclusive sisterhood that reached out to women of all races and ethnicities. On the other, it utilized the bonds of race and ethnicity to gain support for temperance among white, native-born women.

Regarding the first point, there is no question that the organization under Willard became more racially inclusive and made greater efforts to reach out to African Americans and to immigrants. The WCTU actively tried to include immigrants in their work and to counter stereotypes about them. In the 1880's, the organization's motto, "For God and Home and Native Land," was changed to read, "Every Land," because the former phrase "shuts out all foreign born citizens and causes them to feel like aliens."[113] Willard urged her constituents to abandon negative attitudes towards immigrants, whom she deemed "intelligent and well-intentioned people."[114] The WCTU also organized among African Americans in both the North and the South. For reformers working with blacks, temperance was a necessary part of a more general uplift. Black women worked actively in the organization, even in leadership positions, and addressed WCTU conventions. Their white counterparts viewed them as indispensable to the reform of black men, for whom drunkenness was thought to be a significant problem, and pledged to give black women reformers "all the aid in our power."[115] At the WCTU's 1880 convention, the chairwoman of the WCTU committee on work with immigrants and blacks, Sarah Morrison, bestowed high praise on an African American woman she called "Sister" Davis, who was active in the California chapter. In her speech, Morrison went so far as to speak out against racial prejudice, asking her audience to consider "what it is to rest under the damnation of color." She concluded her remarks: "Forgive us, Sister Davis; we acknowledge our fault by calling you 'Sister.'"[116]

Morrison's words were a rather remarkable statement of racial enlightenment; however, the WCTU simultaneously forwarded policies and rhetoric that ran counter to a message of equality. Reformers urged a wholesale cultural conversion for immigrants, and African American women joined the national organization in segregated units.[117] Willard engaged in a four-year debate in the 1890's with black activist Ida B. Wells over the South's treatment of African Americans. Wells actually agreed with the view that alcohol was a danger for black men and supported the WCTU's efforts for prohibition. But she was enraged by Willard's contention that southern race relations were positive on the whole and that racial miscegenation resulted from the immorality of black men.[118] Willard's motivation in forwarding this view was mostly due to her desire to win southern support.[119] This was also her motivation in a speech in which she contrasted the opposing sides in the Civil War with those of the war against alcohol in ethnic terms; the former conflict may have put immigrants and northern reformers on the same side, but in the latter conflict—the "final factor" in American politics—southerners and northerners joined together in opposing immigrants.

While the "bayonets" of reformers and immigrants "no longer point one way," "all through the North and South the men once at sword's points are now . . . sworn allies."[120]

Frances Willard's address at the WCTU's 1881 convention illustrated the joining of these two opposing discourses within the context of the Crusader image and for the purpose of garnering broad support for prohibition. First, she spoke glowingly of the South's "acceptance in good faith of the issues of the war." She went on to paint a rosy picture of race relations in the South and made the argument that the common goal of prohibition was the source of the harmony. She claimed to have heard accounts of "ex-masters" and "ex-slaves" joining together for prohibitory legislation and of "ballots from white hands and black for prohibitory law" erasing the "color line." This point forwarded both the affirmation of a multi-racial electorate and society and the argument that the race problem had ended. Then, in an explicitly racial appeal to white southerners, she declared her belief that the nation was finally ready "for a party along the lines of longitude; a party that shall wipe Mason and Dixon's line out of the hearts as well as off the map, weld the Anglo-Saxons of the New World into one royal family, and give us a really re-United States." The party she proposed to do this was the WCTU-backed Home Protection Party, which argued for prohibition through the rhetoric of domesticity. Confronting the threat to the home posed by alcohol was something Americans of all kinds could agree upon. At the core of the party were the women—the "Home Guards . . . who, upon a moral battle-ground, can march side by side with the gallant and the strong." She ended by urging the Prohibition Party to merge with the Home Protection Party and adopt its name because it would "enlist more of our women workers." In other words, the Home Protection Party might officially make the domestic, feminine image of the Crusader a political vehicle that would solve racial and sectional divisions and confront the alcohol industry with moral might.[121]

But Home Protection Party or not, the WCTU itself performed that function quite well. Its success was largely due to its embodiment of the Crusader image. Within the organization, the careful cultivation of that image and the elevation of that icon allowed the WCTU to house a variety of reformers with differing positions on prohibition, women's rights, class, and race. Beyond the organization, the Crusader built bridges between male reformers and the WCTU, even where there were real ideological differences. The Crusader also allowed the WCTU to contribute to the larger political struggle for national prohibition. Most notably, it helped the movement to both address and distract from the knottiest issues relating to race and the political integration of North and South.

In her address at the 1882 WCTU convention, Mary Lathrap of Michigan spoke poignantly of the tragedy of war and the sacrifices women of both North and South bore. "When the war was finished and the scarred banners hung in every State," she said, "The women of this Republic lifted their eyes to face the future, and said, with that chrism of suffering on their brows, 'Oh, God! What next?'" She then asked, "Is it any wonder that the womanhood of to-day is a different womanhood from that of the last century? Is it any wonder that the women . . . are solving a difficult problem in the center of this Republic?" She went on to discuss the day's major problem: "Our great civilization," which faced dangers from all sides. It confronted "the crooked-eyed Chinaman," "the European immigrants of the Northwest," "an empire of lust," "our freedmen coming up into a liberty they know little how to use," and of course, "the rum shop that destroys the home." She concluded, "In the baptism of suffering that passed over us, we found out what the Nation was worth, and it is just like a woman to stand by this Republic until this greatest danger is swept down into the sea of oblivion."[122]

Lathrap's address illustrates several points relating to the creation and elevation of the Crusader as an icon for the movement. First, it speaks to the reconstruction of the temperance movement after the Civil War as an almost cosmic political and cultural war for the nation. No longer was it a male struggle for identity, it was a national struggle to rescue and define American "civilization." Lathrap's words also demonstrate the relationship between this transition within temperance, the trauma of war and subsequent political and cultural change, and the construction of new female roles within the movement. In the Crusader, and the WCTU by extension, the temperance movement found a potent political weapon in its fight with alcohol. It gave the cause a moral edge and united reformers of various stripes into a coalition.

How the self-made man bled into the crusading woman is a complex tale of the intersections between race, gender, and class within the temperance movement and in American thought and culture. The self-made man revealed an antebellum temperance movement tied to an assertion of white, middle-class male identity and authority. The challenges to that icon revealed temperance as a major arena for debating the racial and gendered exclusions supporting that identity and the justice and competence of that authority. In the antebellum period, temperance helped define and was defined by a meaningful dialogue concerning the nature and rights of the individual.

The crusading woman represented in many ways the obfuscation and submersion of this dialogue in the aftermath of the Civil War. As the

A "Knitting Together of Hearts"

movement mounted a wholesale political drive towards prohibition, the exclusivity and visible polarity of the antebellum movement gave way to the appearance of unity and greater inclusion amidst continued diversity of background and opinion. The drive for consensus and coalition, of which the crusading woman was a symbol and vehicle, made the ideological grounding of the movement, as well as contests over its definition, somewhat ambiguous and contained. Temperance became a way to explore social issues in a safe environment, where any disagreements might dissipate in the common foe of alcohol.

In a larger sense, then, the two icons of the movement demonstrate the relationship of temperance, and its use of gender, to the great issues of war and reconstruction. While the self-made man led temperance forces into a bloody and destructive conflict, the crusading woman resurrected them, redeemed them, and reunited them. She promoted what David Blight has described as the two warring cultural drives of the late nineteenth century—"healing and justice."[123] She helped the temperance movement simplify and harmonize these goals by making the destruction of alcohol the primary mode of healing and the only measure of justice.

Notes

NOTES TO THE INTRODUCTION

1. *The Age of Reform: From Bryan to FDR* (New York: Alfred A. Knopf, 1955), 289–90.
2. Ian R. Tyrrell, *Sobering Up: From Temperance to Prohibition in Antebellum America, 1800–1860* (Westport, CT: Greenwood Press, 1979); Jed Dannenbaum, *Drink and Disorder: Temperance Reform in Cincinnati from the Washingtonian Revival to the WCTU* (Urbana: University of Illinois Press, 1984); Jack S. Blocker, *American Temperance Movements: Cycles of Reform* (Boston: Twayne Publishers, 1989); Thomas Pegram, *Battling Demon Rum: The Struggle for a Dry America, 1800–1933* (Chicago: Ivan R. Dee, 1998); W.J. Rorabaugh, *The Alcoholic Republic: An American Tradition* (New York: Hill and Wang, 1978). These historians and most others focus on the more prolific movement in the northern states. For southern temperance, see Ian R. Tyrrell, "Drink and Temperance in the Antebellum South: An Overview and Interpretation," *Journal of Southern History* 48 (1982): 485–510; Douglas W. Carlson, "'Drinks he to his own undoing:' Temperance Ideology in the Deep South," *Journal of the Early Republic* 18 (1998): 659–91.
3. Clifford S. Griffin, *Their Brothers' Keepers: Moral Stewardship in the United States, 1800–1865* (New Brunswick, NJ: Rutgers University Press, 1960); Joseph R. Gusfield, *Symbolic Crusade: Status Politics and the American Temperance Movement*, 2nd edition (Urbana: University of Illinois Press, 1986); Paul Boyer, *Urban Masses and Moral Order in America, 1820–1920* (Cambridge, MA: Harvard University Press, 1978); Robert L. Hampel, *Temperance and Prohibition in Massachusetts, 1813–1852* (Ann Arbor: UMI Research Press, 1982); John J. Rumbarger, *Profits, Power and Prohibition: Alcohol Reform and the Industrializing of America, 1800–1933* (Albany: SUNY Press, 1989); Mary P. Ryan, *Cradle of the Middle-Class: The Family in Oneida County, New York, 1790–1865* (Cambridge: Cambridge University Press, 1981); John S. Gilkeson, *Middle-Class Providence, 1820–1940* (Princeton: Princeton University Press, 1986). Joyce

Appleby noted the more personal motivations connected to larger class, religious, and gendered motivations within the movement, whereby "personal struggles against self-indulgence metamorphosed into crusades to save the nation;" see "The Personal Roots of the First American Temperance Movement," *Proceedings of the American Philosophical Society* 141 (1997): 141–59, quote on p. 143.

4. Timothy L. Smith, *Revivalism in Mid-Nineteenth Century America* (New York: Abingdon Press, 1957); Carroll Smith-Rosenberg, *Religion and the Rise of the American City: The New York City Mission Movement, 1812–1870* (Ithaca: Cornell University Press, 1971); Lois W. Banner, "Religion and Reform in the Early Republic: The Role of Youth," *American Quarterly* 23 (1971): 677–95; Paul E. Johnson, *A Shopkeeper's Millennium: Society and Revivals in Rochester, New York, 1815–1837* (New York: Hill and Wang, 1978); Robert H. Abzug, *Cosmos Crumbling: American Reform and the Religious Imagination* (New York: Oxford University Press, 1994). For the link between antebellum reform and secular perfectionism, see John L. Thomas, "Romantic Reform in America, 1815–1865," *American Quarterly* 17 (1965): 656–81.

5. Ruth Bordin, *Woman and Temperance: The Quest for Power and Liberty, 1873–1900* (Philadelphia: Temple University Press, 1981); Barbara Leslie Epstein, *The Politics of Domesticity: Women, Evangelism and Temperance in Nineteenth-Century America* (Middletown, CT: Wesleyan University Press, 1981); Janet Zollinger Giele, *Two Paths to Women's Equality: Temperance, Suffrage and the Origins of Modern Feminism* (Boston: Twayne Publishers, 1995); Suzanne M. Marilley, *Woman Suffrage and the Origins of Liberal Feminism in the United States, 1820–1920* (Cambridge, MA: Harvard University Press, 1996), ch. 4; Catherine Gilbert Murdock, *Domesticating Drink: Women, Men and Alcohol in America, 1870–1940* (Baltimore: Johns Hopkins University Press, 1998); Marsha Wedell, *Elite Women and the Reform Impulse in Memphis, 1875–1915* (Knoxville: University of Tennessee Press, 1991), ch. 3; Karen J. Blair, *The Clubwoman as Feminist: True Womanhood Redefined, 1868–1914* (New York: Holmes and Meier, 1980). Although Blair does not deal with the WCTU, her model of "domestic feminism" in examining women's clubs in the Gilded Age fits well with these assessments of the WCTU's brand of feminism. The term "domestic feminism" was first used by Daniel Scott Smith in describing late nineteenth-century women; "Family Limitation, Sexual Control and Domestic Feminism in Victorian America," *Clio's Consciousness Raised*, ed. Mary S. Hartmann and Lois Banner (New York: Harper and Row, 1974), 119–36.

6. Lori D. Ginzberg, *Women and the Work of Benevolence: Morality, Politics and Class in the Nineteenth Century United States* (New Haven: Yale University Press, 1990), 202–207; Louise Michelle Newman, *White Women's Rights: Racial Origins of Feminism in the United States* (Oxford: Oxford University Press, 1999), 66–69; Alison M. Parker, *Purifying America: Women, Cultural Reform, and Pro-Censorship Activism, 1873–1933* (Urbana: University of Illinois Press, 1997); David J. Pivar, *Purity Crusade:*

Sexual Morality and Social Control, 1868–1900 (Westport, CT: Greenwood Press, 1973); Ian R. Tyrrell, *Woman's World, Woman's Empire: The WCTU in International Perspective, 1880–1930* (Chapel Hill: University of North Carolina Press, 1991); Jonathan Zimmerman, *Distilling Democracy: Alcohol Education in America's Public Schools, 1880–1925* (Lawrence: University of Kansas Press, 1999).

7. Blocker, *American Temperance Movements;* Dannenbaum, *Drink and Disorder;* Ian R. Tyrrell, "Women and Temperance in Antebellum America, 1830–1860," *Civil War History* 28 (1982): 128–52.

8. The work that has most inspired my understanding and use of this term is Gail Bederman, *Manliness and Civilization: A Cultural History of Gender and Race in the United States, 1860–1917* (Chicago: University of Chicago Press, 1995). She defines discourse as "a set of ideas and practices, which taken together, organize the way a society defines certain truths about itself and the way it deploys social power" (24). She sees "civilization" as a discourse related to male dominance and white supremacy and contested by various groups and individuals. In particular, she discusses discourses as being "dominant" or "counterhegemonic," the former reinforcing societal assumptions, the latter subverting them by using the same language and ideas for a different end. A related work is Linda Frost, *Never One Nation: Freaks, Savages, and Whiteness in U.S. Popular Culture, 1850–1877* (Minneapolis: University of Minnesota Press, 2005), which examines competing discourses of race, gender, and class in the construction of American identity.

9. For a good general discussion of these trends, see Russell Jacoby, "A New Intellectual History?" *American Historical Review* 97 (1992): 405–24; William J. Bouwsma, "Intellectual History in the 1980's: From the History of Ideas to the History of Meaning," *Journal of Interdisciplinary History* 12 (1981): 279–91. For their ramifications for the study of gender, see Nancy Isenberg, "The Personal is Political: Gender, Feminism, and the Politics of Discourse Theory," *American Quarterly,* 44 (1992): 449–58; Kathleen M. Brown, "Brave New Worlds: Women's and Gender History," *William and Mary Quarterly* 50 (1993): 311–28; Joan Wallach Scott, "Deconstructing Equality-Versus-Difference: or, The Uses of Poststructuralist Theory for Feminism," *Feminist Studies* 14 (1988): 34–38 and "Gender: A Useful Category of Historical Analysis," *American Historical Review* 91 (1986): 1053–75.

10. The body of work demonstrating this is enormous. On masculinity in the nineteenth century, see E. Anthony Rotundo, *American Manhood: Transformations in Masculinity from the Revolution to the Modern Era* (New York: Basic Books, 1993); Michael Kimmel, *Manhood in America: A Cultural History* (New York: Free Press, 1996), ch. 1–2; David G. Pugh, *Sons of Liberty: The Masculine Mind in Nineteenth-Century America* (Westport, CT: Greenwood Press, 1983); David Leverenz, *Manhood and the American Renaissance* (Ithaca: Cornell University Press, 1989); Mark C. Carnes and Clyde Griffen, eds., *Meanings for Manhood: Constructions of Masculinity in Victorian America* (Chicago: University of Chicago Press, 1990);

Stephen M. Frank, *Life with Father: Parenthood and Masculinity in the Nineteenth Century American North* (Baltimore: Johns Hopkins University Press, 1998); Mark C. Carnes, *Secret Ritual and Manhood in Victorian America* (New Haven: Yale University Press, 1989); Joseph Pleck and Elizabeth Pleck, eds., *The American Man* (Englewood Cliffs, NJ: Prentice-Hall, 1980). For studies that examine the relationship of masculinity and femininity, see Nancy Isenberg, *Sex and Citizenship in Antebellum America* (Chapel Hill: University of North Carolina Press, 1998); Catherine Clinton and Nina Silber, eds. *Divided Houses: Gender and the Civil War* (New York: Oxford University Press, 1992) and *Battle Scars: Gender and Sexuality in the American Civil War* (New York: Oxford University Press, 2006); Brian Roberts, *American Alchemy: The California Gold Rush and Middle-Class Culture* (Chapel Hill: University of North Carolina Press, 2000). For studies that combine the study of gender and class, see Catherine E. Kelly, *In the New England Fashion: Reshaping Women's Lives in the Nineteenth Century* (Ithaca: Cornell University Press, 1999); Thomas Winter, *Making Men, Making Class: The YMCA and Workingmen, 1877–1920* (Chicago: University of Chicago Press, 2002); Shawn Johansen, *Family Men: Middle-Class Fatherhood in Early Industrializing America* (New York: Routledge, 2001); Mary Ann Clawson, *Constructing Brotherhood: Class, Gender and Fraternalism* (Princeton: Princeton University Press, 1989); Ginzberg, *Women and the Work of Benevolence;* Ryan, *Cradle of the Middle-*Class. For studies that combine gender and race, see Bederman, *Manliness and Civilization;* Newman, *White Women's Rights;* Stephanie McCurry, *Masters of Small Worlds: Yeoman Households, Gender Relations, and the Political Culture of the Antebellum South Carolina Low Country* (New York: Oxford University Press, 1995); Karen Sanchez-Eppler, *Touching Liberty: Abolition, Feminism and the Politics of the Body* (Los Angeles, Oxford: University of California at Berkeley Press, 1993).

11. *Reforming Men and Women: Gender in the Antebellum City* (Ithaca: Cornell University Press, 2002), 90–135.

12. *Manhood Lost: Fallen Drunkards and Redeeming Women in the Nineteenth-Century United States* (Baltimore: Johns Hopkins University Press, 2003).

13. George M. Fredrickson, *The Inner Civil War: Northern Intellectuals and the Crisis of the Union* (Urbana: University of Illinois Press, 1965); Ginzberg, *Women and the Work of Benevolence;* Gaines M. Foster, *Moral Reconstruction: Christian Lobbyists and the Federal Legislation of Morality, 1865–1920* (Chapel Hill: University of North Carolina Press, 2002); Anne C. Rose, *Victorian Americans and the Civil War* (Cambridge: Cambridge University Press, 1992); Morton Keller, *Affairs of the State: Public Life in Late Nineteenth-Century America* (Cambridge, MA: Belknap Press of Harvard University Press, 1977); Louis Menand, *The Metaphysical Club: A Story of Ideas in America* (New York: Farrar, Straus and Giroux, 2002).

14. Ginzberg, *Women and the Work of Benevolence;* William Leach, *True Love and Perfect Union: The Feminist Reform of Self and Society* (New

York: Basic Books, 1980); Judith Ann Giesurg, *Civil War Sisterhood: The U.S. Sanitary Commission and Women's Politics in Transition* (Boston: Northeastern University Press, 2000); Mary P. Ryan, *Women in Public: Between Banners and Ballots, 1825–1880* (Baltimore: Johns Hopkins University Press, 1990); Bederman, *Manliness and Civilization;* Barbara Cutter, *Domestic Devils, Battlefield Angels: The Radicalism of American Womanhood, 1830–1865* (DeKalb, IL: Northern Illinois University Press, 2003).
15. James M. McPherson, *The Abolitionist Legacy: From Reconstruction to the NAACP* (Princeton: Princeton University Press, 1975); David W. Blight, *Race and Reunion: The Civil War in American Memory* (Cambridge, MA: Harvard University Press, 2001); Heather Cox Richardson, *The Death of Reconstruction: Race, Labor and Politics in the Post-Civil War North, 1865–1901* (Cambridge, MA: Harvard University Press, 2001); Eric Foner, *Reconstruction: America's Unfinished Revolution, 1863–1877* (New York: Harper and Row, 1988).

NOTES TO CHAPTER ONE

1. For historical descriptions of the "self-made man," see Charles E. Rosenberg, "Sexuality, Class and Role in Nineteenth-Century America," *American Quarterly* 25 (1973): 131–53; E. Anthony Rotundo, "Learning About Manhood: Gender Ideals and the Middle-Class Family in Nineteenth-Century America," *Manliness and Morality: Middle-Class Masculinity in Britain and America, 1800–1940*, ed. J.A. Mangan and James Walvin (New York: St. Martin's Press, 1987), 35–51 and *American Manhood: Transformations in Masculinity from the Revolution to the Modern Era* (New York: Basic Books, 1993), 3–5, 18–25; Karen Halttunen, *Confidence Men and Painted Women: A Study of Middle-Class Culture in America, 1830–1870* (New Haven: Yale University Press, 1982); David G. Pugh, *Sons of Liberty: The Masculine Mind in Nineteenth-Century America* (Westport, CT: Greenwood Press, 1983); Michael Kimmel, *Manhood in America: A Cultural History* (New York: Free Press, 1996), 13–80. These studies primarily focus on the gender and class components of the self-made man. For the racial aspects of the self-made man, see Bruce Dorsey, *Reforming Men and Women: Gender in the Antebellum City* (Ithaca: Cornell University Press, 2002),113–24, 126–94; David R. Roediger, *The Wages of Whiteness: Race and the Making of the American Working Class* (New York: Verso, 1991); Gail Bederman, *Manliness and Civilization: A Cultural History of Gender and Race in the United States, 1880–1917* (Chicago: University of Chicago Press, 1995).
2. Recent studies of temperance and masculinity have emphasized the image of the self-made man; see Elaine Frantz Parsons, *Manhood Lost: Fallen Men and Redeeming Women in Nineteenth-Century America* (Baltimore: Johns Hopkins University Press, 2003), particularly 18–74; Dorsey, *Reforming Men and Women*, 90–135; Judith N. McArthur, "Demon Rum on the Boards: Temperance Melodrama and the Tradition of Antebellum Reform," *Journal of the Early Republic* 9 (1989): 517–40.

3. W.J. Rorabaugh, *The Alcoholic Republic: An American Tradition* (New York: Oxford University Press, 1979), ch. 1 and 3.
4. Ronald G. Walters, *American Reformers, 1815–1860* (New York: Hill and Wang, 1978), 124–25; Robert L. Hampel, *Temperance and Prohibition in Massachusetts, 1813–1852* (Ann Arbor: UMI Research Press, 1982).
5. Walters, *American Reformers,*127; Sixth Annual Report for 1833, *Permanent Temperance Documents of the American Temperance Society* (New York: American Temperance Union, 1843), 30; Fourth Annual Report for 1831, Ibid., 23.
6. For descriptions of this process, see Gordon S. Wood, *The Radicalism of the American Revolution* (New York: Vintage Books, 1991), 229–370 and Charles Sellers, *The Market Revolution: Jacksonian America, 1815–1846* (New York: Oxford University Press, 1991), although the two scholars differ on whether capitalism promoted or undermined social and political democracy.
7. Quoted from Robert H. Abzug, *Cosmos Crumbling: American Reform and the Religious Imagination* (New York: Oxford University Press, 1994), 86.
8. Ibid., particularly 81–104; Walters, *American Reformers;* John L. Thomas, "Romantic Reform in America, 1815–1865," *American Quarterly* 17 (1965): 656–81; Lois W. Banner, "Religion and Reform in the Early Republic: The Role of Youth," *American Quarterly* 23 (1971): 677–95. On the overall importance of religion in antebellum America, see Timothy L. Smith, *Revivalism in Mid-Nineteenth Century America* (New York: Abingdon Press, 1957) and Carroll Smith-Rosenberg, *Religion and the Rise of the American City: The New York City Mission Movement, 1812–1870* (Ithaca: Cornell University Press, 1971). Smith-Rosenberg argues that even class-based social control flowed out of religious conviction.
9. Scholars broadly fall within two groups in their interpretation of the relationship between temperance and the middle-class. Those who emphasize middle-class identity include: Joseph R. Gusfield, *Symbolic Crusade: Status Politics and the American Temperance Movement*, 2nd edition (Urbana: University of Illinois Press, 1986) 13–60; Robert Hampel, *Temperance and Prohibition in Massachusetts;* John S. Gilkeson, *Middle-Class Providence, 1820–1940* (Princeton: Princeton University Press, 1986); Stuart Blumin, *The Emergence of the Middle Class: Social Experience in the American City, 1760–1900* (New York: Cambridge University Press, 1989) and "The Hypothesis of Middle-Class Formation in Nineteenth-Century America: A Critique and Some Proposals," *American Historical Review* 90 (1985): 299–338; Mary P. Ryan, *Cradle of the Middle Class: The Family in Oneida County, New York, 1790–1865* (Cambridge: Cambridge University Press, 1981); Harry Gene Levine, "Demon of the Middle-Class: Self-Control, Liquor and the Ideology of Temperance in Nineteenth-Century America" (Ph.D. dissertation, University of California at Berkeley, 1978). Those who emphasize a class-based social control include: Paul Boyer, *Urban Masses and Moral Order in America, 1820–1920* (Cambridge, MA: Harvard University Press, 1978); Clifford S. Griffin, *Their Brothers' Keepers: Moral Stewardship in the United States,*

1800–1865 (New Brunswick, NJ: Rutgers University Press, 1960); Paul E. Johnson, *A Shopkeeper's Millennium: Society and Revivals in Rochester, New York, 1815–1837* (New York: Hill and Wang, 1978); John J. Rumbarger, *Profits, Power and Prohibition: Alcohol Reform and the Industrializing of America, 1800–1933* (Albany: SUNY Press, 1989). Of these, Rumbarger's is the baldest assertion of class conflict/control; he argues that capitalist classes consciously and actively used the issue of alcohol to create better workers and thereby advance their economic position.

10. An emphasis on the ambiguity of the middle-class relationship to the market is a relatively recent and significant trend; See Bruce Laurie, "'We Are Not Afraid to Work:' Master Mechanics and the Market Revolution in the Antebellum North," *The Middling Sorts: Explorations in the History of the American Middle Class*, ed. Burton J. Bledstein and Robert D. Johnston (New York: Routledge, 2001), 50–68; Elizabeth Alice White, "Charitable Calculations: Fancywork, Charity, and the Culture of the Sentimental Market, 1830–1880," Ibid., 71–85; Robert Johnston, "Conclusion: Historians and the American Middle Class," Ibid., 296–306; Catherine E. Kelly, *In the New England Fashion: Reshaping Women's Lives in the Nineteenth Century* (Ithaca: Cornell University Press, 1999) and "'Well Bred Country People:' Sociability, Social Networks, and the Creation of a Provincial Middle Class, 1820–1860," *Journal of the Early Republic* 19 (1999): 451–479; Brian Roberts, *American Alchemy: The California Gold Rush and Middle-Class Culture* (Chapel Hill: University of North Carolina Press, 2000), esp. 29–65.
11. *Temperance Recorder* (Albany, NY), 5 June 1832.
12. Greeley to Moses Cartland, 14 April 1845, Horace Greeley Papers, Library of Congress Manuscripts Division, Washington, DC, box 1, folder 7.
13. "History of Peter and John Hay," Tract No. 112, *The Temperance Volume: Embracing the Temperance Tracts of the American Tract Society* (New York: American Tract Society, 1845), 2–3.
14. The Council of the Massachusetts Temperance Society, *The Doings of a Sprit Shop; or, The Story of James and Mary Duffil: A Tale of Real Life* (Boston: John S. March, 1840).
15. "The Rewards of Drunkenness," Tract No. 159, *The Temperance Volume*, 4.
16. Ibid., 4.
17. Bruce Dorsey has written about the theme of male usefulness in temperance; see *Reforming Men and Women*, 109–124.
18. "History of Peter and John Hay," 2.
19. Contrast, for example, Rumbarger, *Profits, Power and Prohibition* with Roberts, *American Alchemy*.
20. "The Well-Conducted Farm," Tract No. 176, *Temperance Volume*, 4.
21. Mark Kann has argued that liberalism required republicanism, that there was always inherent in individualism a fear of social chaos and a need to temper it with republican values. See *On the Man Question: Gender and Civic Virtue* (Philadelphia: Temple University Press, 1991).
22. Fifth Report of the ATS for 1832, *Permanent Temperance Documents*, 132.

23. *Genius of Temperance, Philanthropist and People's Advocate* (New York), 16 May 1832.
24. *Temperance Mirror* (Dover, NH), Nov. 1837. On this issue, see also McArthur, "Demon Rum on the Boards," 517–40.
25. Albert Barnes, *Barnes on the Traffic in Ardent Spirits* (New York: American Tract Society, 1840–49), 6–8.
26. *Temperance Recorder*, 6 March 1832.
27. The literature on "separate spheres" is substantial. See, for example, Linda K. Kerber, "Separate Spheres, Female Worlds, Woman's Place: The Rhetoric of Women's History," *Journal of American History* 75 (1988): 9–39; Nancy Cott, *The Bonds of Womanhood: "Woman's Sphere" in New England, 1780–1835* (New Haven: Yale University Press, 1977); Ryan, *Cradle of the Middle Class*; Karen Halttunen, *Confidence Men and Painted Women: A Study of Middle-Class Culture in America, 1830–1870* (New Haven: Yale University Press, 1982); Barbara Welter, "The Cult of True Womanhood: 1820–1860," *American Quarterly* 18 (1966): 151–74; Kathryn Kish Sklar, *Catherine Beecher: A Study in American Domesticity* (New York: W.W. Norton, 1976); Carroll Smith-Rosenberg, "Beauty, the Beast, and the Militant Woman: A Case of Sex Roles and Social Stress in Jacksonian America," *American Quarterly* 23 (1971): 562–84; Carl Degler, *At Odds: Women and the Family in America from the Revolution to the Present* (New York: Oxford University Press, 1980). For more recent works that emphasize the non-existence of actual separate spheres, see Lori D. Ginzberg, *Women and the Work of Benevolence: Morality, Politics, and Class in the Nineteenth-Century United States* (New Haven: Yale University Press, 1990); Barbara Cutter, *Domestic Devils and Battlefield Angels: The Radicalism of American Womanhood, 1830–1865* (DeKalb, IL: Northern Illinois University Press, 2003); White, "Charitable Calculations;" Kelly, *In the New England Fashion;* Mary P. Ryan, *Women in Public: Between Banners and Ballots, 1825–1880* (Baltimore: Johns Hopkins University Press, 1990); Elizabeth R. Varon, *We Mean to be Counted: White Women and Politics in Antebellum Virginia* (Chapel Hill: University of North Carolina Press, 1998); Roberts, *American Alchemy*; Fredrika J. Teute, "Roman Matron on the Banks of Tiber Creek: Margaret Bayard Smith and the Politicization of Spheres in the Nation's Capital," *A Republic for the Ages: The United States Capitol and the Political Culture of the Early Republic*, ed. Donald Kennon (Charlottesville: University of Virginia, 1999), 89–121; Jan Lewis, "Politics and the Ambivalence of the Private Sphere: Women in Early Washington, D.C." Ibid., 122–151 and "Motherhood and the Construction of the Male Citizen in the United States, 1750–1850," *Constructions of the Self*, ed. George Levine (New Brunswick, NJ: Rutgers University Press, 1992), 143–64; Shawn Johansen, *Family Men: Middle-Class Fatherhood in Early Industrializing America* (New York: Routledge, 2001); Mary Chapman and Glenn Hendler, eds., *Sentimental Men: Masculinity and the Politics of Affect in American Culture* (Berkeley: University of California Press, 1999); Samuel Watson, "Flexible Gender Roles During the Market Revolution: Family, Friendship, Marriage and Masculinity among U.S. Army Officers, 1815–1846," *Journal of Social History* 29 (1995): 81–106; Christopher Dixon,

"'A True Manly Life:' Abolitionism and the Masculine Ideal," *History of the American Abolitionist Movement: A Bibliography of Scholarly Articles*, vol 4, *Abolitionism and Issues of Race and Gender*, ed.John R. McKivigan (New York: Garland Publishing, 1999), 267–90.
28. Cutter, *Domestic Devils;* Roberts, *American Alchemy,* 255.
29. Amy Dru Stanley, "Home Life and the Market," *The Market Revolution in American Social, Political and Religious Expressions, 1800–1880*, ed. Melvyn Stokes and Stephen Conway (Charlottesville: University of Virginia Press, 1996), 74–96; Roberts, *American Alchemy,* 183; Toby L. Ditz, "Shipwrecked; or, Masculinity Imperiled: Mercantile Representations of Failure and the Gendered Self in Eighteenth-Century Philadelphia," *Journal of American History* 81 (1994): 51–80. Lori Merish, "Representing the 'Deserving Poor:' The 'Sentimental Seamstress' and the Feminization of Poverty in Antebellum America," *Our Sisters' Keepers: Nineteenth-Century Benevolence Literature by American Women,* ed. Jill Bergman and Debra Bernard (Tuscaloosa: University of Alabama Press, 2005), 49–79.
30. Dorsey, *Reforming Men and Women,* 102–112; Parsons, *Manhood Lost,* 53–74.
31. *Genius of Temperance, Philanthropist and People's Advocate* (New York), 11 Jan. 1832.
32. See Carroll Smith-Rosenberg, "The Hysterical Woman: Sex Roles and Role Conflict in Nineteenth-Century America," *Disorderly Conduct: Visions of Gender in Victorian America* (New York: A.A. Knopf, 1985), 197–216.
33. *American Temperance Intelligencer* (Albany, NY), Jan. 1836.
34. "History of Peter and John Hay," 8.
35. *American Temperance Magazine* (Albany, NY), May 1833; *Temperance Recorder,* 1 May 1832.
36. *Temperance Recorder,* 1 May 1832.
37. *Genius of Temperance,* 11 Jan. 1832.
38. *Temperance Mirror* (Dover, NH), Oct. 1837.
39. *Genius of Temperance,* 11 Jan. 1832; *National Philanthropist* (Boston), 23 Dec. 1826. Jerome Nadelhaft examines how antebellum temperance literature portrayed the brutalizing effects of alcohol on previously respectable middle-class husbands in "Alcohol and Wife Abuse in Antebellum Male Temperance Literature," *Canadian Review of American Studies* 25 (1995): 15–43.
40. There is disagreement among historians on which model more greatly informed antebellum, middle-class masculinity. Those who emphasize the "self-made man" include Rotundo, *American Manhood;* Kimmel, *Manhood in America,* ch. 1–2; Pugh, *Sons of Liberty;* David Leverenz, *Manhood and the American Renaissance* (Ithaca: Cornell University Press, 1989). For those who emphasize domesticity, Christianity and more feminine qualities, see Donald Yacovone, "Abolitionists and the Language of Fraternal Love," *Meanings for Manhood: Constructions of Masculinity in Victorian America,* ed. Mark C. Carnes and Clyde Griffen (Chicago: University of Chicago Press, 1990), 85–95; Clyde Griffen, "Reconstruction Masculinity from the Evangelical Revival to the Waning of Progressivism: A Speculative

Synthesis," Ibid., 183–204; Stephen Frank, *Life with Father: Parenthood and Masculinity in the Nineteenth-Century American North* (Baltimore: Johns Hopkins University Press, 1998). For more on different constructions of masculinity in the nineteenth century and "role strain" within it see Watson, "Flexible Gender Roles During the Market Revolution," 81–106; Rosenberg, "Sexuality, Class and Role in Nineteenth-Century America," 219–54; Rotundo, "Learning about Manhood," 35–51; Roberts, *American Alchemy,* esp. ch. 8.

41. G.J. Barker-Benfield posits an extreme version of male antagonism towards female influence in *Horrors of the Half-Known Life: Male Attitudes toward Women and Sexuality in Nineteenth-Century America* (New York: Harper and Row, 1976). He argues that men saw women as parasites that fed off their resources and undermined their ability to compete with other men, a view that resulted in deep hatred for women and even violence against them by male gynecologists. On fraternal orders, see Mary Ann Clawson, *Constructing Brotherhood: Class, Gender and Fraternalism* (Princeton: Princeton University Press, 1989); Mark C. Carnes, *Secret Ritual and Manhood in Victorian America* (New Haven: Yale University Press, 1989). For female antagonism to fraternal orders, see Carroll Smith-Rosenberg, "The Cross and the Pedestal: Women, Anti-Ritualism, and the Emergence of the American Bourgeoisie," *Disorderly Conduct,* 129–64. On the saloon as a foil for middle-class masculinity, also see Roy Rosenzweig, *Eight Hours for What We Will: Workers and Leisure in an Industrial City, 1870–1920* (Cambridge: Cambridge University Press, 1983) and Jon M. Kingsdale, "The 'Poor Man's Club:' Social Functions of the Urban Working-Class Saloon," *American Quarterly* 25 (1973), 255–84.
42. Fourth Report for 1831, *Permanent Temperance Documents,* 54.
43. This is the general consensus of historians of the movement: Jack S. Blocker, *American Temperance Movements: Cycles of Reform* (Boston: Twayne Publishers, 1989), ch. 1; Ian R. Tyrrell, *Sobering Up: From Temperance to Prohibition in Antebellum America, 1800–1860* (Westport, CT: Greenwood Press, 1979); Jed Dannenbaum, *Drink and Disorder,* ch. 6–7 and "The Origins of Temperance Activity and Militancy Among American Women," *Journal of Social History* 15 (1981): 235–52; Ian R. Tyrrell, "Women and Temperance in Antebellum America, 1830–1860," *Civil War History* 28 (1982): 128–52. Most recently, Bruce Dorsey has supported this view; *Reforming Men and Women,* 132.
44. Ibid.
45. Cott, *The Bonds of Womanhood;* Dorsey, *Reforming Men and Women;* Cutter, *Domestic Devils.*
46. Teute, "Roman Matron;" Varon, *We Mean to be Counted;* Lewis, "Politics and the Ambivalence of the Private Sphere."
47. Seventh Report for 1834, *Permanent Temperance Documents,* 3.
48. *Genius of Temperance,* 1 Feb. 1832.
49. Fourth Annual Report of the New York State Society for the Promotion of Temperance, *The American Quarterly Magazine,* May 1833.

Notes to Chapter One

50. *Genius of Temperance,* 11 Apr. 1832.
51. *National Philanthropist,* 7 Oct. 1826.
52. *American Temperance Intelligencer,* Feb. 1835.
53. *Temperance Recorder,* 1 Jan. 1833.
54. Seventh Annual Report for 1834, *Permanent Temperance Documents,* 13.
55. Fourth Annual Report for 1831, Ibid., 17.
56. *Temperance Recorder,* 1 May 1832.
57. Cott, *The Bonds of Womanhood,* 84–98.
58. Eighth Report for 1835, *Permanent Temperance Documents,* 92.
59. Thomas Sewall, M.D., "Address on the Effects of Intemperance on the Intellectual, Moral and Physical Powers," *Temperance Volume,* 19–20.
60. *Temperance Recorder,* 1 May 1832.
61. Address by Mr. Cooke, *The American Quarterly Temperance Magazine,* May 1833.
62. *Temperance Recorder,* 5 June 1832.
63. Fifth Report for 1832, *Permanent Temperance Documents,* 140.
64. Massachusetts Temperance Society, *The Doings of a Spirit Shop.*
65. George Cheever to Charlotte Cheever, 23 Jan. 1834, Cheever Family Papers, American Antiquarian Society, Worcester, MA, box 3, folder 5; George B. Cheever, *The Dream, or The True History of Deacon Giles's Distillery and Deacon Jones's Brewery* (New York: Printed for the publishers, 1846); George Cheever to Charlotte Cheever, 7 Feb. 1835, Cheever Family Papers, box 4, folder 2.
66. *American Temperance Intelligencer,* March 1835.
67. Charlotte Cheever to George Cheever, 8 June 1833, Cheever Family Papers, box 3, folder 5.
68. Charlotte Cheever to George Cheever, 15 Feb. 1835, Ibid., box 4, folder 2.
69. Charlotte Cheever to George Cheever, 15 Feb. 1835, Ibid., box 4, folder 2.
70. Robert M. York, *George Barrell Cheever, Religious and Social Reformer, 1807–1910* (Orono, ME: University Press, 1955), 17.
71. George Cheever to Charlotte Cheever, 20 Feb. 1835, Cheever Family Papers, box 4, folder 2.
72. George Cheever to Charlotte Cheever, 13 Oct. 1836, Ibid., box 5, folder 2.
73. 7 Jan. 1836, Ibid., box 5, folder 1.
74. George B. Cheever, *A defense in abatement of judgment for an alleged libel, before the Massachusetts Supreme Court, Dec. 4, 1835* (Salem, MA: John W. Archer, 1836), 28.
75. Fourth Annual Report for 1831, *Permanent Temperance Documents,* 7.
76. Introduction to *Permanent Temperance Documents.*
77. Address by Dr. Fisk, *Temperance Record,* 6 March 1832.
78. Ibid., 3 Apr. 1832.
79. Sixth Report for 1833, *Permanent Temperance Documents,* 284.
80. Justin Edwards to Gerrit Smith, 17 Oct. 1833, Gerrit Smith Papers (microfilm), Library of Congress Manuscripts Division, Washington, DC, reel 8.
81. John Marsh, *Temperance Recollections, Labors, Defeats, Triumphs. An Autobiography* (New York: Charles Scribner and Co., 1867), 65.

82. Ibid., 64; Report of the ATU for 1838, *Permanent Temperance Documents*, 32.
83. Report of the ATU for 1840, Ibid., 27.
84. Edward C. Delavan to Gerrit Smith, 20 Apr. 1852, Gerrit Smith Papers, reel 5.
85. Daniel Walker Howe, *The Political Culture of the American Whigs* (Chicago: University of Chicago Press, 1979).
86. See for example, Morton Horwitz, *The Transformation of American Law, 1780–1860* (Cambridge, MA: Harvard University Press, 1977); William Nelson, *The Americanization of the Common Law, 1780–1860* (Cambridge, MA: Harvard University Press, 1975); Stanley Kutler, *Privilege and Creative Destruction: The Charles River Bridge Case* (Philadelphia, New York and Toronto: J.B. Lippincott Co., 1971); Hendrik Hartog, *Public Property and Private Power: The Corporation of the City of New York in American Law* (Ithaca: Cornell University Press, 1983); Christopher Tomlins, *Law, Labor and Ideology in the Early American Republic* (Cambridge: Cambridge University Press, 1993). Most of these works follow an economic interpretation, arguing that legal developments worked to reinforce the emergence of capitalism and the pre-eminence of capitalist classes. A recent revision of this argument is Peter Karsten, *Heart versus Head: Judge-Made Law in Nineteenth-Century America* (Chapel Hill: University of North Carolina Press, 1997), which contends that judges in the nineteenth century often bent the common law in order to aid "the weak and the poor" (3).
87. Gusfield, *Symbolic Crusade*.
88. Michael Grossberg, *Governing the Hearth: Law and the Family in Nineteenth-Century America* (Chapel Hill: University of North Carolina Press, 1985); Hendrik Hartog, *Man and Wife in America: A History* (Cambridge, MA: Harvard University Press, 2000); Norma Basch, *Framing American Divorce: From the Revolutionary Generation to the Victorians* (Berkeley: University of California Press, 1999); Merril D. Smith, *Breaking the Bonds: Marital Discord in Pennsylvania, 1730–1830* (New York: New York University Press, 1991); Richard H. Chused, *Private Acts in Public Places: A Social History of Divorce in the Formative Era of American Family Law* (Philadelphia: University of Pennsylvania Press, 1994). These works also discuss the impact of companionate marriage on antebellum views of marriage and divorce. For more on women's property rights, see Elizabeth Bowles Warbasse, *The Changing Legal Rights of Married Women, 1800–1861* (New York: Garland, 1987); Marylynn Salmon, *Women and the Law of Property in Early America* (Chapel Hill: University of North Carolina Press, 1986). From the 1820's to the 1860's several states did indeed pass laws giving property rights to married women.
89. Nancy Cott, *Public Vows: A History of Marriage and the Nation* (Cambridge, MA: Harvard University Press, 2000), 50.
90. Basch, *Framing American Divorce,* ch. 3.
91. Marsh, *Half Century,* 15, 18.
92. *Journal of the American Temperance Union* (New York), May 1853.
93. *New York People's Organ* (New York), 27 Aug. 1853.

Notes to Chapter One

94. Ibid., 17 Feb. 1855.
95. Ibid., 10 June 1854.
96. *Young Men's Journal and Advocate of Temperance* (Detroit, MI), 3 Sept. 1859, Microfilm Edition of the Temperance and Prohibition Papers, joint project of the Ohio Historical Society, the Michigan Historical Collections, and the Woman's Christian Temperance Union, series I, reel 2. For a good, basic account of these events, see Dannenbaum, *Drink and Disorder,* 180–211.
97. *New York People's Organ,* 10 June 1854.
98. Ibid., 30 Sept. 1854.
99. Ibid.
100. *Western Temperance Almanac for 1833* (Cincinnati: Truman and Smith, 1833), 20; for more on the comparison of alcoholism and slavery, see John W. Crowley, "Slaves to the Bottle: Gough's *Autobiography* and Douglass's *Narrative,*" and Robert W. Levine, "'Whiskey, Blacking and All:' Temperance and Race in William Wells Brown's *Clotel,*" both in *Serpent in the Cup: Temperance in American Literature,* ed. David Reynolds and Debra J. Rosenthal (Amherst, MA: University of Massachusetts Press, 1997), 115–135 and 93–114, respectively; Debra J. Rosenthal, *Race Mixture in Nineteenth-Century U.S. and Spanish American Fictions: Gender, Culture, and Nation Building* (Chapel Hill: University of North Carolina Press, 2004), 52–68.
101. Nancy Shoemaker, "How Indians Got to Be Red," *American Historical Review* 102 (1997): 625–44; Alden T. Vaughan, "From White Man to Redskin: Changing Anglo-American Perceptions of the American Indian," *American Historical Review* 87 (1982): 917–53. Shoemaker argues that Indians as well as whites constructed this racial category.
102. Quoted in Glenn Hendler, "Bloated Bodies and Sober Sentiments: Masculinity in 1840's Temperance Narratives," *Sentimental Men: Masculinity and the Politics of Affect in American Culture,* ed. Glenn Hendler and Mary Chapman (Berkeley: University of California Press, 1999), 132.
103. Michael Paul Rogin, *Fathers and Children: Andrew Jackson and the Subjugation of the American Indian* (New Brunswick, NJ: Transaction Publishers, 1995), 113–125, 165–205; Eugene Genovese, *Roll, Jordan, Roll: The World the Slaves Made* (New York: Pantheon Books, 1975).
104. *Western Temperance Almanac for 1835* (Cincinnati: Truman and Smith, 1835), frontispiece.
105. There has been very little historical study of the southern movement, but see Ian R. Tyrrell, "Drink and Temperance in the Antebellum South: An Overview and Interpretation," *Journal of Southern History* 48 (1982): 485–510; Douglas W. Carlson, "'Drinks he to his own undoing:' Temperance Ideology in the Deep South," *Journal of the Early Republic* 18 (1998): 659–91.
106. The next chapter discusses this point further.
107. Stephanie McCurry, *Masters of Small Worlds: Yeoman Households, Gender Relations, and the Political Culture of the Antebellum South Carolina Low Country* (New York: Oxford University Press, 1995); Christine Heyrman, *Southern Cross: The Beginnings of the Bible Belt* (Chapel Hill: University

of North Carolina Press, 1997). McCurry's work discusses the link between race and gender in the southern idea of masterhood/patriarchy. Heyrman's work discusses how evangelical Christianity was adapted to southern needs of bolstering white male supremacy. Temperance, too, achieved any success it did in the antebellum South through a similar process. See Carlson, "'Drinks he to his own undoing,'" 659–91.
108. Ibid.; Tyrrell, "Drink and Temperance in the Antebellum South," 489, although Tyrrell finds that southern supporters of temperance, while strong defenders of slavery, were more often professional, "middling" classes.
109. South Carolina State Temperance Society, *Permanent Documents,* vol. 1 (Columbia, SC: I.C. Morgan's Letter Press, 1846), 150–51, 39, 437.
110. Ibid., 154. For paternalism, see Genovese, *Roll, Jordan, Roll.*
111. South Carolina State Temperance Society, *Permanent Documents,* 41.

NOTES TO CHAPTER TWO

1. 26 June 1853, Blackwell Family Papers (microfilm), Library of Congress Manuscripts Division, Washington, DC, reel 63.
2. Jack S. Blocker, *American Temperance Movements: Cycles of Reform* (Boston: Twayne Publishers, 1989), 21–29. The disputes over abstinence mainly concerned the use of wine for communion.
3. Sean Wilentz, *Chants Democratic: New York and the Rise of the American Working Class* (Oxford: Oxford University Press, 1984), 307. Wilentz attributes the success of the movement to the depression, saying that temperance acted as a "balm" (314).
4. Among the six founders were a blacksmith, a wheelwright, a coachmaker, a silverplater, a carpenter and a tailor. Philip S. White and Ezra Stiles Ely, *Vindication of the Order of the Sons of Temperance* (New York: Oliver and Brothers, Publishers, 1848), 20.
5. *Report of the Executive Committee of the American Temperance Union* (New York: American Temperance Union, 1842), 13.
6. Blocker, *American Temperance Movements,* 30–60; Wilentz, *Chants Democratic,* 306–314; Joseph R. Gusfield, *Symbolic Crusade: Status Politics and the American Temperance Movement,* 2nd edition (Urbana: University of Illinois Press, 1986), 44–51; A member of the society, *The Foundation, Progress and Principles of the Washingtonian Temperance Society of Baltimore and the Influence it has had on the Temperance Movements in the United States* (Baltimore: John D. Toy, 1842), 62.
7. Report of the ATU for 1842, *Permanent Temperance Documents of the American Temperance Society* (New York: American Temperance Union, 1843), 9; *Temperance Offering* (Salem, MA), Dec. 1845.
8. *The Washingtonian* (Augusta, ME), 2 June 1841.
9. 30 June 1841; *Michigan Washingtonian* (Jackson, MI), 15 July 1846.
10. *The Washingtonian,* 23 June 1841.
11. Lorenzo Dow Johnson, *Martha Washingtonianism, or History of the Ladies Temperance Benevolent Societies* (New York: Saxton and Miles, 1843), 9.
12. White and Ely, *Vindication,* 20.

13. Although she deals mainly with print culture and Washingtonian narratives were usually spoken, Ann Fabian's analysis of personal narratives in the nineteenth century fits the Washingtonian meetings quite well. She argues that the tellers of such stories asserted a kind of cultural authority that was otherwise beyond their reach. She states, too, that the telling of such stories was "a means of building bonds among people, a means of making visible to themselves and to others the history of those whose voices counted little." *The Unvarnished Truth: Personal Narratives in Nineteenth-Century America* (Berkeley: University of California Press, 2000), quote on p. 7.
14. Quoted in Glenn Hendler, "Bloated Bodies and Sober Sentiments: Masculinity in 1840's Temperance Narratives," in *Sentimental Men: Masculinity and the Politics of Affect in American Culture*, ed. Mary Chapman and Glenn Hendler (Berkeley: University of California Press, 1999), 125.
15. *Foundation, Progress and Principles*, 38.
16. *The Washingtonian*, 28 July 1841. Glenn Hendler argues that working-class Washingtonians constructed gendered spheres much differently than did middle-class Americans due to the lack of separation between domestic and work spaces, leisure and working hours. See "Bloated Bodies and Sober Sentiments," 125–48; Teresa Anne Murphy, *Ten Hours' Labor: Religion, Reform, and Gender in Early New England* (Ithaca: Cornell University Press, 1992); Roy Rosenzweig, *Eight Hours for What We Will: Workers and Leisure in an Industrial City* (Cambridge: Cambridge University Press, 1983); Lawrence W. Levine, *Highbrow/Lowbrow: The Emergence of Cultural Hierarchy in America* (Cambridge, MA: Harvard University Press, 1988). There are striking similarities between the sentimentalized manhood of Washingtonians and that of abolitionists; see Lawrence Friedman, *Gregarious Saints: Self and Community in Antebellum American Abolitionism, 1830–1870* (Cambridge: Cambridge University Press, 1982); Christopher Dixon, "'A True Manly Life:' Abolitionism and the Masculine Ideal," *Mid-America* 77 (1995): 267–90; Lewis Perry, *Childhood, Marriage and Reform: Henry Clarke Wright, 1797–1870* (Chicago: University of Chicago, 1980); Donald Yacovone, "Abolitionists and the Language of Fraternal Love," *Meanings for Manhood: Constructions of Masculinity in Victorian America*, ed. Mark C. Carnes and Clyde Griffen (Chicago: University of Chicago Press, 1990), 85–95.
17. *The Washingtonian*, 9 June 1841, 1 September 1841.
18. W.K. Scott, Address before the Ladies' Temperance Society, Sandy Hill, NY, 21 April 1832, *The American Quarterly Temperance Magazine* (Albany, NY), May 1833; *Worcester County Cataract and Massachusetts Washingtonian* (Worcester, MA), 29 March 1843. The latter did not credit Scott. Also on the issue of working-class gender ideology, see Ruth M. Alexander, "'We Are Engaged as a Band of Sisters:' Class and Domesticity in the Washingtonian Temperance Movement, 1840–1850," *Journal of American History* 75 (1988): 763–87. Also see Barbara Cutter, *Domestic Devils, Battlefield Angels: The Radicalism of American Womanhood, 1830–1865* (DeKalb, IL: Northern Illinois University Press, 2003), who argues that female morality was a concept shared by Americans of all classes and races in the nineteenth century.

19. Ruth Alexander has argued that the Washingtonians attempted to emulate middle-class domesticity, but Barbara Cutter has maintained that the idea of female moral authority pervaded all of American society, not just the white middle-class. See "'We Are Engaged as a Band of Sisters,'" and *Domestic Devils*, respectively.
20. Johnson, *Martha Washingtonianism*, 9.
21. Ibid., 16–17.
22. Ibid., 9.
23. Ibid., 32.
24. Ibid., 28
25. Ibid., 31.
26. Ruth Alexander has identified most of the Martha Washingtonian women as wives of artisans or working-women; "'We are Engaged as a Band of Sisters,'" 765–66.
27. *The Samaritan and Total Abstinence Advocate* (Providence, RI), 25 May 1842.
28. *Michigan Temperance Journal and Washingtonian* (Jackson, MI), 15 July 1847, Microfilm Edition of the Temperance and Prohibition Papers, joint project of the Michigan Historical Collections, Ohio Historical Society, and the Woman's Christian Temperance Union, series I, reel 2; Barbara Cutter, *Domestic Devils*, also bears out this statement.
29. *The Samaritan*, 25 May 1842.
30. This quote comes from a letter from the Directress of the Lady Mt. Vernon Society in New York. Johnson, *Martha Washingtonianism*, 69.
31. *The Fountain, Organ of the Connecticut Washingtonian Total Abstinence Society* (New Haven, CT), 27 March 1841.
32. T.S. Arthur, *Six Nights with the Washingtonians: A Series of Temperance Tales* (Philadelphia: L.A. Godey and Morton McMichael, 1842), 61. Although this account is fictional, it closely mirrors real life incidents. For example, *Cataract*, 22 May 1843.
33. *Cataract*, 5 July 1843.
34. *Chants Democratic*, 309.
35. *Michigan Temperance Journal and Washingtonian*, 15 July 1847; the paper defended itself by saying that often at the stories' ends, the agent of redemption was usually a woman as well.
36. Rev. D.C. Haynes, "The Ungrateful Wife," *The Fountain Organ*, 27 Dec. 1844.
37. On the importance of the saloon to working-class culture in the nineteenth century, see Wilentz, *Chants Democratic*, 306–14; Rosenzweig, *Eight Hours for What We Will*, especially ch. 4; Kingsdale, "The 'Poor Man's Club,'" 485–87. Kingsdale more directly describes the gendered importance of the saloon for working-class men.
38. *Michigan Temperance Journal and Washingtonian*, 15 July 1846. For an examination of the gendered cooperation within working-class temperance, see Murphy, *Ten Hours' Labor*, especially ch. 5; Alexander, "'We are Engaged as a Band of Sisters,'" 763–87.
39. *The Washingtonian*, 24 Nov. 1841.

Notes to Chapter Two 141

40. D.C. Bloomer, *The Life and Writings of Amelia Bloomer* (Boston: Arena Publishing, 1895), 20.
41. Ibid., 26.
42. Ibid., 39; *The Lily* (Seneca Falls, NY), 1 Jan. 1849.
43. Ibid.
44. Mary E. Livermore, *The Story of My Life, or Sunshine and Shadow of Seventy Years* (Hartford, CT: A.D. Worthington and Co., Publishers, 1899), 365.
45. Ellen Carol DuBois, ed., *Elizabeth Cady Stanton, Susan B. Anthony: Correspondence, Writings, Speeches* (New York: Schocken Books, 1981), 15–22.
46. Bloomer, *Life and Writings*, 36.
47. Ibid., 20.
48. *Lily*, March 1849.
49. Bloomer, *Life and Writings*, 20.
50. *Lily*, Oct. 1849.
51. Ibid., March 1849.
52. Ibid., Apr. 1850.
53. Ibid., July 1850.
54. Susan B. Anthony to Amelia Bloomer, 26 Aug. 1852, *Stanton, Anthony*, 37–40.
55. Susan B. Anthony, "Expediency," 27 June 1853, Susan B. Anthony Papers (microfilm), Library of Congress Manuscripts Division, Washington, DC, reel 7.
56. Susan B. Anthony to Bloomer, 26 Aug. 1852, *Stanton, Anthony*, 37–40.
57. *Lily*, 2 Jan. 1854.
58. Other historians who have noted a connection between women's work in temperance and women's rights reforms include: Barbara Leslie Epstein, *The Politics of Domesticity: Women, Evangelism and Temperance in Nineteenth-Century America* (Middletown, CT: Wesleyan University Press, 1981); Janet Zollinger Giele, *Two Paths to Women's Equality: Temperance, Suffrage, and the Origins of Liberal Feminism in the United States, 1820–1920* (Cambridge, MA: Harvard University Press, 1996); Ruth Bordin, *Woman and Temperance: The Quest for Power and Liberty, 1873–1900* (Philadelphia: Temple University Press, 1991), 3–14, 156–62; Mary P. Ryan, *Women in Public: Between Banners and Ballots, 1825–1880* (Baltimore: Johns Hopkins University Press, 1990); Nancy Isenberg, *Sex and Citizenship in Antebellum America* (Chapel Hill: University of North Carolina Press, 1998), ch. 6; Paula Baker, *The Moral Frameworks of Public Life: Gender, Politics, and the State in Rural New York, 1870–1930* (New York: Oxford University Press, 1991) and "The Domestication of Politics: Women and American Political Society, 1780–1920," *American Historical Review* 89 (1984): 620–47; Suzanne Marilley, *Woman Suffrage and the Origins of Liberal Feminism in the United States, 1820–1920* (Cambridge, MA: Harvard University Press, 1996), ch. 4; Elizabeth Battelle Clark, "The Politics of God and the Woman's Vote: Religion in the American Suffrage Movement, 1848–95" (Ph.D. dissertation, Princeton University, 1989);

Michael McGerr, "Political Style and Women's Power, 1830–1930," *Journal of American History* 77 (1990): 864–85.
59. *Lily*, 2 Jan. 1854.
60. Amelia Bloomer, "A New Era has Dawned," 7 Feb. 1853, in *Hear Me Patiently: The Reform Speeches of Amelia Jenks Bloomer*, ed. Anne C. Coon (Westport, CT: Greenwood Press, 1994), 41–56.
61. Historians see the blurring of the boundaries between the public and private as an essential step in attacking female subjugation; see Mary P. Ryan, *Women in Public: Between Banners and Ballots, 1825–1880* (Baltimore: Johns Hopkins University Press, 1990); Isenberg, *Sex and Citizenship in Antebellum America*; Ellen Carol DuBois, "The Radicalism of the Woman Suffrage Movement," *Woman Suffrage and Women's Rights* (New York: New York University Press, 1998), 30–42.
62. On Anthony, see DuBois, *Stanton, Anthony*, 15–22; Bloomer, *Life and Writings*, 34.
63. Elizabeth Cady Stanton, Susan B. Anthony et al, *History of Woman's Suffrage*, vol. I (New York: Arno Press, 1969), 76.
64. Ibid., 480–92.
65. Ibid., 118–82.
66. Ibid.
67. *Frederick Douglass Paper* (Rochester, NY), 10 June 1853.
68. 2 Apr. 1852, *Stanton, Anthony*, 54–55.
69. Stanton to Anthony, 20 June 1853, Ibid., 56–57.
70. *Lily*, 1 Nov. 1854.
71. Jane Grey Swisshelm, *Half a Century*, 2nd edition (Chicago: Jansen, McClurg and Co., 1880), 147; *Lily*, June 1849.
72. Ibid., Sept. 1852.
73. Bloomer, "A New Era Has Dawned."
74. *Lily*, June 1849.
75. *Journal of the American Temperance Union* (New York), 1 Sept. 1852.
76. Anthony to Bloomer, 26 Aug. 1852, *Stanton, Anthony*, 37–40.
77. Bloomer concurred with this view, see Bloomer to T.S.Arthur, 1853, *Life and Writings*, 61.
78. Stone to Antoinette Brown, 11 July 1855, Blackwell Family Papers, reel 63; *Anti-Slavery Bugle* (Salem, OH), 10 June 1852 (reprint of a circular by Stanton "To the Women of New York"). Feminist implications drawn from temperance were probably even more disturbing than abolitionist ones. See Kristin Hoganson, "Garrisonian Abolitionists and the Rhetoric of Gender, 1850–1860," *American Quarterly* 45 (1993): 292–329; Michael D. Pierson, *Free Hearts and Free Homes: Gender and American Antislavery Politics* (Chapel Hill: University of North Carolina Press, 2003), 97–114.
79. *Frederick Douglass Paper*, 10 June 1853.
80. Bloomer, "Most Terribly Bereft," *Hear Me Patiently*, 77–82.
81. Bloomer, *Life and Writings*, 55.
82. *Lily*, June 1849.
83. Ibid., June 1849 and 15 March 1854.

84. Ibid., Sept. 1852.
85. Karen Sanchez-Eppler, "Bodily Bonds: The Intersecting Rhetorics of Feminism and Abolition," *Representations* 24 (1988): 28–59.
86. Bloomer, "A New Era has Dawned;" Amelia Bloomer to T.S. Arthur in 1853, in response to his book *Ruling a Wife,* in which he argued that even in unjust conditions, women had the duty of submission; *Life and Writings,* 61. On the similarities between feminism and abolitionism with regard to legal and bodily dispossession, see Karen Sanchez-Eppler, "Bodily Bonds," 28–59; Jennifer Putzi, *Identifying Marks: Race, Gender, and the Marked Body in Nineteenth-Century America* (Athens: University of Georgia Press, 2006).
87. Susan B. Anthony, speech on the Maine Law first delivered in Monroe County, New York on 17 Apr. 1853, Susan B. Anthony Papers, reel 6.
88. For the overlap of feminism and abolition/racial egalitarianism, see Karen Sanchez-Eppler, *Touching Liberty: Abolition, Feminism and the Politics of the Body* (Los Angeles, Oxford: University of California at Berkeley, 1993) and "Bodily Bonds," 28–50; Gretchen Murphy, "Enslaved Bodies: Figurative Slavery in the Temperance Fiction of Harriet Beecher Stowe and Walt Whitman," *Genre* 28 (1995): 95–118; Hoganson, "Garrisonian Abolitionists and the Rhetoric of Gender," 292–329; Dixon, "'A True Manly Life,'" 267–90. On women within the abolitionist movement and the conflict over the women's rights issue within it, see Ira Brown, "'Am I not a Woman and a Sister?' The Anti-Slavery Convention and American Women, 1837–1839," *History of the American Abolitionist Movement,* vol. 4, *Abolitionism and Issues of Race and Gender,* ed. John R. McKivigan (New York: Garland, 1999), 185–203; Donald R. Kennon, "'An Apple of Discord:' The Woman Question at the World's Anti-Slavery Convention of 1840," *Slavery and Abolition* 5 (1984): 244–66; Julie Roy Jeffrey, *The Great Silent Army of Abolitionism: Ordinary Women in the Antislavery Movement* (Chapel Hill: University of North Carolina Press, 1998); Michael Pierson, "Between Antislavery and Abolition: The Politics and Rhetoric of Jane Grey Swisshelm," *Pennsylvania History* 60 (1993): 305–21; Blanche Glassman Hersh, *The Slavery of Sex: Feminist-Abolitionists in America* (Urbana: University of Illinois Press, 1978); Keith Melder, *The Beginnings of Sisterhood: The American Woman's Rights Movement, 1800–1850* (New York: Schocken Books, 1977); Debra Gold Hansen, *Strained Sisterhood: Gender and Class in the Boston Female Anti-Slavery Society* (Amherst: University of Massachusetts Press, 1993); Jean Fagan Yellin, *Women and Sisters: Antislavery Feminists in American Culture* (New Haven: Yale University Press, 1989). Of these, Sanchez-Eppler offers the most unique perspective; she argues that the shared status of women and blacks derived from society's biological categorization of them. Women and slaves (as well as free blacks in many instances) were divested of their very personhood and their individuality on the basis of their physical natures. Race and sex were biological indicators of social, political, and economic function, and the bodies of women and African Americans marked them for roles of "reproduction and production," not for those of power and domination.

89. Douglass quoted his own speech in a letter to Samuel Cox, 30 Oct. 1846 in *Frederick Douglass: Selected Speeches and Writings*, ed. Philip Foner (Chicago: Lawrence Hill Books, 1975), 40–48.
90. Ibid.
91. Ibid.
92. *Journal of the American Temperance Union*, October 1846.
93. Literature on black abolitionists and northern blacks addresses temperance in part, although no thorough study has been done: James Oliver Horton and Lois E. Horton, *In Hope of Liberty: Culture, Community, and Protest among Northern Free Blacks, 1700–1860* (New York: Oxford University Press, 1997), 221–24; William Gienapp, "Abolitionism and the Nature of Antebellum Reform," *Courage and Conscience: Black and White Abolitionists in Boston*, ed. Donald Jacobs (Bloomington: Indiana University Press, 1993), 21–46; Waldo E. Marton, Jr., *The Mind of Frederick Douglass* (Chapel Hill: University of North Carolina Press, 1984), 139, 166, 174, 185–90; William McFeely, *Frederick Douglass* (New York: Simon and Schuster, 1991); Jane H. Pease and William H. Pease, *They Who Would be Free: Blacks' Search for Freedom, 1830–1860* (New York: Athenaeum, 1974), 56–57, 121, 124–26; Benjamin Quarles, *Black Abolitionists*, 2nd edition (New York: Norton, 1973), 91–100; Patrick Rael, *Black Identity and Protest in the Antebellum North* (Chapel Hill: University of North Carolina Press, 2002), 67–68, 194; Donald Yacovone, "The Transformation of the Black Temperance Movement, 1827–1854: An Interpretation," *Journal of the Early Republic* 8 (1988): 281–97; Frederick Cooper, "Elevating the Race: The Social Thought of Black Leaders, 1827–1850," *American Quarterly* 24 (1972): 604–25.
94. Douglass himself described these occurrences, but also see Robert S. Levine, "Disturbing Boundaries: Temperance, Black Elevation, and Violence in Frank J. Webb's *The Garies and Their Friends*," *Prospects* 19 (1994): 358; Julie Winch, *Philadelphia's Black Elite: Activism, Accommodation, and the Struggle for Autonomy* (Philadelphia: Temple University Press, 1988), 148–49. Levine offers evidence to suggest that respectability exhibited by blacks in Philadelphia (such as participation in a temperance society) actually heightened racial hostility toward them.
95. Douglass to Garrison from Dublin, September 29, 1845, Frederick Douglass Papers (microfilm), Library of Congress Manuscripts Division, Washington, DC, reel 1.
96. Ibid.; Douglass, "The Right to Criticize American Institutions," before the American Anti-Slavery Society, 11 May 1847, *Frederick Douglass*, 76–83.
97. Editorial in the *North Star*, Jan. 1848, Frederick Douglass Papers, reel 13.
98. Editorial in the *North Star*, July 1848, Ibid.
99. 4 March 1837, in Peter C. Ripley, *Witness for Freedom: African American Voices on Race, Slavery and Emancipation* (Chapel Hill: University of North Carolina Press, 1993), 51–53.
100. "To the Free Colored Inhabitants of These United States," *Witness for Freedom*, 49–51.
101. Essay by Jacob W. White, 24 March 1854, Ibid., 55–56.

102. Editorial by Samuel Cornish, *Colored American* (New York), 4 March 1837.
103. 25 Aug 1841, Elizur Wright Papers, Library of Congress Manuscripts Division, Washington, DC, folio vol. 1. He spoke of the Liberty Party, to be discussed later in this chapter.
104. Henry Mayer, *All on Fire: William Lloyd Garrison and the Abolition of Slavery* (New York: St. Martin's Press, 1998), 49–50. The motto of the paper was printed on the front page of each issue. Garrison edited the paper from 1828 to 1829.
105. Almost every issue during this time period included reports from southern societies. On the presence of southerners at conventions, see for example, September 1841. Ian R. Tyrrell, "Drink and Temperance in the Antebellum South," *Journal of Southern History* 48 (1982): 485–510.
106. Ibid., 485.
107. Ibid., 487.
108. *Journal of the American Temperance Union,* April 1837.
109. Delavan to Smith, 30 Nov. 1837, Gerrit Smith Papers (microfilm), Library of Congress Manuscripts Division, Washington, DC, reel 5.
110. Tyrrell, "Drink and Temperance in the Antebellum South," 487.
111. Delavan to Smith, 23 July 1840, Gerrit Smith Papers, reel 5.
112. 25 March 1851, Ibid.
113. John Stauffer, *The Black Hearts of Men: Radical Abolitionists and the Transformation of Race* (Cambridge, MA: Harvard University Press, 1998), 95; Mayer, *All on Fire;* Bertram Wyatt-Brown, *Lewis Tappan and the Evangelical War Against Slavery* (Cleveland: Case-Western Reserve University Press, 1969); Hugh Davis, *Joshua Leavitt: Evangelical Abolitionist* (Baton Rouge: Louisiana State University Press, 1990).
114. For more on the political climate of the 1850's and the growth of radicalism within the abolitionist movement, see David M. Potter, *The Impending Crisis, 1848–1861* (New York: HarperCollins, 1977); Jane Pease and William Pease, "Confrontation and Abolition in the 1850's," *Journal of American History* 58 (1972): 923–37; Richard Newman, "The Transformation of American Abolition: Tactics, Strategies and the Changing Meanings of Activism, 1780's-1830's," (Ph.D. dissertation, SUNY Buffalo, 1998); Michael Holt, *The Political Crisis of the 1850's* (New York: W.W. Norton, 1983).
115. Including the *Investigator and General Intelligencer* (Providence, Rhode Island); the *National Philanthropist, Investigator and Genius of Temperance,* which had formerly been simply the *National Philanthropist* and edited by William Lloyd Garrison; and the *Genius of Temperance, Philanthropist and People's Advocate* (New York).
116. Paul Goodman, *Of One Blood: Abolitionism and the Origins of Racial Equality* (Berkeley: University of California Press, 1998), ch. 7.
117. Goodell to Josiah Cady, April 1831, William Goodell Family Papers, Historical Collections of Berea College, Berea, KY, box 13, folder 15.
118. Jan 20, 1829 and June 4, 1829.
119. *Genius of Temperance, Philanthropist and People's Advocate,* 1 Jan. 1832.

120. His chief differences (and those of Smith and most others in their circle) with Garrison concerned his belief in the Constitution as an anti-slavery document and in political tactics. The historiography concerning the differences between these two groups of abolitionists is large. Most historians seem to agree that the issue of political reform, not women's rights, was the chief difference. Historians seem to be moving away from the moderate/radical method of categorization, as many anti-Garrisonians were very radical indeed and against what became the "one idea" method of the Liberty Party. Goodell and Smith definitely fit this mould. See Lawrence Friedman, "The Gerrit Smith Circle: Abolitionism in the Burned Over District," *History of the American Abolitionist Movement,* vol. 3, *Abolitionism and American Politics and Government,* ed. John McKivigan (New York: Garland Publishing, 1999), 12–32; Aileen Kraditor, *Means and Ends in American Abolitionism: Garrison and His Critics on Strategy and Tactics* (New York: Random House, 1967); James Brewer Stewart, *Holy Warriors: The Abolitionists and American Slavery,* revised edition (New York: Hill and Wang, 1997), ch. 3–4; Ronald G. Walters, *The Antislavery Appeal: American Abolitionism after 1830* (Baltimore: Johns Hopkins University Press, 1976); William W. Wiecek, *The Sources of Antislavery Constitutionalism in America* (Ithaca: Cornell University Press, 1977); John Stauffer, *The Black Hearts of Men;* Goodman, *Of One Blood,* ch. 7; Lewis Perry, "Versions of Anarchism in the Antislavery Movement," *American Quarterly* 20 (1968): 768–82. For more on the specific constitutional views of Goodell and other anti-Garrisonians, see M. Leon Perkal, "The American Abolition Society: A Viable Alternative to the Republican Party?," *Journal of Negro History* 65 (1980): 57–71 and Randy Barnett, "Was Slavery Unconstitutional Before the Thirteenth Amendment?: Lysander Spooner's Theory of Interpretation," *Pacific Law Journal* 28 (1997): 977–1014. Also see Goodell's own writing on the subject, such as *Views of American constitutional law in its bearing upon American slavery* (Utica, NY: Lawson & Chaplin, 1845).

121. For more on "comeouterism" and the religious side of abolition, see James D. Essig, *The Bonds of Wickedness: American Evangelicals against Slavery, 1770–1808* (Philadelphia: Temple University Press, 1982); Victor B. Howard, *The Evangelical War against Slavery and Caste: The Life and Times of John G. Fee* (Selinsgrove, PA: Susquehanna University Press, 1996); James Brewer Stewart, *Holy Warriors;* Robert H. Abzug, *Cosmos Crumbling: American Reform and the Religious Imagination* (New York: Oxford University Press, 1994); Lawrence Friedman, *Gregarious Saints;* John R. McKivigan, *The War Against Proslavery Religion: Abolitionism and the Northern Churches, 1830–1865* (Ithaca: Cornell University Press, 1984) and "The Antislavery 'Comeouter' Sects: A Neglected Dimension of the Abolitionist Movement," *Civil War History* 26 (1980): 142–60; Anne C. Loveland, "Evangelicalism and 'Immediate Emancipation' in American Antislavery Thought," *Journal of Southern History* 32 (May 1966): 172–88; Donald G. Mathews, *Slavery and Methodism: A Chapter in American Morality, 1780–1845* (Princeton: Princeton University Press, 1965), 677–695; Douglas Strong, *Perfectionist*

Politics: Abolitionism and the Religious Tensions of American Democracy (Syracuse, NY: Syracuse University Press, 1999). Strong gives Goodell much attention as a reformer who led the way in ecclesiastical abolitionism. He sees the Liberty Party as an outgrowth of perfectionist evangelical religion, which stressed the experience of personal sanctification and the belief in human frailty as necessitating human political structures.

122. William Goodell to J. Cady, 6 July 1846, Goodell Family Papers, box 13, folder 16; "In Memoriam. William Goodell" (Chicago: Guilbert and Winchell Printers, 1879), Frederick Douglass Papers, reel 11.

123. Smith's own reform career closely paralleled and intertwined with that of Goodell. His hometown of Peterboro, New York was rife with intemperance, and Smith had been an early temperance proponent. He had been a moderate on that issue and on slavery (he was in favor of colonization), until the late 1830's, when his path turned toward militant abolitionism and other radical reforms. One historian attributed this transition and that made by other reformers to the shock of the financial collapse of 1837. Smith's own fortune suffered, and his ideas seemed markedly affected. Stauffer, *Black Hearts of Men*, 95; Friedman, "The Gerrit Smith Circle."

124. Goodell to J. Cady, 4 April 1846, Goodell Family Papers, box 13, folder 17. For more on the Liberty Party, see Richard H. Sewell, *Ballots for Freedom: Antislavery Politics in the United States, 1837–1860* (New York: Oxford University Press, 1976); Strong, *Perfectionist Politics*. The only thorough history of the Liberty Party is Vernon Volpe's *Forlorn Hope of Freedom: The Liberty Party in the Old Northwest, 1838–1848* (Kent, OH: Kent State University Press, 1990), which views the Liberty Party as the closest thing in American politics to an abolitionist party and an evangelical party. He notes the religious roots of the party; most members were, like Goodell, anti-Garrisonian Protestant Christians, who had been involved in the "comeouter" movements in the major denominations. The Liberty Party's radical egalitarianism, including attacks on the American tax system and the "land monopoly," seems to counter the interpretation of abolitionists as conservatives who reinforced class hegemony. For more on this debate, see David Brion Davis, "Reflections on Abolitionism and Ideological Hegemony," *American Historical Review* 92 (1987): 797–812; Thomas Haskell, "Capitalism and the Origins of Humanitarian Sensibility, Part I," *American Historical Review* 90 (1985): 339–61 and Part 2 *American Historical Review* 90 (1985): 457–566; Betty Fladeland, *Abolitionists and Working-Class Problems in the Age of Industrialization* (Baton Rouge: Louisiana State University Press, 1984); James Brewer Stewart, "The Aims and Impact of Garrisonian Abolitionism, 1840–1860," *Civil War History* 15 (1969): 197–209; Kraditor, *Means and Ends in American Abolitionism*; James L. Huston, "The Experiential Basis of the Northern Antislavery Impulse," *Journal of Southern History* 56 (1990): 192–215.

125. The Liberty Party did not include women's rights in its platform, but subsequent political efforts by Goodell and Gerrit Smith did. The two men went on in 1856 and 1858 to form a New York state equal rights party with an "omnibus" reform platform that featured women's rights more prominently.

In addition, John Stauffer has called Smith a "gender radical," and Goodell's anti-clerical stance had feminist ramifications, since the clerical system blocked women's participation in church leadership. See Stauffer, *Black Hearts of Men*, 211; Isenberg, *Sex and* Citizenship, ch. 4; *Gerrit Smith Banner* (New York), 16 and 21 October 1858. In addition, Michael Pierson identifies a "jumble" of gendered views in the Liberty Party, some of them radical; see *Free Hearts and Free Homes*, 20, 25–70.

126. "Address of the Macedon Convention," (Albany: S.W. Green, 1847), quote on 6, 9. With this address, Goodell split from the Liberty Party and formed the Liberty League because he believed the Liberty Party was too single-minded in its pursuit of abolition.
127. "Christian Temperance," delivered in Arcadia, NY in Aug. 1858, Goodell Family Papers, box 8, folder 39; "The Condition and Refuge of our Country," 9 Oct. 1859 at Williamsburg, Ibid., box 8, folder 37.
128. "Address of the Macedon Convention," 6–7.
129. This view is based on an interpretation of liberalism that emphasizes its radical potentials, as expressed in moral reform movements. Abolitionists, feminists, and other radical egalitarians emphasized individualism not for economic self-interest, but on the basis of human rights. See Louis S. Gerteis, *Morality and Utility in American Antislavery Reform* (Chapel Hill: University of North Carolina Press, 1987); Peter F. Walker, *Moral Choices: Memory, Desire, and Imagination in Nineteenth Century American Abolition* (Baton Rouge: Louisiana State University Press, 1978); Isenberg, *Sex and Citizenship*; Linda K. Kerber, *No Constitutional Right to be Ladies: Women and the Obligations of Citizenship* (New York: Hill and Wang, 1998); Amy Dru Stanley, *From Bondage to Contract: Wage Labor, Marriage, and the Market in the Age of Slave Emancipation* (Cambridge: Cambridge University Press, 1998); Sylvia Hoffert, *When Hens Crow: The Woman's Rights Movement in Antebellum America* (Bloomington: Indiana University Press, 1995); Rosemarie Zagarri, "Gender and the New Liberal Synthesis," *American Quarterly* 53 (2001): 123–30; Stauffer, *Black Hearts of Men*; David F. Ericson, *The Debate over Slavery: Antislavery and Proslavery Liberalism in Antebellum America* (New York: New York University Press, 2000).
130. For other historical accounts of the events described here, see Elizabeth Cazden, *Antoinette Brown Blackwell: A Biography* (Old Westbury, NY: The Feminist Press, 1983), ch. 2, 3, 5; Isenberg, *Sex and Citizenship*, 99–101; Hoffert, *When Hens Crow*, 20–21.
131. *New York Tribune*, 13 May 1853; *New York Times*, 13 May 1853.
132. *Anti-Slavery Bugle* (Salem, OH), 2 July 1853.
133. *New York Tribune*, 3 Sept. 1853.
134. Ibid.
135. *Journal of the American Temperance Union*, June 1853.
136. Ibid., Oct. 1853
137. *New York People's Organ, A Family Companion* (New York), 15 Oct. 1853.
138. *New York Tribune*, 7 Sept. 1853.

139. *Una* (Providence, RI), 1 September 1853.
140. *New York Tribune*, 7 Sept. 1853.
141. Ibid., 9 Sept. 1853.
142. Ibid., 7 Sept. 1853.
143. *Anti-Slavery Bugle*, 17 Sept. 1853.
144. *New York Tribune*, 7 Sept. 1853; *New York Times*, 7–8 Sept. 1853.
145. Ibid., 8–10 Sept. 1853.

NOTES TO CHAPTER THREE

1. John Marsh, *Temperance Recollections, Labors, Defeats, Triumphs. An Autobiography* (New York: Charles Scribner & Co., 1867), 296–97.
2. Quote from *National Temperance Advocate* (New York), Jan. 1866; *Journal of the American Temperance Union* (New York), July 1865, Aug. 1865; Marsh, *Temperance Recollections*, 351.
3. E.C. Delavan to Gerrit Smith, 23 May 1865, Gerrit Smith Papers (microfilm), Library of Congress Manuscripts Division, Washington, DC, reel 5.
4. E.C. Delavan to Gerrit Smith, 11 April 1866, Ibid.
5. E.C. Delavan to Gerrit Smith, 13 Jan. 1868, Ibid.
6. George Washington Adams, *Doctors in Blue: The Medical History of the Union Army* (New York: Henry Schuman, 1952), 128, 140, 144. Adams asserts that "alcohol was the sovereign remedy of the Civil War, rivaled only by quinine" (140). *Harper's Weekly* maintained that alcohol and quinine were "very efficient safeguards against the diseases of the camp;" 11 March 1865.
7. *Journal of the American Temperance Union*, Feb. 1863.
8. Jack S. Blocker, *American Temperance Movements: Cycles of Reform* (Boston: Twayne Publishers, 1989), 64–67; W. J. Rorabaugh, *Alcoholic Republic: An American Tradition* (New York: Oxford University Press, 1979), appendix one; Stanley Wade Baron, *Brewed in America: A History of Beer and Ale in the United States* (Boston: Little, Brown Co., 1962); Mark Lender and James Kirby Martin, *Drinking in America: A History* (New York: Free Press, 1982), 87–132; James R. Turner, "The American Prohibition Movement, 1865–1897" (Ph.D. dissertation, University of Wisconsin, 1972).
9. *The Rescue* (Sacramento, CA), Feb. 1864.
10. Oct. 1866.
11. Glenn Hendler, "Bloated Bodies and Sober Sentiments: Masculinity in 1840's Temperance Narratives," *Sentimental Men: Masculinity and the Politics of Affect in American Culture*, ed. Glenn Hendler and Mary Chapman (Berkeley: University of California Press, 1999), 125–48; Blocker, *Cycles of Reform*, 12–20, 32, 42–46, 77, 87, 99–106, 150.
12. D.R. Thomason, *Reply to Dr. Marsh on Teetotalism, including a letter from Howard Crosby, D.D.* (New York: Richardson and Company, 1867).
13. *National Temperance Advocate*, Sept. 1866.
14. *Temperance Host* (Franklin, IN), 5 April 1866. Also see the *National Temperance Advocate*, Feb. 1869, Feb. 1866; *Journal of the American Temperance Union and New York Prohibitionist*, July 1865.

15. John Joseph Coffey, "A Political History of the Temperance Movement in New York State, 1808–1920," (Ph.D. dissertation, Pennsylvania State University, 1976), 99.
16. Morton Keller, *Affairs of State: Public Life in Late Nineteenth-Century America* (Cambridge, MA: Belknap Press of Harvard University Press, 1977), 129; Jed Dannenbaum, *Drink and Disorder: Temperance Reform in Cincinnati from the Washingtonian Revival to the WCTU* (Urbana and Chicago: University of Illinois Press, 1984), 156–79.
17. *National Temperance Advocate,* June 1873.
18. *Journal of the American Temperance Union,* Sept. 1864.
19. For more on the Civil War's impact on concepts of masculinity, see Clyde Griffen, "Reconstructing Masculinity from the Evangelical Revival to the Waning of Progressivism: A Speculative Synthesis," *Meanings for Manhood: Constructions of Masculinity in Victorian America,* ed. Mark C. Carnes and Clyde Griffen (Chicago: University of Chicago Press, 1990), 190–93; E. Anthony Rotundo, "Body and Soul: Changing Ideals of American Middle-Class Manhood, 1770–1920," *Journal of Social History* 16 (1983): 23–38 and *American Manhood: Transformations in Masculinity from the Revolution to the Modern Era* (New York: Basic Books, 1993), 21, 36, 42, 227, 233–35, 254, 271; Michael Kimmel, *Manhood in America: A Cultural History* (New York: The Free Press, 1996), 72–78, 94, 151; Joe L. Dubbert, *A Man's Place: Masculinity in Transition* (Englewood Cliffs, NJ: Prentice-Hall, 1979), ch. 3.
20. *Journal of the American Temperance Union,* Apr. 1863.
21. Ibid., Aug. 1863.
22. Ibid., Jan. 1863.
23. Ibid., Feb. 1864.
24. Ibid., Dec. 1863, May 1863, Sept. 1862.
25. Ibid., April 1863. Newspapers reported numerous instances of drunken officers; see *Harper's Weekly,* 28 June 1862, 8 Nov. 1862, 13 June 1863, 29 Aug. 1863, 23 Jan. 1864.
26. *Journal of the American Temperance Union,* May 1861.
27. Ibid., Sept. 1863.
28. Ibid.
29. Lyle W. Dorsett, "The Problem of Grant's Drinking During the Civil War," *Hayes Historical Journal* 4 (1983): 37–48.
30. Bruce Catton, *Grant Moves South* (Boston: Little, Brown and Co., 1960), 371.
31. *Journal of the American Temperance Union,* Oct 1863.
32. Ibid., Sept. 1863.
33. Ibid., Sept. 1864.
34. Ibid., July 1864, Aug, 1864.
35. Elaine Parsons notes how temperance was discussed using war metaphors during this time; *Manhood Lost: Fallen Drunkards and Redeeming Women in the Nineteenth-Century United States* (Baltimore: Johns Hopkins University Press, 2003), 126–56. She argues this was part of a new discourse of invasion, inspired by the Civil War, that minimized individual volition and

looked to the state to protect men from alcohol. Edward Blum also notes the movement's use of Civil War imagery and rhetoric; *Reforging the White Republic: Race, Religion and American Nationalism, 1865–1898* (Baton Rouge: Louisiana State University Press, 2005), 174–208.

36. *The Transcript, Young Men's Journal and Advocate of Temperance* (Detroit, MI), 8 March 1862, Microfilm Edition of the Temperance and Prohibition Papers, joint project of the Michigan Historical Collections, Ohio Historical Society, and the Woman's Christian Temperance Union, series I, reel 2.
37. Jan. 1866.
38. *The Rescue*, Dec. 1864.
39. *Journal of the American Temperance Union*, May 1861, April 1861.
40. *National Temperance Advocate*, May 1867.
41. "Self-Denial," Ibid., May 1869.
42. *National Temperance Advocate*, Jan. 1868.
43. Rev. George Lansing Taylor, "The Cold Water Battle Hymn," Ibid., July 1867.
44. Gaines Foster argues that the Civil War established a precedent for numerous reform movements, including temperance, for looking to the state to counter social evils and regulate individual behavior. *Moral Reconstruction: Christian Lobbyists and the Federal Legislation of Morality, 1865–1920* (Chapel Hill: University of North Carolina Press, 2002).
45. *Templar's Magazine* (Philadelphia), June 1868.
46. *National Temperance Advocate*, Nov. 1872.
47. Ibid., Nov. 1870.
48. Blocker, *Cycles of Reform*, 71–79, 85–94.
49. Gaines Foster sees the general push for moral legislation during the Gilded Age in these terms as well; *Moral Reconstruction*, 77–85.
50. Historians have noted middle-class ambivalence to the growing wealth and political power of big business and the identification between the middle and working classes during this time period. See Alan Trachtenberg, *The Incorporation of America: Culture and Society in the Gilded Age* (New York: Hill and Wang, 1982), ch. 3; Thomas Winter, *Making Men, Making Class: The YMCA and Workingmen, 1877–1920* (Chicago: University of Chicago, 2002); Gail Bederman, *Manliness and Civilization: A Cultural History of Gender and Race in the United States, 1880–1917* (Chicago: University of Chicago, 1995). Bederman points out that there was a dramatic drop in the number of middle-class men who were self-employed; the common status of middle-class and working-class men as wage workers helps account for the growing identification between them (12).
51. One of the primary reasons for their growth during the war was most likely their openness to women. While men were preoccupied with the war, women took up leadership positions within the movement. This will be discussed in greater detail later in the chapter. See David Fahey, *Temperance and Racism: John Bull, Johnny Reb and the Good Templars* (Lexington: University of Kentucky Press, 1996), also *National Temperance Advocate*, Sept. 1868. William Dodge, the president of the NTS, noted that secret

societies owed their war-era success to "the cooperation of women they secure." More will be said on this point below.
52. John Marsh, *Letter on the Promotion of Moral Reforms by Secret Societies; Addressed to William Dodge* (New York: New York Tract Office, 1868); *National Temperance Advocate*, April 1866.
53. *National Temperance Advocate*, Feb. 1872.
54. Ibid., June 1872.
55. *Templar's Magazine*, Jan. 1868.
56. Mary Dwinell Chellis, *Wealth and Wine* (New York: National Temperance Society and Publication House, 1874); *Templar's Magazine*, Feb. 1869.
57. *Journal of the American Temperance Union*, June 1861.
58. "Drinking for Health," *Temperance Sermons* (New York: National Temperance Society and Publication House, 1873), 328.
59. *National Temperance Advocate*, Feb. 1874.
60. Ibid., Nov. 1868.
61. J.H. Hartwell, "Outlaw or Legalize the Liquor Traffic—Which?" (1874), Microfilm Edition of the Temperance and Prohibition Papers, series I, reel 1.
62. *National Temperance Advocate*, March 1869.
63. Ibid., Apr. 1872; see also Sept. and Oct. 1869, and Albert Williams, *Prohibition and Woman Suffrage* (Lansing, 1874, no other publication information given), *History of Women* (microform collection) (New Haven: Research Publications, 1975–79), reel 418, no. 3057.
64. *National Temperance Advocate*, Sept. 1870.
65. For works on the influence of immigration and ethnicity on Gilded Age politics, see Matthew Frye Jacobsen, *Barbarian Virtues: The United States encounters foreign peoples at home and abroad, 1876–1917* (New York: Hill and Wang, 2000); Richard Jensen, *Grass Roots Politics: Parties, Issues and Voters, 1854–1893* (Westport, CT: Greenwood Press, 1983); Paul Kleppner, *The Third Electoral System, 1853–1892: Parties, Voters and Political Cultures* (Chapel Hill: University of North Carolina Press, 1979); Robert Kelley, *The Cultural Pattern in American Politics: The First Century* (New York: Alfred A. Knopf, 1979); Mary P. Ryan, *Civic Wars: Democracy and Public Life in the American City during the Nineteenth Century* (Berkeley: University of California Press, 1997); Roy Rosenzweig, *Eight Hours for What We Will: Workers and Leisure in an Industrial City, 1870–1920* (Cambridge: Cambridge University Press, 1983), especially ch. 4–6; Bederman, *Manliness and Civilization*, 12–30. Elaine Parsons argues that the concern with immigrants did not surround the immigrants themselves as much as it did the political and economic support they might provide to the alcohol industry; *Manhood Lost*, 129.
66. Ibid., Aug. 1867.
67. Ibid., June 1868, Nov. 1870.
68. Ibid., Aug. 1870.
69. Ibid., Jan. 1872.
70. Ibid., March 1870, Dec. 1867.
71. Ibid., Sept. 1874, July 1872.

Notes to Chapter Three

72. There was abundant use of this comparison in the temperance movement in general; see for example, Schuyler Colfax, *Example and Effort. An Address delivered before the Congressional Temperance Society at Washington, D.C.* (New York: National Temperance Society and Publishing House, 1872), 3; *National Temperance Advocate,* March 1866, Apr. 1870; *Templar's Magazine,* June 1868.
73. This tract was written by George Bungay and advertised in the *National Temperance Advocate,* Nov. 1868.
74. Ibid., Jan. 1869.
75. Ibid., June 1874.
76. Eric Foner, *Reconstruction: America's Unfinished Revolution, 1863–1877* (New York: Harper and Row, 1988), 277–280; David W. Blight, *Race and Reunion: The Civil War in American Memory* (Cambridge, MA: Harvard University Press, 2001); Heather Cox Richardson, *The Death of Reconstruction: Race, Labor and Politics in the Post-Civil War North, 1865–1901* (Cambridge, MA: Harvard University Press, 2001).
77. Smith to the Anti-Dramshop Party, 6 Nov. 1872, Gerrit Smith Papers, reel 74; *National Temperance Advocate,* Nov. 1874.
78. Ibid., July 1872, Sept. 1868.
79. David Fahey has written the only book-length study on the Good Templars and recounts the controversy over black lodges. He argues that the organization compromised their democratic principles for the sake of expediency on this issue. See *Temperance and Racism*. The pragmatic sacrifice of a dialogue on racial equality in the interest of other issues in the postwar period has received much attention from historians. See, for example, Richardson, *The Death of Reconstruction;* Blight, *Race and Reunion,* esp. ch. 4. See also Nina Silber, *The Romance of Reunion: Northerners and the South, 1865–1900* (Chapel Hill: University of North Carolina Press, 1993); David Montgomery, *Beyond Equality: Labor and the Radical Republicans, 1862–1872* (New York: Alfred A. Knopf, 1967); John G. Sproat, *"The Best Men:" Liberal Reformers in the Gilded Age* (Oxford: Oxford University Press, 1968). James M. McPherson offers a different view, emphasizing the continuance of a racial egalitarian tradition in American reform; see *The Struggle for Equality: Abolitionists and the Negro in the Civil War and Reconstruction* (Princeton: Princeton University Press, 1964), *The Abolitionist Legacy: From Reconstruction to the NAACP* (Princeton: Princeton University Press, 1975) and "Abolitionists and the Civil Rights Act of 1875," *Journal of American History* 52 (1965): 493–510.
80. Fahey, *Temperance and Racism; National Temperance Advocate,* June 1868, Nov. 1871, Aug. 1872, Nov. 1872, May 1873, Sept. 1873.
81. Ibid., July 1872.
82. Ibid.
83. For more on the gendered implications of citizenship and political definitions of manhood, see Nancy Isenberg, *Sex and Citizenship in Antebellum America* (Chapel Hill: University of North Carolina Press, 1998), ch. 5 discusses the racial aspects of this; Paula Baker, *The Moral Frameworks of Public Life: Gender, Politics and the State in Rural New York, 1870–1930*

(New York: Oxford University Press, 1991); Bederman, *Manliness and Civilization*; Mark Kann, *On the Man Question: Gender and Civic Virtue in America* (Philadelphia: Temple University Press, 1991).
84. *National Temperance Advocate,* Nov. 1870, Sept. 1872.
85. Rev. John Hall, "The Active Pity of a Queen," *Temperance Sermons,* 167.
86. *National Temperance Advocate,* May 1869, Aug. 1870.
87. Ibid., July 1872, Aug. 1870, May 1869. Elaine Parsons also examines temperance reformers' interest in Native Americans' alcohol problem; she interprets it as both exhibiting the guilt of American civilization and the fearsome power of alcohol's destruction; *Manhood Lost,* 143–45.
88. *National Temperance Advocate,* Dec. 1868.
89. This idea is explored in Parsons, *Manhood Lost.* She argues that the theme of male "volition" was prominent in temperance discourse; prohibition resulted from that volition being called into doubt; see especially 18–52.
90. *Journal of the American Temperance Union,* July 1864; "Col. Freiedrich Hecker on the New Temperance Law," (1880? No other publishing information given), Microfilm Edition of the Temperance and Prohibition Papers, series I, reel 1.
91. Dr. Stephen Smith, "Effects of the Drinking Usages of Society among Women," *National Temperance Advocate,* Feb. 1874.
92. *Templar's Magazine,* June 1868.
93. For works on women's expanded public role during and after the Civil War, see Nancy M. Theriot, *Mothers and Daughters in Nineteenth-Century America: The Biosocial Construction of Femininity* (Lexington: University of Kentucky, 1996); Barbara Cutter, *Domestic Devils, Battlefield Angels: The Radicalism of American Womanhood, 1830–1865* (DeKalb, IL: Northern Illinois University Press, 2003); Jeanie Attie, *Patriotic Toil: Northern Women and the American Civil War* (Ithaca: Cornell University Press, 1998); Judith Ann Giesberg, *Civil War Sisterhood: The U.S. Sanitary Commission and Women's Politics in Transition* (Boston: Northeastern University Press, 2000); Lori D.Ginzberg, *Women and the Work of Benevolence: Morality, Politics and Class in the Nineteenth-Century United States* (New Haven: Yale University Press, 1994). Ginzberg sees the Civil War as expanding women's roles in the context of class solidarity, as opposed to the continued notion of female morality; the other works mentioned emphasize the continued belief in female morality.
94. Nina Baker Brown, *Cyclone in Calico: The Story of Mary Ann Bickerdyke* (Boston: Little, Brown and Co., 1952), 160.
95. Barbara Cutter has argued that nineteenth-century Americans were not as concerned with women's actual roles and behavior as they were with how well that behavior meshed with the notion of female morality and self-sacrifice. Women's Civil War activity, though in settings often seen as male, actually fit perfectly with these expectations for women. *Domestic Devils,* 154–95.
96. Blocker, *American Temperance Movements,* 73. The Sons doubled their membership in the three years after the war, while the Good Templars increased theirs almost five-fold. Blocker attributes this success to inroads

made in the southern states. David Fahey claims the groups' openness to women accounted for this; *Temperance and Racism*.
97. *Lily* (Seneca Falls, NY), 15 July 1854.
98. *Templar's Magazine*, Jan. 1868.
99. J.H. Hartwell, "There is no exclusion," (1869), Microfilm Edition of the Temperance and Prohibition Papers, series I, reel 2.
100. *National Temperance Advocate*, April 1867, Sept. 1872.
101. Ibid., Aug. 1870, Oct. 1870; *Templar's Magazine*, Nov. 1868.
102. Speech by Miss J.S. Maloney, 6 May 1868, Ibid., Nov. 1868.
103. *National Temperance Advocate*, Feb. 1874.
104. Sept. 1872.
105. Ibid., April 1867.
106. 14 March 1868.
107. *National Temperance Advocate*, Nov. 1866.
108. Ibid., May 1870. This was at the anniversary meeting of the Philadelphia Sons of Temperance.
109. Ibid., Aug. 1873.
110. Williams, "Prohibition and Woman Suffrage," 21.
111. Ibid.
112. James Black, *Brief History of Prohibition and of the Prohibition Reform Party* (New York: National Committee of the Prohibition Reform Party, 1872), 26.
113. James McPherson, "Abolitionists, Woman Suffrage, and the Negro, 1865–1869," *Mid-America* 47 (1965): 40–47; Nancy Cott, *Public Vows: A History of Marriage and the Nation* (Cambridge, MA: Harvard University Press, 2000); Carl Degler, *At Odds: Women and the Family from the Revolution to the Present* (New York: Oxford University Press, 2000); Louise Michelle Newman, *White Women's Rights: Racial Origins of Feminism in the United States* (New York: Oxford University Press, 1999); Sandra F. VanBurkleo, *"Belonging to the World:" Women's Rights and American Constitutional Culture* (New York: Oxford University Press, 2001), ch. 7; Suzanne Marilley, *Woman Suffrage and the Origins of Liberal Feminism in the United States, 1820–1920* (Cambridge, MA: Harvard University Press, 1996), ch. 3; Ellen Carol DuBois, "Outgrowing the Compact of the Fathers: Equal Rights, Woman Suffrage, and the United States Constitution, 1820–1878," *Journal of American History* 74 (1987): 844–52. On the loss of a dialogue on individual equality within women's rights, see William Leach, *True Love and Perfect Union: The Feminist Reform of Sex and Society* (New York: Basic Books, 1980); Karen J. Blair, *The Clubwoman as Feminist: True Womanhood Redefined, 1868–1914* (New York: Holmes and Meier, 1980); Janet Zollinger Giele, *Two Paths to Women's Equality: Temperance, Suffrage and the Origins of Liberal Feminism in the United States, 1820–1920* (Cambridge, MA: Harvard University Press, 1996); Elizabeth Battelle Clark, "The Politics of God and the Woman's Vote: Religion in the American Suffrage Movement, 1848–1895" (Ph.D. dissertation, Princeton University, 1989); Barbara Leslie Epstein, *The Politics of Domesticity: Women,*

Evangelism and Temperance in Nineteenth-Century America (Middletown, CT: Wesleyan University Press, 1981). Many of these works refer to the growth of "domestic feminism," describing the new context of women's rights and public roles within the traditional family. This term was first used by Daniel Scott Smith, "Family Limitation, Sexual Control, and Domestic Feminism in Victorian America," *Clio's Consciousness Raised*, ed. Mart Hartman and Lois Banner (New York: Harper and Row, 1974), 4–5.

114. This quote is from Cott, *Public Vows*, 96. Also see Lori Ginzberg, "Pernicious Heresies: Female Citizenship and Sexual Respectability in the Nineteenth Century," *Women and the Unstable State in Nineteenth-Century America*, ed. Alison M. Parker and Stephanie Cole (College Station, TX: Texas A&M University Press, 2000), 139–62; Degler, *At Odds*, 329.

115. George M. Frederickson, *The Inner Civil War: Northern Intellectuals and the Crisis of the Union* (Urbana: University of Illinois Press, 1965); Ginzberg, *Women and the Work of Benevolence*; Nancy Cohen, *The Reconstruction of American Liberalism, 1865–1914* (Chapel Hill: University of North Carolina Press, 2002); Foster, *Moral Reconstruction*.

116. For this counterpoint, see Anne C. Rose, *Victorian America and the Civil War* (Cambridge: Cambridge University Press, 1992); Louis Menand, *The Metaphysical Club: A Story of Ideas in America* (New York: Farrar, Straus and Giroux, 2001); Judith Ann Giesburg, *Civil War Sisterhood: The U.S. Sanitary Commission and Women's Politics in Transition* (Boston: Northeastern University Press, 2000); Morton Keller, *Affairs of the State: Public Life in the Nineteenth Century America* (Cambridge, MA: Harvard University Press, 1977); Alan Trachtenberg, *The Incorporation of America: Culture and Society in the Gilded Age* (New York: Hill and Wang, 1982). Trachtenberg gives both sides of this, depicting a deep ambivalence in American culture after the Civil War.

117. Michael McGerr asserts that "men's and women's politics developed in tandem;" "Political Style and Women's Power," *Journal of American History* 77(1990): 864. Works that discuss women's expanded public role in terms of the new political situation include Theriot, *Mothers and Daughters*; Cott, *Public Vows*; Sarah Barringer Gordon, "Introduction: Politics, Marriage and the Texture of History," *Women and the Unstable State*, 3–14; Rebecca Edwards, *Angels in the Machinery: Gender in American Party Politics from the Civil war to the Progressive Era* (New York: Oxford University Press, 1997); Ryan, *Women in Public*, 172. Lori Ginzberg views women's expanded public roles in terms of a class alliance with men rather than a racial/ethnic one; she also argues that the notion of female morality declined after the Civil War; *Women and the Work of Benevolence*, 133–213.

NOTES TO CHAPTER FOUR

1. Quoted in J.E. Stebbins, *Fifty Years History of the Temperance Cause* (Hartford, CT: J.P. Fitch, 1876), 311.

Notes to Chapter Four

2. *New York Times*, 14 February 1874.
3. For general accounts of the Crusade, see Jack S. Blocker, *American Temperance Movements: Cycles of Reform* (Boston: Twayne Publishers, 1989), ch. 3 and *"Give to the Winds Thy Fears:" The Women's Temperance Crusade, 1873–1874* (Westport, CT: Greenwood Press, 1985). According to Blocker, Washington Courthouse was actually the fourth community where the Crusade was inaugurated, the first three being Fredonia and Jamestown, New York and Hillsboro, Ohio.
4. Blocker, "*Give to the Winds Thy Fears*," 18.
5. See for example, Blocker, "*Give to the Winds Thy Fears;*" Jed Dannenbaum, *Drink and Disorder: Temperance Reform in Cincinnati from the Washingtonian Revival to the WCTU* (Urbana: University of Illinois Press, 1984); Ruth Bordin, *Woman and Temperance: The Quest for Power and Liberty, 1873–1900* (Philadelphia: Temple University Press, 1981); Barbara Leslie Epstein, *The Politics of Domesticity: Women, Evangelism and Temperance in Nineteenth-Century America* (Middletown, CT: Wesleyan University Press, 1981). A slight departure from this interpretation is Elaine Franz Parsons, *Manhood Lost: Fallen Drunkards and Redeeming Women in the Nineteenth-Century United States* (Baltimore: Johns Hopkins University Press, 2003). She views the Crusade in terms of a discourse of "female invasion" and redemption; however, she does not note the depth of male participation.
6. *National Temperance Advocate* (New York), March 1870; this is from the proceedings of the Pennsylvania State Temperance Society convention, which debated the issue.
7. Ibid.
8. Ibid., Sept. 1869.
9. Ibid., March 1872, Dec. 1869.
10. Ibid., Dec. 1869, Nov. 1869.
11. 19 Nov. 1869 in Gerrit Smith Papers (microfilm), Library of Congress Manuscripts Division, Washington, DC, reel 5.
12. *National Temperance Advocate*, Nov. 1869, Dec. 1869. By the early 1870's, Smith had reversed his own position on the Prohibition Party, of which he was a founding member, first based on his belief in limited government, then based on his belief that the Prohibition Party only helped the Democrats, whom he abhorred. In the former case, he founded the Anti-Dram Shop Party, which sought only the prohibition of saloons; in the latter case, in 1872, he dispensed with third parties altogether and endorsed the Republican Party.
13. Ibid., Dec. 1869.
14. Ibid., Jan. 1869.
15. Ibid., May 1868; *Templar's Magazine* (Philadelphia), Jan. 1869; *The Rescue* (Sacramento), 23 May 1868.
16. *National Temperance Advocate*, Oct. 1872.
17. Ibid., June 1873. Almost this entire issue, as well as subsequent issues, was consumed with discussion of the Dix veto.
18. Ibid., Sept. 1873.

19. Ibid., Nov. 1869.
20. Ibid., Dec. 1869.
21. Ibid., March 1871.
22. Ibid., Dec. 1870.
23. Dio Lewis, *Prohibition a Failure, or the True Solution of the Temperance Question* (Boston: James R. Osgood and Co., 1875), 82.
24. Ibid., 5–6, 12–15, 44, 69.
25. Dio Lewis, *Our Girls* (New York: Harper and Brothers, 1871), 197–98, 115, 50, 86–87.
26. Introduction by Lewis to J.H. Beadle, *The Women's War on Whisky* (Cincinnati: Wilstach, Baldwin and Co., 1874).
27. Blocker says that Frances Willard started and perpetuated this myth, but does not really say why; "Give to the Winds Thy Fears," 27 (fn16). I have my own interpretation of the Willard-Thompson relationship in the next chapter.
28. Frances Willard's manuscript for the introduction of Thompson's memoirs, the Thompson and Tuttle Family Papers, 1812–1915, Ms. 1511, Western Reserve Historical Society, Cleveland, OH, container 1, folder 1.
29. Blocker, "Give to the Winds Thy Fears," 114–16.
30. Letter from Allen Trimble to James Henry Thompson, July 1861, James Henry Thompson Papers, Mss qT473, box 1, item 4, Cincinnati Museum Center.
31. Allen Trimble to James Henry Thompson, 3 July 1864, James Henry Thompson Papers, box 1, item 8.
32. Eliza Jane Thompson, *Hillsboro Crusade Sketches and Family Records* (Cincinnati: Cranston and Curts, 1896), 59–60.
33. Blocker argues that personal reasons came into play for many of the Crusaders; "*Give to the Winds Thy Fears.*"
34. Eliza Daniel Stewart, *Memories of the Crusade*, 2nd edition (Columbus, OH: William G. Hubbard, 1889), 93–94; Thompson, *Hillsboro Crusade Sketches*, 59–60.
35. Stewart, *Memories*, 104.
36. Thompson, *Hillsboro Crusade Sketches*, 62.
37. This is an account from the Boston *Watchman and Reflector* included in Thompson, *Hillsboro Crusade Sketches*, 94–95.
38. Ibid., 76–77.
39. Ibid., 114–15.
40. "Notice to the Ladies of Hillsborough," in the Thompson and Tuttle Family Papers, container 9, folder 4.
41. *New York Times*, 14 February 1874.
42. Thompson, *Hillsboro Crusade Sketches*, 114–15.
43. Ibid., 135.
44. *National Temperance Advocate*, May 1874.
45. Annie Wittenmyer, "The Work of the Woman's Christian Temperance Union," *The Dissenters: America's Voices of Opposition*, ed. John Gabriel Hunt (New York: Gramercy Books, 1993), 123–25; Stewart, *Memories*, 424.

Notes to Chapter Four

46. Annie Wittenmyer, *History of the Woman's Temperance Crusade* (Philadelphia: Office of the Christian Woman, 1878), 33.
47. Stewart, *Memories*, 164.
48. 12 February 1874.
49. *New York Times*, 12 February 1874.
50. *Cincinnati Enquirer*, 6 March 1874.
51. Beadle, *Women's War*, 34.
52. Wittenmyer, *History*, 156.
53. Ibid.
54. Ibid., 455.
55. *National Temperance Advocate*, March 1874; Beadle, *Women's War*, 35–37.
56. *National Temperance Advocate*, May 1874.
57. T.A.H. Brown, "A Full Description of the Origin and Progress of the New Plan of Labor by the Women up to the Present Time," in Stebbins, *Fifty Years*, 365.
58. *National Temperance Advocate*, June 1874.
59. Ibid., May 1874.
60. W.C. Steel, *The Woman's Temperance Movement* (New York: National Temperance Society and Publishing House, 1874), 8–9.
61. Blocker certainly downplays male involvement, beginning with Dio Lewis's own role. He writes that the fact that the Crusade was begun by a male orator is ironic (*"Give to the Winds Thy Fears,"* 7). Blocker says Crusaders included men only because they had needed resources, but that they were ambivalent towards male presence and feared men would "take over." He says they often excluded men, men organized separately, or women allowed men some degree of participation while maintaining control themselves (Ibid., 72). Ruth Bordin, Barbara Epstein and Jed Dannenbaum also portray the Crusade as fundamentally a women's movement.
62. Beadle, *Women's War*, 45.
63. *New York Times*, 22 February 1874.
64. Ibid., 18 February 1874.
65. Ibid., 21 February 1874. This is a letter published from Lewis to the "Friends of the Woman's Temperance Movement."
66. Beadle, *Women's War*, 78–81.
67. *Cincinnati Enquirer*, 6 March 1874.
68. *New York Times*, 22 and 24 February 1874.
69. Ibid., 24 and 28 February 1874.
70. Ibid., 18 February 1874.
71. Matilda Gilruth Carpenter, *The Crusade: its origin and development at Washington Court House and its results* (Columbus, OH: W.G. Hubbard and Co., 1893), 196.
72. Beadle, *Women's War*, 35–37.
73. Stewart, *Memories*, 147, 219, 234, 289; *New York Times*, 12 February 1874.
74. *Springfield Daily Republic*, 9 March 1874.
75. *National Temperance Advocate*, March 1874.

76. *Cincinnati Enquirer,* 14 March 1874.
77. For various examples of this work, see *New York Times,* 20–21 February 1874, 6 March 1874; *Cincinnati Enquirer,* 6 March 1874; Beadle, *Women's War,* 55.
78. *National Temperance Advocate,* June 1874. This is from the minutes of the NTS annual meeting; also included in this issue are reports of the prohibition work in which the society engaged.
79. Ibid., October 1874.
80. Carpenter, *The Crusade,* 66–67.
81. The culmination of such political activity was the formation of the Anti-Saloon League in 1892, a highly effective lobbying organization. Blocker, *American Temperance Movements,* 99–111.
82. Account by Sarah Knowles Bolton in Wittenmyer, *History,* 154.
83. Wittenmyer, *History,* 403–404.
84. Stewart, *Memories,* 354.
85. *National Temperance Advocate,* June 1874.
86. Blocker, "*Give to the Winds Thy Fears,*" 62–64. Charles Isetts did a statistical study of the class and ethnic make-up of Hillsboro, Ohio Crusaders and found the vast majority of them to be upper-middle-class and native-born; "A Social Profile of the Women's Temperance Crusade: Hillsboro, Ohio," *Alcohol, Reform and Society: The Liquor Issue in Social Context,* ed. Jack S. Blocker (Westport, CT: Greenwood Press, 1979), 101–109.
87. Wittenmyer, *History,* 771–72.
88. Blocker, "*Give to the Winds Thy Fears,*" 62–64. Barbara Epstein in *The Politics of Domesticity* disagrees, saying that the Crusade did contain a nativist element (90).
89. Wittenmyer, *History,* 771.
90. Stewart, *Memories,* 385–86.
91. Thompson, *Hillsboro Sketches,* 123.
92. *Cincinnati Enquirer,* 18 March 1874.
93. T.A.H. Brown, "A Full Description," 435–39. Nancy Garner does an excellent job in discussing the gender wars between temperance and anti-temperance forces in "A Prayerful Public Protest: The Significance of Gender in the Kansas Woman's Crusade of 1874," *Kansas History* 20 (1997): 214–29.
94. See Blocker, "*Give to the Winds Thy Fears,*" 50–51.
95. Dr. D.H. Mann, *The Woman's Crusade; or, A Novel Temperance Movement in Delhi, New York* (New York: National Temperance Society and Publication House, 1874).
96. *New York Times,* 26 February 1874.
97. Stewart, *Memories,* 388.
98. Brown, "A Full Description," 392–94, 433.
99. 3 March 1874; also see 26 February 1874.
100. Stewart, *Memories,* 388.
101. Ibid., 62; Stewart, *Memories,* 388–90.

Notes to Chapter Five

102. M.E. Winslow, *A More Excellent Way, and other stories of the Crusade* (New York: National Temperance Society and Publication House, 1876), quotes on 18, 20, 46.
103. *New York Times,* 26 Feb. 1874. Jane Grey Swisshelm was another vocal critic of the Crusade, see J.H. Beadle, *Women's War on Whisky,* 93–95. Susan B. Anthony, who kept up her temperance work throughout her career, also eventually cooperated with the Crusade. See Ellen Carol DuBois, ed., *Elizabeth Cady Stanton, Susan B. Anthony: Correspondence, Writings, Speeches* (New York: Schocken Books, 1981), 172. Also, Anthony's diary entries for 1874 demonstrate her continued temperance activism. See, for example, 20 March, 6 April, 23 June, 12 July, 2 August, Susan B. Anthony Papers (microfilm), Library of Congress Manuscripts Division, Washington, DC, reel 2.
104. Stewart, *Memories,* 23.
105. Ibid., 26.
106. Ibid., 27–32.
107. Ibid., 32–39.
108. Ibid., 54–56; Beadle, *Women's War,* 7–11.
109. Stewart, *Memories,* 67–81.
110. Ibid., 107, 182.
111. Ibid., 125–26.
112. Ibid., 39; Beadle, *Women's War on Whisky,* 52.

NOTES TO CHAPTER FIVE

1. WCTU, *Minutes of the Woman's National Christian Temperance Union, at the Annual Meeting, held in Baltimore, November 6–11, 1878* (5th convention) (Cincinnati: A.H. Pugh, 1879), 51, Microfilm Edition of the Temperance and Prohibition Papers, a joint project of the Ohio Historical Society, the Michigan Historical Collections, and the Woman's Christian Temperance Union, series III, reel 1.
2. Eliza Jane Thompson, "The Relation of the WCTU to the Crusade," written for the Friday Club of Hillsboro, Ohio in Oct. 1898, E.J. Thompson Papers, The Library of Congress Manuscripts Division, Washington, DC; Ruth Bordin, *Woman and Temperance: The Quest for Power and Liberty, 1873–1900* (Philadelphia: Temple University Press), 33–51.
3. Ibid.; Thompson, "The Relation of the WCTU to the Crusade;" Eliza Jane Thompson, *Hillsboro Crusade Sketches and Family Records* (Cincinnati: Cranston and Curts, 1896), 128–29.
4. Eliza Daniel Stewart, *Memories of the Crusade,* 2nd edition (Columbus, OH: William G. Hubbard, 1889), 424; WCTU, *Minutes of the First Convention of the National Woman's Christian Temperance Union, Held in Cleveland, Ohio, November 17, 18, and 19, 1874* (Chicago: Woman's Temperance Publication Association, 1889), 29, Microfilm Edition of the Temperance and Prohibition Papers, series III, reel 1; Bordin, *Woman and Temperance,* 33–51.
5. Annie Turner Wittenmyer, *History of the Woman's Temperance Crusade* (Philadelphia: Office of the Christian Woman, 1878), 771–72; Jed Dannenbaum,

Drink and Disorder: Temperance Reform in Cincinnati from the Washingtonian Revival to the WCTU (Urbana: University of Illinois Press, 1984), 224.
6. Annie Turner Wittenmyer, "The Work of the Woman's Christian Temperance Union," *The Dissenters: America's Voices of Opposition,* ed. John Gabriel Hunt (New York: Gramercy Books, 1993), 122.
7. WCTU, *Minutes of the Third Convention of the National WCTU* (Chicago: Woman's Temperance Publishing Association, 1889), 89, 104, Microfilm Edition of the Temperance and Prohibition Papers, series III, reel 1.
8. *The Reform* (published by the Woman's Temperance Union in Philadelphia), volume 4, no. 9, 1875 (no other date is given for this issue; it is at the American Antiquarian Society in Worcester, MA).
9. WCTU, *1st Convention,* 6.
10. Ibid., 20.
11. WCTU, *Minutes of the Second Convention of the National Women's Christian Temperance Union held in Cincinnati, Ohio, November 17, 18, and 19, 1875* (Chicago: Woman's Temperance Publication Association, 1889) 53, Microfilm Edition of the Temperance and Prohibition Papers, series III, reel 1.
12. Ibid.
13. Bordin, *Woman and Temperance,* 57–58, 119–21.
14. Gaines M. Foster, *Moral Reconstruction: Christian Lobbyists and the Federal Legislation of Morality, 1865–1920* (Chapel Hill: University of North Carolina Press, 2002). Foster demonstrates this as an issue in other movements form moral reform during this period.
15. Jack S. Blocker, *American Temperance Movements: Cycles of Reform* (Boston: Twayne Publishers, 1989), 85.
16. Howard Crosby et al, *Moderation vs. Total Abstinence; or Dr. Crosby and His Reviewers* (New York: National Temperance Society and Publication House, 1881).
17. Dio Lewis and John B. Finch, *Prohibition. For and Against. Containing the correspondence between and speeches of Dr. Dio Lewis, of New York; and Hon. John B. Finch, of Nebraska, on the great question.* (New York: J.W. Cummings Publisher, 1884), 1–5.
18. Wittenmyer, *History,* 590–605; Mary Livermore, *The Story of My Life, or Sunshine and Shadow of Seventy Years* (Hartford, CT: A.D. Worthington, 1899), 482, 490, 578–84.
19. Stewart, *Memories,* 125–26.
20. WCTU, *2nd Convention,* 61.
21. Frances Willard to Annie Wittenmyer, 24 May 1876, Microfilm Edition of the Temperance and Prohibition Papers, series III, reel 11, folder 3.
22. Susan B. Anthony to Frances Willard, 18 Sept. 1876, Susan B. Anthony Papers (microfilm), Library of Congress Manuscripts Division, Washington, DC, reel 18. Stanton remained rather aloof from the WCTU; see Ellen Carol DuBois, ed., *Elizabeth Cady Stanton, Susan B. Anthony: Correspondence, Writings, Speeches* (New York: Schocken Books, 1981), 109.
23. Bordin, *Woman and Temperance,* 56–63.
24. WCTU, *3rd Convention,* 93. For more on this issue within the WCTU, see Leslie Kathrin Dunlap, "In the Name of the Home: Temperance, Women

Notes to Chapter Five

and Southern Grass-Roots Politics, 1873–1933" (Ph.D. dissertation, Northwestern University, 2001). On the issue of gender in the Reconstruction South, see Laura F. Edwards, *Gendered Strife and Confusion: The Political Culture of Reconstruction* (Urbana: University of Illinois Press, 1997).

25. Frances Willard to Annie Wittenmyer, 26 June 1875, Microfilm Edition of the Temperance and Prohibition Papers, series III, reel 11, folder 3.
26. *National Temperance Advocate*, Jan. 1882.
27. Anna Gordon to Mrs. Willard, 27 May 1880, Microfilm Edition of the Temperance and Prohibition Papers, series III, reel 12, folder 8.
28. Feb. 1882.
29. Bordin, *Woman and Temperance;* Michael McGerr, "Political Style and Women's Power, 1830–1930," *Journal of American History* 77 (1990): 864–85.
30. Bordin, *Woman and Temperance*, 58.
31. Frances Willard, *How to Win: A Book for Girls* (New York and London: Funk and Wagnalls, 1886), 54. For more on "domestic feminism," and the expansion of domesticity into the public sphere, see Daniel Scott Smith, "Family Limitation, Sexual Control, and Domestic Feminism in Victorian America," *Clio's Consciousness Raised*, ed. Mary Hartman and Lois W. Banner (New York: Harper and Row, 1974), 119–36; Karen J. Blair, *The Clubwoman as Feminist: True Womanhood Redefined, 1868–1914* (New York: Holmes and Meier, 1980); William O'Neill, *Everyone Was Brave: The Rise and Fall of Feminism in America* (Chicago: Quadrangle Books, 1969); McGerr, "Political Style and Women's Power, 1830–1930," 864–85; David J. Pivar, *Purity Crusade: Sexual Morality and Social Control, 1868–1900* (Westport, CT: Greenwood Press, 1973); Mary P. Ryan, *Women in Public: Between Banners and Ballots, 1825–1880* (Baltimore: Johns Hopkins University Press, 1990); Barbara Leslie Epstein, *The Politics of Domesticity: Women, Evangelism and Temperance in Nineteenth-Century America* (Middletown, CT: Wesleyan University Press, 1981); Aileen Kraditor, *The Ideas of the Woman Suffrage Movement* (New York: Columbia University Press, 1965); Lori D. Ginzberg, *Women and the Work of Benevolence: Morality, Politics and Class in the Nineteenth-Century United States* (New Haven: Yale University Press, 1990); Janet Zollinger Giele, *Two Paths to Women's Equality: Temperance, Suffrage and the Origins of Liberal Feminism in the United States, 1820–1920* (Cambridge, MA: Harvard University Press, 1996); Elizabeth Batelle Clark, "The Politics of God and the Woman's Vote: Religion in the American Suffrage Movement, 1848–1895" (Ph.D. dissertation, Princeton University, 1989). Ellen Carol DuBois resents any qualification of this kind of feminism as "domestic" and has argued that suffrage was always a radical reform in "The Radicalism of the Woman Suffrage Movement," *Woman Suffrage and Women's Rights* (New York: New York University Press, 1998), 30–42.
32. Willard, *How to Win*, 54; Livermore, *The Story of My Life*, 579; Frances Willard, "The Ballot for the Home," *Equal Suffrage Leaflet* (Boston: *The Woman's Journal*, 1898), 1; Rev. C.C. Harrah, "Jesus Christ the Emancipator

of Women," *Equal Suffrage Leaflet* (Boston: *The Woman's Journal*, 1888), 1; Frances Willard, "Christ in Government," *Union Signal*, 4 Jan. 1883; Frances Willard, *Annual Address at the World's and National Woman's Christian Temperance Union Convention, 1890* (Atlanta: *Constitution* Job Office, 1890), 57–58.
33. WCTU, *3rd Convention*, 102.
34. *Union Signal*, 1 February 1883; Livermore, *The Story of My Life*, 579; Frances Willard, *Do Everything: A Handbook for White Ribboners* (Chicago: The Woman's Temperance Publishing Association, 1895), 23–24; Willard, *How to Win*, 48. This public usage of female sacrifice demonstrates well Nancy Theriot's thesis that in the postwar period, public service replaced private suffering as a basis for femininity; see *The Biosocial Construction of Femininity: Mothers and Daughters in Nineteenth-Century America* (Westport, CT: Greenwood Press, 1988).
35. 29 March 1883.
36. Willard, *Do Everything*, 181–82. On the use of gender difference and the celebration of femininity, see Suzanne Marilley, *Woman Suffrage and the Origins of Liberal Feminism in the United States, 1820–1920* (Cambridge, MA: Harvard University Press, 1996), ch. 4; Epstein, *The Politics of Domesticity*.
37. Frances Willard, "Work of the WCTU," *Woman's Work in America*, ed. Annie Nathan Myer (New York: Henry Holt and Co., 1891), 404.
38. Many historians distinguish between two types of woman suffrage agitation, one based on natural rights and the other on the use of woman suffrage towards larger ends; see Kraditor, *The Ideas of the Woman Suffrage Movement*, 43–46, 52–56, 66–71; Giele, *Two Paths*; Ginzberg, *Women and the Work of Benevolence*; DuBois, "The Radicalism of the Woman Suffrage Movement."
39. Willard, "The Ballot for the Home."
40. M.E. Winslow, "Woman's Temperance Work," *Essays written for the National Temperance Convention in Saratoga, June 21, 1881* (New York, [n.p.], 1881), 11.
41. Willard, *How to Win*, 66–75.
42. Ibid., 30–31.
43. Ibid., 105–16.
44. Ibid., 121.
45. Bordin, *Woman and Temperance*, 114–15. Historians have noted that marriage reforms were truly the most revolutionary within women's rights; see Carl Degler, *At Odds: Women and the Family in America from the Revolution to the Present* (New York: Oxford University Press, 1980).
46. Livermore, *The Story of My Life*, 674–76.
47. Mary Livermore, "Woman and the State," *Woman's Work in America*, 110–17.
48. Nancy F. Cott, *Public Vows: A History of Marriage and the Nation* (Cambridge, MA: Harvard University Press, 2000), 105–107, 110–11.
49. Samuel Dike to D. Paddock, date unknown, Samuel Warren Dike Papers, Library of Congress Manuscripts Division, Washington, DC, box 1, folder

Notes to Chapter Five

3; Dike to Joseph Cook, 21 Jan. 1879, Ibid., box 1, folder 2; Samuel Dike, "An Address on Divorce," delivered at Montpelier, VT, 10 Nov. 1880, Ibid., box 19, folder 1.
50. Ibid; Samuel Dike, "The Divorce Question and its Problems," delivered before Hartford Theological Seminary, 10 May 1882, Ibid., box 19, folder 9.
51. Dike to Joseph Cook, 21 Jan. 1879, Ibid., box 1, folder 2.
52. Willard to Dike, 23 Sept. 1887 and 17 March 1888, Ibid., box 2, folder 2.
53. Willard, *Do Everything,* 130 (quote), 90–106.
54. Frances Willard, "Annual Address, 1881," *"Do Everything" Reform: The Oratory of Frances E. Willard,* ed. Richard Leeman (Westport, CT: Greenwood Press, 1992), 143. Here Willard discussed the formation of the Home Protection Party and stated that woman suffrage was not required as a plank for southern states who wanted to remain "aloof" from the issue.
55. Ibid., 109.
56. Willard, "Work of the WCTU," 410.
57. Ibid., 403.
58. Willard, *Do Everything,* 90–106.
59. Esther Pugh to Anna Gordon, 3 June 1880, Microfilm Edition of the Temperance and Prohibition Papers, series III, reel 12, folder 8.
60. Frances Willard to Eliza Jane Thompson, 17 September 1889, The Thompson and Tuttle Family Papers, 1812–1915, Ms. 1511, Western Reserve Historical Society, Cleveland, OH, container 2, folder 2.
61. 25 October 1890, Ibid., container 2, folder 3.
62. 3 June 1892, Ibid.
63. 13 March 1890, James Henry Thompson Papers, Mss qT473, box 1, item 136, Cincinnati Museum Center.
64. Frances Willard, "My friend Mrs. Thompson and the Present Condition of the Temperance Work," in Thompson, *Hillsboro Crusade Sketches,* 200.
65. Letter from Alice Briggs on behalf of Frances Willard, 27 Dec. 1888 and pamphlet, both in Thompson and Tuttle Family Papers, container 2, folder 2.
66. 1 Nov. 1887, Ibid., container 2, folder 2.
67. WCTU, *Minutes of the Woman's National Christian Temperance Union at the Seventh Annual Meeting* (New York: National Temperance Society and Publishing House, 1880), 16, Microfilm Edition of the Temperance and Prohibition Papers, series III, reel 1; WCTU, *Minutes of the Woman's National Christian Temperance Union, at the Eighth Annual Meeting* (Brooklyn: Union-Argus Steam Printing Establishment, 1881), xxxi, Ibid.
68. Eliza Jane Thompson to Mary Tuttle, 24 June 1885, Thompson and Tuttle Family Papers, container 3, folder 1.
69. 5 March 1893, Ibid., container 3, folder 5.
70. 27 Aug. 1892, Ibid., container 2, folder 2; also see Anna Gordon to Eliza Jane Thompson, 5 Nov. 1890, Ibid., container 2, folder 2.
71. 29 June 1895, Ibid., container 2, folder 4.
72. Clipping from the *Ohio Messenger,* Ibid., container 11, folder 5.
73. These are the words of her nephew, Nicholas Longworth, writing to Marie Thompson Rives, 4 Nov. 1905, James Henry Thompson Papers, box 1, item 163.

74. WCTU, *8th Convention*, 22.
75. 1 Dec. 1879, Microfilm Edition of the Temperance and Prohibition Papers, series III, reel 11, folder 5.
76. WCTU, *8th Convention*, 23.
77. *National Temperance Advocate*, Feb. 1882.
78. Ibid.
79. Crosby, *Moderation vs. Total Abstinence*, 10, 61.
80. For example, May 1881, in which a WCTU lady addresses Crosby's claim that wine use never produced alcoholism. She claimed that the son of a New York Crusader had become a drunk through his father's offerings of wine. For another example, see Elizabeth Cleveland's short story "A Woman's Cry," written in response to Dr. Crosby, also May 1881.
81. Thompson, *Hillsboro Crusade Sketches*, 146, 200; Matilda Gilruth Carpenter, *The Crusade: Its origin and development at Washington Court House and its results* (Columbus, OH: W.G. Hubbard and Co., 1893), 251–52.
82. For examples, WCTU, *3rd Convention*, 85, 88–90; WCTU, *Minutes of the Fourth Convention of the National Woman's Christian Temperance Union* (Chicago: Woman's Temperance Publication Association, 1889), Microfilm Edition of the Temperance and Prohibition Papers, series III, reel 1; WCTU, *5th convention*, 74; WCTU, *8th convention*, lxxvii-lxxx; *National Temperance Advocate*, May 1881, March 1882, May 1882.
83. For more on the cooperation between the WCTU and labor, see Dawn Michelle Dyer, "'Combating the Fiery Flood:' The WCTU's Approach to Labor and Socialism" (Ph.D. dissertation, Auburn University, 1998); Ronald M. Benson, "American Workers and Temperance Reform, 1866–1933" (Ph.D. dissertation, Notre Dame, 1974); Leon Fink, *Workingmen's Democracy: The Knights of Labor and American Politics* (Urbana: University of Illinois Press, 1983), 12, 46–47, 62; Roy Rosenzweig, *Eight Hours for What We Will: Workers and Leisure in an Industrial City, 1870–1920* (Cambridge: Cambridge University Press, 1983), ch. 4–6. Rozensweig argues that temperance represented a threat to working-class autonomy; Benson argues that temperance was genuinely appealing to workers because of the challenges of the new industrial economy.
84. Willard, *Do Everything*, 4.
85. Willard, *How to Win*, 95–101
86. Willard, *Address, 1890*, 76–77, 39.
87. Dyer argues that Willard used domesticity to peddle socialism to a conservative, middle-class base, just as she did woman suffrage; "Combating the Fiery Flood."
88. WCTU, *Minutes of the Woman's National Christian Temperance Union at the Sixth Annual Meeting* (Cleveland: Fairbanks and Co., 1879), 148–153, Microfilm Edition of the Temperance and Prohibition Papers, series III, reel 1.
89. From an address by Mrs. McCabe, WCTU, *1st convention*, 23.
90. WCTU, *6th Convention*, 16.
91. WCTU, *7th Convention*, 109.

Notes to Chapter Five

92. *National Temperance Advocate,* Feb. 1882, May 1881. For the growth of southern support for prohibition and other "moral legislation," see also Foster, *Moral Reconstruction,* 240–42.
93. David W. Blight, *Race and Reunion: The Civil War in American Memory* (Cambridge, MA: Harvard University Press, 2001); Heather Cox Richardson, *The Death of Reconstruction: Race, Labor and Politics in the Post-Civil War North, 1865–1900* (Cambridge, MA: Harvard University Press, 2001); Nina Silber, *The Romance of Reunion: Northerners and the South, 1865–1900* (Chapel Hill: University of North Carolina Press, 1993).
94. Silber, *Romance of Reunion,* 103–105; Dunlap, "In the Name of the Home."
95. WCTU, *7th Convention,* 113; WCTU, *8th Convention,* xxxi.
96. Ibid., lxxxviii.
97. Ibid., 32.
98. Ibid., lxxviii.
99. WCTU, *7th Convention,* 16.
100. Ibid.
101. WCTU, *8th Convention,* 24–28.
102. Ibid., 25–26.
103. *National Temperance Advocate,* May 1881.
104. Ibid.
105. Ibid., Feb. 1882.
106. Ibid., June 1882.
107. Eric Foner, *Reconstruction: America's Unfinished Revolution, 1863–1877* (New York: Harper and Row, 1988), 425–59, 564–601
108. *National Temperance Advocate,* June 1882.
109. Ibid., Feb. 1882.
110. Ibid., March 1882.
111. *Christian Recorder* (Philadelphia), 22 Apr. 1871.
112. Ibid., 25 July 1878 and 10 Oct. 1878.
113. Willard, *Do Everything,* 19–22; *Union Signal,* 19 June 1884.
114. WCTU, *7th Convention,* 16.
115. Dunlap, "In the Name of the Home;" Carolyn Gifford De Swarte, ed., *"Writing out my Heart:" Selections from the Journal of Frances E. Willard, 1855–1896,* (Urbana: University of Illinois Press, 1995) 396; WCTU, *8th Convention,* 35 (quote), 45 52.
116. WCTU, *7th Convention,* 64–65.
117. *Union Signal,* 18 Jan. 1883, 22 March 1883, 5 June 1884, 10 May 1888.
118. Gail Bederman, *Manliness and Civilization: A Cultural History of Race and Gender in the United States, 1860–1917* (Chicago: University of Chicago Press, 1995), 45–76; Louise Michelle Newman, *White Women's Rights: Racial Origins of Feminism in the United States* (Oxford: Oxford University Press, 1999), 66–69; Dunlap, "In the Name of the Home;" Silber, *The Romance of Reunion,* 102–105; Edward Blum, *Reforging the White Republic: Race, Religion and American Nationalism, 1865–1898* (Baton Rouge: Louisiana State University Press, 2005), 174–208. Dunlap, Blum,

and Silber argue that the WCTU was part of a larger process of sectional reunion after Reconstruction that glossed over racial issues.
119. Willard's true views on race are difficult to discern; she made statements of racial equality and of racism both, and there are different interpretations among historians. For example, Bordin, *Woman and Temperance*, 57, 87, 122–23, 78, 82–85, 159–60 vs. Bederman, *Manliness and Civilization*, 45–76; Newman, *White Women's Rights,* 66–69. Brian Donovan provides a more nuanced view, arguing that Willard's racial views were highly complex, and while the WCTU was "a model of interracial cooperation," Willard used racism to agitate against white slavery and for woman suffrage; *White Slave Crusades: Race, Gender, and Anti-Vice Activism, 1887–1917* (Urbana and Chicago: University of Illinois Press, 2006), 37–55 (quote on p. 44). My own view is that Willard pursued a pragmatic and intentionally ambiguous course on this issue and others for the purpose of building support for the organization.
120. WCTU, *8th Convention*, lxxvi.
121. WCTU, *7th Convention*, lxxv-lxxix.
122. WCTU, *8th Convention*, 29–32.
123. *Race and Reunion*, 3.

Bibliography

MANUSCRIPT COLLECTIONS

Susan B. Anthony Papers (microfilm). Manuscripts Division, Library of Congress. Washington, DC.
Blackwell Family Papers (microfilm). Manuscripts Division, Library of Congress. Washington, DC.
Cheever Family Papers. American Antiquarian Society. Worcester, Massachusetts.
Samuel Warren Dike Papers. Manuscripts Division, Library of Congress. Washington, DC.
Frederick Douglass Papers (microfilm). Manuscripts Division, Library of Congress. Washington, DC.
William Goodell Family Papers. Historical Collections, Berea College. Berea, Kentucky.
Horace Greeley Papers. Manuscripts Division, Library of Congress. Washington, DC.
Gerrit Smith Papers (microfilm). Manuscripts Division, Library of Congress. Washington, DC.
Microfilm Edition of the Temperance and Prohibition Papers. Joint project of the Michigan Historical Collections, the Ohio Historical Society, and the Woman's Christian Temperance Union. Ann Arbor: University of Michigan, 1977.
E.J. Thompson Papers. Manuscripts Division, Library of Congress. Washington, DC.
James Henry Thompson Papers. Mss qT473. Cincinnati Museum Center. Cincinnati, Ohio.
Thompson and Tuttle Family Papers, 1812–1915. Ms. 1511. Western Reserve Historical Society. Cleveland, Ohio.
Elizur Wright Papers. Manuscripts Division, Library of Congress. Washington, DC.

NEWSPAPERS AND PERIODICALS

American Quarterly Temperance Magazine (Albany, NY)
American Temperance Intelligencer (Albany, NY)

American Temperance Magazine (Albany, NY)
Anti-Slavery Bugle (Salem, OH)
Christian Recorder (Philadelphia)
Cincinnati Enquirer
The Colored American (New York)
Family Favorite and Temperance Journal (Adrian, MI)
The Fountain, Organ of the Connecticut Washingtonian Total Abstinence Society (New Haven, CT)
Frederick Douglass Paper (Rochester, NY)
Genius of Temperance, Philanthropist and People's Advocate (New York)
Gerrit Smith Banner (New York)
Harper's Weekly
Journal of the American Temperance Union (Philadelphia)
Journal of the American Temperance Union and The New York Prohibitionist (New York)
The Lily (Seneca Falls, NY)
Michigan Temperance Advocate (Marshall, MI)
Michigan Temperance Journal and Washingtonian (Jackson, MI)
Michigan Washingtonian (Jackson, MI)
National Philanthropist (Boston)
National Temperance Advocate (New York)
New York Evangelist (New York)
New York People's Organ, A Family Companion (New York)
New York Times
New York Tribune
The Reform (Philadelphia)
The Rescue (Sacramento, CA)
The Samaritan and Total Abstinence Advocate (Providence, RI)
Springfield Daily Republic (Springfield, OH)
Temperance Banner (Albion, NY)
Temperance Host (Franklin, IN)
Temperance Mirror (Dover, NH)
Temperance Offering (Salem, MA)
Temperance Recorder (Albany, NY)
The Templar's Magazine (Philadelphia)
The Transcript, Young Men's Journal and Temperance Advocate (Detroit, MI)
The Una (Providence, RI)

Bibliography

Union Signal (Evanston, IL)
The Washingtonian (Augusta, ME)
Western Temperance Almanac (Cincinnati)
Worcester County Cataract and Massachusetts Washingtonian (Worcester, MA)
Young Men's Journal and Advocate of Temperance (Detroit, MI)

PUBLISHED PRIMARY SOURCES

American Temperance Union. *Report of the Executive Committee of the American Temperance Union.* New York: American Temperance Union, 1842.
———. *Permanent Temperance Documents of the American Temperance Society.* New York: American Temperance Union, 1843.
American Tract Society. *The Temperance Volume: Embracing the Temperance Tracts of the American Tract Society.* New York: American Tract Society, 1845.
Arthur, T.S. *Six Nights with the Washingtonians: A Series of Temperance Tales.* Philadelphia: L.A. Godey and Morton McMichael, 1842.
Barnes, Albert. *Barnes on the Traffic in Ardent Spirits.* New York: American Tract Society, 1840–1849.
Beadle, J.H. *The Women's War on Whisky.* Cincinnati: Wilstach, Baldwin and Co., 1874.
Black, James. *Brief History of Prohibition and of the Prohibition Reform Party.* New York: National Committee of the Prohibition Reform Party, 1872.
Bloomer, D.C. *The Life and Writings of Amelia Bloomer.* Boston: Arena Publishing, 1895.
Carpenter, Matilda Gilruth. *The Crusade: Its origin and development at Washington Court House and its results.* Columbus, OH: W.G. Hubbard and Co., 1893.
Cheever, George B. *A defense in abatement of judgment for an alleged libel, before the Massachusetts Supreme Court, Dec. 4, 1835.* Salem, MA: John W. Archer, 1836.
———. *The Dream, or The True History of Deacon Giles's Distillery and Deacon Jones's Brewery.* New York: Printed for the publisher, 1846.
Chellis, Mary Dwinell. *Wealth and Wine.* New York: National Temperance Society and Publication House, 1874.
Colfax, Schuyler. *Example and effort: An address delivered before the Congressional Temperance Society at Washington, D.C.* New York: National Temperance Society and Publication House, 1872.
Coon, Anne C., ed. *Hear Me Patiently: The Reform Speeches of Amelia Jenks Bloomer.* Westport, CT: Greenwood Press, 1994.
The Council of the Massachusetts Temperance Society. *The Doings of a Sprit Shop; or, The Story of James and Mary Duffil: A Tale of Real Life.* Boston: John S. March, 1840.
Crosby, Howard et al. *Moderation vs. total abstinence; or, Dr. Howard Crosby and his reviewers.* New York: National Temperance Society and Publication House, 1881.
DuBois, Ellen Carol, ed. *Elizabeth Cady Stanton, Susan B. Anthony: Correspondence, Writings, Speeches.* New York: Schocken Brooks, 1981.

Foner, Philip, ed. *Frederick Douglass: Selected Speeches and Writings*. Chicago: Lawrence Hill Books, 1975.

Gifford, Carolyn De Swarte, ed. *"Writing out my Heart:" Selections from the Journal of Frances E. Willard, 1855–1896*. Urbana: University of Illinois Press, 1995.

Goodell, William. *Views of American constitutional law in its bearing upon American slavery*. Utica, NY: Lawson & Chaplin, 1845.

———. *Address of the Macedon Convention*. Albany, NY: S.W. Green, 1847.

Gordon, Ann, ed. *The Selected Papers of Elizabeth Cady Stanton and Susan B. Anthony*. Vol. I. New Brunswick, NJ: Rutgers University Press, 1997.

Harrah, C.C. "Jesus Christ the Emancipator of Women." *Equal Suffrage Leaflet*. Boston: *The Woman's Journal*, 1888.

Hunt, John Gabriel, ed. *The Dissenters: America's Voices of Opposition*. New York: Gramercy Books, 1993.

Johnson, Lorenzo Dow. *Martha Washingtonianism, or History of the Ladies Temperance Benevolent Societies*. New York: Saxton and Miles, 1843.

Leeman, Richard, ed. *"Do Everything" Reform: The Oratory of Frances Willard*. Westport, CT: Greenwood Press, 1992.

Lewis, Dio. *Our Girls*. New York: Harper and Brothers, 1871.

———. *Prohibition a Failure, or, The True Solution of the Temperance Question*. Boston: James R. Osgood and Co., 1875.

Lewis, Dio and John B. Finch. *Prohibition. For and Against. Containing the correspondence between and speeches of Dr. Dio Lewis, of New York; and Hon. John B. Finch, of Nebraska, on the great question*. New York: J.W. Cummings Publisher, 1884.

Livermore, Mary A. *The Story of My Life, or The Sunshine and Shadow of Seventy Years*. Hartford, CT: A.D. Worthington and Co., Publishers, 1899.

Mann, D.H. *The Woman's Crusade; or, A Novel Temperance Movement in Delhi, New York*. New York: National Temperance Society and Publication House, 1874.

Marsh, John. *Temperance, Recollections, Labor, Defeats, Triumphs: An Autobiography*. New York: Charles Scribner and Co., 1867.

———. *Letter on the Promotion of Moral Reforms by Secret Societies; Addressed to William Dodge*. New York: New York Tract Office, 1868.

A member of the society. *The Foundation, Progress and Principles of the Washingtonian Temperance Society of Baltimore and the Influence it has had on the Temperance Movements in the United States*. Baltimore: John D. Troy, 1842.

Moss, Lemuel. *Annals of the United States Christian Commission*. Philadelphia: J.B. Lippincott and Co., 1868.

Myer, Annie Nathan, ed. *Woman's Work in America*. New York: Henry Holt and Co., 1891.

National Prohibition Party. *An Adequate Remedy for a National Evil; or, a Vindication of the National Prohibition Party by the Rev. John Russell, also the Platform of the Prohibition Party*. Detroit: New World Book and Job Print, 1872.

National Temperance Convention. *Essays written for the National Temperance Convention in Saratoga, June 21, 1881*. New York, [n.p.], 1881.

National Temperance Society and Publication House. *Temperance Sermons delivered in response to an invitation by the National Temperance Society and Publication House*. New York: National Temperance Society and Publication House, 1873.

Ripley, Peter C., ed. *Witness for Freedom: African American Voices on Race, Slavery and Emancipation*. Chapel Hill: University of North Carolina Press, 1993.

South Carolina State Temperance Society. *Permanent Documents*. Vol. 1. Columbia, SC: I.C. Morgan's Letter Press, 1846.

Stanton, Elizabeth Cady, Susan B. Anthony et al. *History of Woman Suffrage*. Vol. I. New York: Arno Press, 1969.

Stebbins, J.E. *Fifty Years History of the Temperance Cause*. Hartford, CT: J.P. Fitch, 1876.

Steel, W.C. *The Woman's Temperance Movement*. New York: National Temperance Society and Publication House, 1874.

Stewart, Eliza Daniel. *Memories of the Crusade*. 2nd edition. Columbus, OH: William G. Hubbard, 1889.

Swisshelm, Jane Grey. *Half a Century*. 2nd edition. Chicago: Jansen, McClurg and Co., 1980.

Thomason, D.R. *Reply to Dr. Marsh on Teetotalism, including a letter from Howard Crosby, D.D.* New York: Richardson and Company, 1867.

Thompson, Eliza Jane. *Hillsboro Crusade Sketches and Family Records*. Cincinnati: Cranston and Curts, 1896.

Waggenspack, Beth M., ed. *The Search for Self-Sovereignty: The Oratory of Elizabeth Cady Stanton*. Westport, CT: Greenwood Press, 1989.

White, Philip S. and Ezra Stiles Ely. *Vindication of the Order of the Sons of Temperance*. New York: Oliver and Brothers, Publishers, 1848.

Willard, Frances E. *Hints and Helps in our Temperance Work*. New York: National Temperance Society and Publication House, 1875.

———. *How to Win: A Book for Girls*. New York and London: Funk and Wagnalls, 1886.

———. *Annual Address at the World's and National Woman's Christian Temperance Union Convention, 1890*. Atlanta: The *Constitution* Job Office, 1890.

———. *Do Everything: A Handbook for The World's White Ribboners*. Chicago: The Woman's Temperance Publishing Association, 1895.

———. "The Ballot for the Home." *Equal Suffrage Leaflet*. Boston: *The Woman's Journal*, 1898.

Williams, Albert. *Prohibition and Woman Suffrage*. Lansing, MI, 1874. *History of Women* (microform collection). New Haven, CT: Research Publications, 1977–79. Reel 418, No. 3057.

Winslow, M.E. *A More Excellent Way, and other stories of the Crusade*. New York: National Temperance Society and Publication House, 1876.

Wittenmyer, Annie Turner. *History of the Woman's Temperance Crusade*. Philadelphia: Office of the Christian Woman, 1878.

PUBLISHED SECONDARY SOURCES

Abzug, Robert H. *Cosmos Crumbling: American Reform and the Religious Imagination*. New York: Oxford University Press, 1994.

Adams, George Washington. *Doctors in Blue: The Medical History of the Union Army*. New York: Henry Schuman, 1952.

Alexander, Ruth M. "'We Are Engaged as a Band of Sisters:' Class and Domesticity in the Washingtonian Temperance Movement, 1840–1850." *Journal of American History* 75 (1988): 763–87.
Appleby, Joyce. "The Personal Roots of the First American Temperance Movement." *Proceedings of the American Philosophical Society* 141 (1997): 141–59.
Attie, Jeanie. *Patriotic Toil: Northern Women and the American Civil War*. Ithaca: Cornell University Press, 1998.
Baker, Paula. "The Domestication of Politics: Women and American Political Society, 1780–1920." *American Historical Review* 89 (1984): 620–47.
———. *The Moral Frameworks of Public Life: Gender, Politics and the State in Rural New York, 1870–1930*. New York: Oxford University Press, 1991.
Banner, Lois W. "Religion and Reform in the Early Republic: The Role of Youth." *American Quarterly* 23 (1971): 677–95.
Banner, Lois W. and Mary Hartman, eds. *Clio's Consciousness Raised*. New York: Harper and Row, 1974.
Barker-Benfield, G.J. *Horrors of the Half-Known Life: Male Attitudes toward Women and Sexuality in Nineteenth-Century America*. New York: Harper and Row, 1976.
Barnett, Randy. "Was Slavery Unconstitutional Before the Thirteenth Amendment?: Lysander Spooner's Theory of Interpretation." *Pacific Law Journal* 28 (1997): 977–1014.
Baron, Stanley Wade. *Brewed in America: A History of Beer and Ale in the United States*. Boston: Little, Brown and Co., 1962.
Basch, Norma. *Framing American Divorce: From the Revolutionary Generation to the Victorians*. Berkeley: University of California Press, 1999.
Bederman, Gail. *Manliness and Civilization: A Cultural History of Gender and Race in the United States, 1860–1917*. Chicago: University of Chicago Press, 1995.
Bergman, Jill and Debra Bernard, eds. *Our Sisters' Keepers: Nineteenth-Century Benevolence Literature by American Women*. Tuscaloosa: University of Alabama Press, 2005.
Blair, Karen J. *The Clubwoman as Feminist: True Womanhood Redefined, 1868–1914*. New York: Holmes and Meier, 1980.
Bledstein, Burton J. and Robert D. Johnston, eds. *The Middling Sorts: Explorations in the History of the American Middle Class*. New York: Routledge, 2001.
Blight, David W. *Race and Reunion: The Civil War in American Memory*. Cambridge, MA: Harvard University Press, 2001.
Blocker, Jack S., ed. *Alcohol, Reform and Society: The Liquor Issue in Social Context*. Westport, CT: Greenwood Press, 1979.
———. *"Give to the Winds Thy Fears:" The Women's Temperance Crusade, 1873–1874*. Westport, CT: Greenwood Press, 1985.
———. *American Temperance Movements: Cycles of Reform*. Boston: Twayne Publishers, 1989.
Blum, Edward. *Reforging the White Republic: Race, Religion and American Nationalism, 1865–1898*. Baton Rouge: Louisiana State University Press, 2005.
Blumin, Stuart. "The Hypothesis of Middle-Class Formation in Nineteenth-Century America: A Critique and Some Proposals." *American Historical Review* 90 (1985): 299–388.

———. *The Emergence of the Middle Class: Social Experience in the American City, 1760–1900*. New York: Cambridge University Press, 1989.

Bordin, Ruth. *Woman and Temperance: The Quest for Power and Liberty, 1873–1900*. Philadelphia: Temple University Press, 1981.

Bouwsma, William J. "Intellectual History in the 1980's: From the History of Ideas to the History of Meaning." *Journal of Interdisciplinary History* 12 (1981): 279–91.

Boyer, Paul. *Urban Masses and Moral Order in America, 1820–1920*. Cambridge, MA: Harvard University Press, 1978.

Brown, Kathleen M. "Brave New Worlds: Women's and Gender History." *William and Mary Quarterly* 50 (1993): 311–28.

Brown, Nina Baker. *Cyclone in Calico: The Story of Mary Ann Bickerdyke*. Boston: Little, Brown and Co., 1952.

Carlson, Douglas W. "'Drinks he to his own undoing:' Temperance Ideology in the Deep South." *Journal of the Early Republic* 18 (1998): 659–91.

Carnes, Mark C. *Secret Ritual and Manhood in Victorian America*. New Haven: Yale University Press, 1989.

Carnes, Mark C. and Clyde Griffen, eds. *Meanings for Manhood: Constructions of Masculinity in Victorian America*. Chicago: Chicago University Press, 1990.

Catton, Bruce. *Grant Moves South*. Boston: Little, Brown and Co., 1960.

Cazden, Elizabeth. *Antoinette Brown Blackwell: A Biography*. Old Westbury, NY: The Feminist Press, 1983.

Chused, Richard H. *Private Acts in Public Places: A Social History of Divorce in the Formative Era of American Family Law*. Philadelphia: University of Pennsylvania Press, 1994.

Clawson, Mary Ann. *Constructing Brotherhood: Class, Gender, and Fraternalism*. Princeton: Princeton University Press, 1989.

Clinton, Catherine and Nina Silber, eds. *Divided Houses: Gender and the Civil War*. New York: Oxford University Press, 1992.

———, eds. *Battle Scars: Gender and Sexuality in the American Civil War*. New York: Oxford University Press, 2006.

Cohen, Nancy. *The Reconstruction of American Liberalism, 1865–1914*. Chapel Hill: University of North Carolina Press, 2002.

Cooper, Frederick. "Elevating the Race: The Social Thought of Black Leaders, 1827–1850." *American Quarterly* 24 (1972): 604–25.

Cott, Nancy. *The Bonds of Womanhood: "Women's Sphere" in New England, 1780–1835*. New Haven: Yale University Press, 1977

———. *Public Vows: A History of Marriage and the Nation*. Cambridge, MA: Harvard University Press, 2000.

Cutter, Barbara. *Domestic Devils, Battlefield Angels: The Radicalism of American Womanhood, 1830–1865*. DeKalb, IL: Northern Illinois University Press, 2003.

Dannenbaum, Jed. "The Origins of Temperance Activity and Militancy Among American Women." *Journal of Social History* 15 (1981): 235–52.

———. *Drink and Disorder: Temperance Reform in Cincinnati from the Washington Revival to the WCTU*. Urbana: University of Illinois Press, 1984.

Davis, David Brion. "Reflections on Abolitionism and Ideological Hegemony." *American Historical Review* 92 (1987): 797–812.

Davis, Hugh. *Joshua Leavitt: Evangelical Abolitionist*. Baton Rouge: Louisiana State University Press, 1990.

Degler, Carl. *At Odds: Women and the Family in America from the Revolution to the Present*. New York: Oxford University Press, 1980.

Ditz, Toby L. "Shipwrecked; or, Masculinity Imperiled: Mercantile Representations of Failure and the Gendered Self in Eighteenth-Century Philadelphia." *Journal of American History* 81 (1994): 51–80.

Dixon, Christopher. "'A True Manly Life:' Abolitionism and the Masculine Ideal." *Mid-America* 77 (1995): 267–90.

Donovan, Brian. *White Slave Crusades: Race, Gender, and Anti-Vice Activism, 1887–1917*. Urbana and Chicago: University of Illinois Press, 2006.

Dorsett, Lyle W. "The Problem of Grant's Drinking During the Civil War." *Hayes Historical Journal* 4 (1983): 37–48.

Dorsey, Bruce. *Reforming Men and Women: Gender in the Antebellum City*. Ithaca: Cornell University Press, 2002.

Dubbert, Joe L. *A Man's Place: Masculinity in Transition*. Englewood Cliffs, NJ: Prentice-Hall, 1979.

DuBois, Ellen Carol. *Feminism and Suffrage: The Emergence of an Independent Women's Movement in America, 1848–1869*. Ithaca: Cornell University Press, 1978.

———. "Outgrowing the Compact of the Fathers: Equal Rights, Woman Suffrage, and the United States Constitution, 1820–1878." *Journal of American History* 74 (1987): 836–62.

———. *Woman Suffrage and Women's Rights*. New York: New York University Press, 1998.

Edwards, Laura F. *Gendered Strife and Confusion: The Political Culture of Reconstruction*. Urbana: University of Illinois Press, 1997.

Edwards, Rebecca. *Angels in Machinery: Gender in American Party Politics from the Civil War to the Progressive Era*. New York: Oxford University Press, 1997.

Epstein, Barbara Leslie. *The Politics of Domesticity: Women, Evangelism and Temperance in Nineteenth-Century America*. Middletown, CT: Wesleyan University Press, 1981.

Ericson, David F. *The Debate over Slavery: Antislavery and Proslavery Liberalism in Antebellum America*. New York: New York University Press, 2000.

Essig, James D. *The Bonds of Wickedness: American Evangelicals against Slavery, 1770–1808*. Philadelphia: Temple University Press, 1982.

Fabian, Ann. *The Unvarnished Truth: Personal Narratives in Nineteenth-Century America*. Berkeley: University of California Press, 2000.

Fahey, David M. *Temperance and Racism: John Bull, Johnny Reb and the Good Templars*. Lexington: University of Kentucky Press, 1996.

Fink, Leon. *Workingmen's Democracy: The Knights of Labor and American Politics*. Urbana: University of Illinois Press, 1983.

Fladeland, Betty. *Abolitionists and Working-Class Problems in the Age of Industrialization*. Baton Rouge: Louisiana State University Press, 1984.

Foner, Eric. *Free Soil, Free Labor, Free Men: The Ideology of the Republican Party before the Civil War*. New York: Oxford University Press, 1970.

———. *Reconstruction: America's Unfinished Revolution, 1863–1877*. New York: Harper and Row, 1988.
Foster, Gaines M. *Moral Reconstruction: Christian Lobbyists and the Federal Legislation of Morality, 1865–1920*. Chapel Hill: University of North Carolina Press, 2002.
Frank, Stephen M. *Life with Father: Parenthood and Masculinity in the Nineteenth-Century American North*. Baltimore: Johns Hopkins University Press, 1998.
Fredrickson, George M. *The Inner Civil War: Northern Intellectuals and the Crisis of the Union*. Urbana: University of Illinois Press, 1965.
Friedman, Lawrence. *Gregarious Saints: Self and Community in Antebellum American Abolitionism, 1830–1870*. Cambridge: Cambridge University Press, 1982.
Frost, Linda. *Never One Nation: Freaks, Savages, and Whiteness in U.S. Popular Culture, 1850–1877*. Minneapolis: University of Minnesota Press, 2005.
Garner, Nancy. "A Prayerful Public Protest: The Significance of Gender in the Kansas Woman's Crusade of 1874." *Kansas History* 20 (1997): 214–29.
Genovese, Eugene. *Roll, Jordan, Roll: The World the Slaves Made*. New York: Vintage Books, 1976.
Gerteis, Louis S. *Morality and Utility in American Antislavery Reform*. Chapel Hill: University of North Carolina Press, 1987.
Giele, Janet Zollinger. *Two Paths to Women's Equality: Temperance, Suffrage, and the Origins of Liberal Feminism in the United States, 1820–1920*. Cambridge, MA: Harvard University Press, 1996.
Giesburg, Judith Ann. *Civil War Sisterhood: The U.S. Sanitary Commission and Women's Politics in Transition*. Boston: Northeastern University Press, 2000.
Gilkeson, John S. *Middle-Class Providence, 1820–1940*. Princeton: Princeton University Press, 1986.
Ginzberg, Lori D. *Women and the Work of Benevolence: Morality, Politics, and Class in the Nineteenth-Century United States*. New Haven: Yale University Press, 1990.
Goodman, Paul. *Of One Blood: Abolitionism and the Origins of Racial Equality*. Berkeley: University of California Press, 1998.
Griffin, Clifford S. *Their Brothers' Keepers: Moral Stewardship in the United States, 1800–1865*. New Brunswick, NJ: Rutgers University Press, 1960.
Griswold, Robert. *Fatherhood in America: A History*. New York: Basic Books, 1993.
Grossberg, Michael. *Governing the Hearth: Law and the Family in Nineteenth-Century America*. Chapel Hill: University of North Carolina Press, 1985.
Gusfield, Joseph R. *Symbolic Crusade: Status Politics and the American Temperance Movement*. 2nd edition. Urbana: University of Illinois Press, 1986.
Halttunen, Karen. *Confidence Men and Painted Women: A Study of Middle-Class Culture in America, 1830–1870*. New Haven: Yale University Press, 1982.
Hampel, Robert L. *Temperance and Prohibition in Massachusetts, 1813–1852*. Ann Arbor: University of Michigan Research Press, 1982.
Hansen, Debra Gold. *Strained Sisterhood: Gender and Class in the Boston Female Anti-Slavery Society*. Amherst: University of Massachusetts Press, 1993.
Hartog, Hendrick. *Public Property and Private Power: The Corporation of the City of New York in American Law*. Ithaca: Cornell University Press, 1983.

———. *Man and Wife in America: A History.* Cambridge, MA: Harvard University Press, 2000.
Haskell, Thomas. "Capitalism and the Origins of Humanitarian Sensibility, Part I." *American Historical Review* 90 (1985): 339–61.
———. "Capitalism and the Origins of Humanitarian Sensibility, Part II." *American Historical Review* 90 (1985): 457–566.
Hendler, Glenn and Mary Chapman, eds. *Sentimental Men: Masculinity and the Politics of Affect in American Culture.* Berkeley: University of California Press, 1999.
Hersh, Blanche Glassman. *The Slavery of Sex: Feminist-Abolitionists in America.* Urbana: University of Illinois Press, 1978.
Heyrman, Christine. *Southern Cross: The Beginnings of the Bible Belt.* Chapel Hill: University of North Carolina Press, 1997.
Hoffert, Sylvia. *When Hens Crow: The Women's Rights Movement in Antebellum America.* Bloomington: Indiana University Press, 1995.
Hofstadter, Richard. *The Age of Reform: From Bryan to FDR.* New York: Alfred A. Knopf, 1955.
Hoganson, Kristin. "Garrisonian Abolitionists and the Rhetoric of Gender, 1850–1860." *American Quarterly* 45 (1993): 292–329.
Holt, Michael. *The Political Crisis of the 1850's.* New York: W.W. Norton, 1983.
Horton, James Oliver and Lois E. Horton. *In Hope of Liberty: Culture, Community, and Protest among Northern Free Blacks, 1700–1860.* New York: Oxford University Press, 1997.
Horwitz, Morton. *The Transformation of American Law, 1780–1860.* Cambridge, MA: Harvard University Press, 1977.
Howard, Victor B. *The Evangelical War against Slavery and Caste: The Life and Times of John G. Fee.* Selinsgrove, PA: Susquehanna University Press, 1996.
Howe, Daniel Walker. *The Political Culture of the American Whigs.* Chicago: University of Chicago Press, 1979.
Huston, James L. "The Experiential Basis of the Northern Antislavery Impulse." *Journal of Southern History* 56 (1990): 192–215.
Isenberg, Nancy. "The Personal is Political: Gender, Feminism, and the Politics of Discourse Theory." *American Quarterly* 44 (1992): 449–58.
———. *Sex and Citizenship in Antebellum America.* Chapel Hill: University of North Carolina Press, 1998.
Jacobs, Donald, ed. *Courage and Conscience: Black and White Abolitionists in Boston.* Bloomington: Indiana University Press, 1993.
Jacobsen, Matthew Frye. *Barbarian Virtues: The United States encounters foreign peoples at home and abroad, 1876–1917.* New York: Hill and Wang, 2000.
Jacoby, Russell. "A New Intellectual History?" *American Historical Review* 97 (1992): 405–24.
Jeffrey, Julie Roy. *The Great Silent Army of Abolitionism: Ordinary Women in the Antislavery Movement.* Chapel Hill: University of North Carolina Press, 1998.
Jensen, Richard. *Grass Roots Politics: Parties, Issues, and Voters, 1854–1893.* Westport, CT: Greenwood Press, 1983.
Johansen, Shawn. *Family Men: Middle-Class Fatherhood in Early Industrializing America.* New York: Routledge, 2001.

Bibliography

Johnson, Paul E. *A Shopkeeper's Millennium: Society and Revivals in Rochester, New York, 1815–1837.* New York: Hill and Wang, 1978.

Kann, Mark. *On the Man Question: Gender and Civic Virtue.* Philadelphia: Temple University Press, 1991.

Karsten, Peter. *Heart versus Head: Judge-Made Law in Nineteenth-Century America.* Chapel Hill: University of North Carolina Press, 1993.

Keller, Morton. *Affairs of State: Public Life in Late Nineteenth-Century America.* Cambridge, MA: Belknap Press of Harvard University Press, 1977.

Kelley, Robert. *The Cultural Pattern in American Politics: The First Century.* New York: Alfred A. Knopf, 1979.

Kelly, Catherine E. "'Well-Bred Country People:' Sociability, Social Networks, and the Creation of a Provincial Middle Class, 1820–1860." *Journal of the Early Republic* 19 (1999): 451–79.

———. *In the New England Fashion: Reshaping Women's Lives in the Nineteenth Century.* Ithaca: Cornell University Press, 1999.

Kennon, Donald R. "'An Apple of Discord:' The Woman Question at the World's Anti-Slavery Convention of 1840." *Slavery and Abolition* 5 (1984): 244–66.

———, ed. *A Republic for the Ages: The United States Capitol and the Political Culture of the Early Republic.* Charlottesville: University of Virginia Press, 1999.

Kerber, Linda K. "Separate Spheres, Female Worlds, Woman's Place: The Rhetoric of Women's History." *Journal of American History* 75 (1988): 9–39.

———. *No Constitutional Right to be Ladies: Women and the Obligations of Citizenship.* New York: Hill and Wang, 1998.

Kimmel, Michael. *Manhood in America: A Cultural History.* New York: Free Press, 1993.

Kingsdale, Jon M. "The 'Poor Man's Club:' Social Functions of the Urban Working-Class Saloon." *American Quarterly* 25 (1973): 255–84.

Kleppner, Paul. *The Third Electoral System, 1853–1892: Parties, Voters, and Political Cultures.* Chapel Hill: University of North Carolina Press, 1979.

Kraditor, Aileen. *The Ideas of the Woman Suffrage Movement.* New York: Columbia University Press, 1965.

———. *Means and Ends in American Abolitionism: Garrison and His Critics on Strategy and Tactics.* New York: Random House, 1967.

Kutler, Stanley. *Privilege and Creative Destruction: The Charles River Bridge Case.* Philadelphia, New York, and Toronto: J.B. Lippincott Co., 1971.

Leach, William. *True Love and Perfect Union: The Feminist Reform of Sex and Society.* New York: Basic Books, 1980.

Leonard, Elizabeth. *Yankee Women: Gender Battles in the Civil War.* New York: W.W. Norton, 1994.

Lender, Mark and James Kirby Martin. *Drinking in America: A History.* New York: Free Press, 1982.

Leverenz, David. *Manhood and the American Renaissance.* Ithaca: Cornell University Press, 1989.

Levine, George, ed. *Constructions of the Self.* New Brunswick, NJ: Rutgers University Press, 1992.

Levine, Lawrence W. *Highbrow/Lowbrow: The Emergence of Cultural Hierarchy in America.* Cambridge, MA: Harvard University Press, 1988.

Levine, Robert S. "Disturbing Boundaries: Temperance, Black Elevation, and Violence in Frank J. Webb's *The Garies and Their Friends.*" *Prospects* 19 (1994): 349–74.

Loveland, Anne C. "Evangelicalism and 'Immediate Emancipation' in American Antislavery Thought." *Journal of Southern History* 32 (1966): 172–88.

Mangan, J.A. and James Walvin, eds. *Manliness and Morality: Middle-Class Masculinity in Britain and America, 1800–1940.* New York: St. Martin's Press, 1987.

Marilley, Suzanne. *Woman Suffrage and the Origins of Liberal Feminism in the United States, 1820–1920.* Cambridge, MA: Harvard University Press, 1996.

Marton, Waldo E., Jr. *The Mind of Frederick Douglass.* Chapel Hill: University of North Carolina Press, 1984.

Mathews, Donald G. *Slavery and Methodism: A Chapter in American Morality, 1780–1845.* Princeton: Princeton University Press, 1965.

Mayer, Henry. *All on Fire: William Lloyd Garrison and the Abolition of Slavery.* New York: St. Martin's Press, 1998.

McArthur, Judith N. "Demon Rum on the Boards: Temperance Melodrama and the Tradition of Antebellum Reform." *Journal of the Early Republic* 9 (1989): 517–40.

McCurry, Stephanie. *Masters of Small Worlds: Yeoman Households, Gender Relations, and the Political Culture of the Antebellum South Carolina Low Country.* New York: Oxford University Press, 1995.

McFeely, William. *Frederick Douglass.* New York: Simon and Schuster, 1991.

McGerr, Michael. "Political Style and Women's Power, 1830–1930." *Journal of American History* 77 (1990): 864–85.

McKivigan, John R. "The Antislavery 'Comeouter' Sects: A Neglected Dimension of the Abolitionist Movement." *Civil War History* 26 (1980): 142–60.

———. *The War Against Proslavery Religion: Abolitionism and the Northern Churches, 1830–1865.* Ithaca: Cornell University Press, 1984.

———, ed. *History of the American Abolitionist Movement.* Vol. 3, *Abolitionism and American Politics and Government.* New York: Garland Publishing, 1999.

———, ed. *History of the American Abolitionist Movement.* Vol. 4, *Abolitionism and Issues of Race and Gender.* New York: Garland Publishing, 1999.

McPherson, James M. *The Struggle for Equality: Abolitionists and the Negro in the Civil War and Reconstruction.* Princeton: Princeton University Press, 1964.

———. "Abolitionists, Woman Suffrage, and the Negro, 1865–1869." *Mid-America* 47 (1965): 40–47.

———. "Abolitionists and the Civil Rights Act of 1875." *Journal of American History* 52 (1965): 493–510.

———. *The Abolitionist Legacy: From Reconstruction to the NAACP.* Princeton: Princeton University Press, 1975.

Melder, Keith. *The Beginnings of Sisterhood: The American Women's Rights Movement, 1800–1850.* New York: Schocken Books, 1977.

Menand, Louis. *The Metaphysical Club: A Story of Ideas in America.* New York: Farrar, Straus and Giroux, 2002.

Montgomery, David. *Beyond Equality: Labor and the Radical Republicans, 1862–1872.* New York: Alfred A. Knopf, 1967.

Murdock, Catherine Gilbert. *Domesticating Drink: Women, Men and Alcohol in America, 1870–1940*. Baltimore: Johns Hopkins University Press, 1998.
Murphy, Gretchen. "Enslaved Bodies: Figurative Slavery in the Temperance Fiction of Harriet Beecher Stowe and Walt Whitman." *Genre* 28 (1995): 95–118.
Murphy, Teresa Anne. *Ten Hours' Labor: Religion, Reform, and gender in Early New England*. Ithaca: Cornell University Press, 1992.
Nadelhaft, Jerome. "Alcohol and Wife Abuse in Antebellum Male Temperance Literature." *Canadian Review of American Studies* 25 (1995): 15–43.
Nelson, William. *The Americanization of the Common Law, 1780–1860*. Cambridge, MA: Harvard University Press, 1975.
Newman, Louise Michelle. *White Women's Rights: Racial Origins of Feminism in the United States*. Oxford: Oxford University Press, 1999.
O'Neill, William. *Everyone Was Brave: The Rise and Fall of Feminism in America*. Chicago: Quadrangle Books, 1969.
Parker, Alison M. and Stephanie Cole, eds. *Women and the Unstable State in Nineteenth-Century America*. College Station: Texas A & M University Press, 2000.
Parker, Allison M. *Purifying America: Women, Cultural Reform, and Pro-Censorship Activism, 1873–1933*. Urbana: University of Illinois Press, 1997.
Parsons, Elaine Frantz. *Manhood Lost: Fallen Drunkards and Redeeming Women in the Nineteenth-Century United States*. Baltimore: Johns Hopkins University Press, 2003.
Pease, Jane H. and William H. Pease. "Confrontation and Abolition in the 1850's." *Journal of American History* 58 (1972): 923–37.
———. *They Who Would Be Free: Blacks' Search for Freedom, 1830–1860*. New York: Athenaeum, 1974.
Pegram, Thomas. *Battling Demon Rum: The Struggle for a Dry America, 1800–1933*. Chicago: Ivan R. Dee, 1998.
Perkal, M. Leon. "The American Abolition Society: A Viable Alternative to the Republican Party?" *Journal of Negro History* 65 (1980): 57–71.
Perry, Lewis. "Versions of Anarchism in the Antislavery Movement." *American Quarterly* 20 (1968): 768–82.
———. *Childhood, Marriage and Reform: Henry Clarke Wright, 1797–1870*. Chicago: University of Chicago Press, 1980.
Pierson, Michael D. "Between Antislavery and Abolition: The Politics and Rhetoric of Jane Grey Swisshelm." *Pennsylvania History* 60 (1993): 305–21.
———. *Free Hearts and Free Homes: Gender and American Antislavery Politics*. Chapel Hill: University of North Carolina Press, 2003.
Pivar, David J. *Purity Crusade: Sexual Morality and Social Control, 1868–1900*. Westport, CT: Greenwood Press, 1973.
Pleck, Joseph H. and Elizabeth H. Pleck, eds. *The American Man*. Englewood Cliffs, NJ: Prentice-Hall, 1980.
Potter, David M. *The Impending Crisis, 1848–1861*. New York: Harper Collins, 1977.
Pugh, David G. *Sons of Liberty: The Masculine Mind in Nineteenth-Century America*. Westport, CT: Greenwood Press, 1983.
Putzi, Jennifer. *Identifying Marks: Race, Gender, and the Marked Body in Nineteenth-Century America*. Athens: University of Georgia Press, 2006.

Quarles, Benjamin. *Black Abolitionists*. New York: W.W. Norton, 1973.
Rael, Patrick. *Black Identity and Protest in the Antebellum North*. Chapel Hill: University of North Carolina Press, 2002.
Reynolds, David S. and Debra J. Rosenthal, eds. *Serpent in the Cup: Temperance in American Literature*. Amherst: University of Massachusetts Press, 1997.
Richardson, Heather Cox. *The Death of Reconstruction: Race, Labor and Politics in the Post-Civil War North, 1865–1901*. Cambridge, MA: Harvard University Press, 2001.
Roberts, Brian. *American Alchemy: The California Gold Rush and Middle-Class Culture*. Chapel Hill: University of North Carolina Press, 2000.
Roediger, David R. *The Wages of Whiteness: Race and the Making of the American Working Class*. Revised edition. New York: Verso Press, 1991.
Rogin, Michael Paul. *Fathers and Children: Andrew Jackson and the Subjugation of the American Indian*. London and New Brunswick: Transaction Publishers, 1995.
Rorabaugh, W.J. *The Alcoholic Republic: An American Tradition*. New York: Hill and Wang, 1978.
Rose, Anne C. *Victorian America and the Civil War*. Cambridge: Cambridge University Press, 1992.
Rosenberg, Charles E. "Sexuality, Class and Role in Nineteenth-Century America." *American Quarterly* 25 (1973): 131–53.
Rosenthal, Debra J. *Race Mixture in Nineteenth-Century U.S. and Spanish American Fictions: Gender, Culture, and Nation Building*. Chapel Hill: University of North Carolina Press, 2004.
Rosenzweig, Roy. *Eight Hours for What We Will: Workers and Leisure in an Industrial City, 1870–1920*. Cambridge: Cambridge University Press, 1983.
Rotundo, E. Anthony. "Body and Soul: Changing Ideals of American Middle-Class Manhood, 1770–1920." *Journal of Social History* 16 (1983): 23–38.
———. *American Manhood: Transformation in Masculinity from the Revolution to the Modern Era*. New York: Basic Books, 1993.
Rumbarger, John J. *Profits, Power, and Prohibition: Alcohol Reform and the Industrializing of America, 1800–1933*. Albany: State University of New York Press, 1989.
Ryan, Mary P. *Cradle of the Middle-Class: The Family in Oneida County, New York, 1790–1865*. Cambridge: Cambridge University Press, 1981.
———. *Women in Public: Between Banners and Ballots, 1825–1880*. Baltimore: Johns Hopkins University Press, 1990.
———. *Civic Wars: Democracy and Public Life in the American City during the Nineteenth Century*. Berkeley: University of California Press, 1997.
Salmon, Marylynn. *Women and the Law of Property in Early America*. Chapel Hill: University of North Carolina Press, 1986.
Sanchez-Eppler, Karen. "Bodily Bonds: The Intersecting Rhetorics of Feminism and Abolition." *Representations* 24 (1988): 28–59.
———. *Touching Liberty: Abolition, Feminism and the Politics of the Body*. Los Angeles: University of California at Berkeley Press, 1993.
Scott, Joan Wallach. "Deconstructing Equality-Versus-Difference: Or, the Uses of Poststructuralist Theory for Feminism." *Feminist Studies* 14 (1988): 34–38.

Bibliography

———. "Gender: A Useful Category of Historical Analysis." *American Historical Review* 91 (1986): 1053–75.
Sellers, Charles. *The Market Revolution: Jacksonian America, 1815–1846.* Oxford: Oxford University Press, 1991.
Sewell, Richard H. *Ballots for Freedom: Antislavery Politics in the United States, 1837–1860.* New York: Oxford University Press, 1976.
Shoemaker, Nancy. "How Indians Got to Be Red." *American Historical Review* 102 (1997): 625–44.
Silber, Nina. *The Romance of Reunion: Northerners and the South, 1865–1900.* Chapel Hill: University of North Carolina Press, 1993.
Sklar, Kathryn Kish. *Catherine Beecher: A Study in American Domesticity.* New York: W.W. Norton, 1976.
Smith, Merril D. *Breaking the Bonds: Marital Discord in Pennsylvania, 1730–1830.* New York: New York University Press, 1991.
Smith, Timothy L. *Revivalism in Mid-Nineteenth Century America.* New York: Abingdon Press, 1957.
Smith-Rosenburg, Carroll. "Beauty, the Beast, and the Militant Woman: A Case of Sex Roles and Social Stress in Jacksonian America." *American Quarterly* 23 (1971): 562–84.
———. *Religion and the Rise of the American City: The New York City Mission Movement, 1812–1870.* Ithaca: Cornell University Press, 1971.
———. *Disorderly Conduct: Visions of Gender in Victorian America.* New York: Alfred A. Knopf, 1985.
Sproat, John G. *"The Best Men:" Liberal Reformers in the Gilded Age.* Oxford: Oxford University Press, 1968.
Stanley, Amy Dru. *From Bondage to Contract: Wage Labor, Marriage, and the Market in the Age of Slave Emancipation.* Cambridge: Cambridge University Press, 1998.
Stauffer, John. *The Black Hearts of Men: Radical Abolitionists and the Transformation of Race.* Cambridge, MA: Harvard University Press, 2002.
Stewart, James Brewer. "The Aims and Impact of Garrisonian Abolitionism, 1840–1860." *Civil War History* 15 (1969): 197–209.
———. *Holy Warriors: The Abolitionists and American Slavery.* Revised edition. New York: Hill and Wang, 1997.
Storms, Roger C. *Partisan Prophets: A History of the Prohibition Party.* Denver: National Prohibition Foundation, Inc., 1972.
Strong, Douglas. *Perfectionist Politics: Abolitionism and the Religious Tensions of American Democracy.* Syracuse, NY: Syracuse University Press, 1999.
Theriot, Nancy. *The Biosocial Construction of Femininity: Mothers and Daughters in Nineteenth-Century America.* Westport, CT: Greenwood Press, 1988.
Thomas, John L. "Romantic Reform in America, 1815–1865." *American Quarterly* 17 (1965): 656–81.
Tomlins, Christopher. *Law, Labor, and Ideology in the Early American Republic.* Cambridge: Cambridge University Press, 1993.
Trachtenberg, Alan. *The Incorporation of America: Culture and Society in the Gilded Age.* New York: Hill and Wang, 1982.

Tyrell, Ian R. *Sobering Up: From Temperance to Prohibition in Antebellum America, 1800–1860*. Westport, CT: Greenwood Press, 1979.

———. "Drink and Temperance in the Antebellum South: An Overview and Interpretation." *Journal of Southern History* 48 (1982): 485–510.

———. "Women and Temperance in Antebellum America, 1830–1860." *Civil War History* 28 (1982): 128–52.

———. *Woman's World, Woman's Empire: The WCTU in International Perspective, 1880–1930*. Chapel Hill: University of North Carolina Press, 1991.

VanBurkleo, Sandra F. *"Belonging to the World:" Women's Rights and American Constitutional Culture*. New York: Oxford University Press, 2001.

Varon, Elizabeth R. *We Mean to be Counted: White Women and Politics in Antebellum Virginia*. Chapel Hill: University of North Carolina Press, 1998.

Vaughan, Alden T. "From White Man to Redskin: Changing Anglo-American Perceptions of the American Indian." *American Historical Review* 87 (1982): 917–53.

Volpe, Vernon. *Forlorn Hope of Freedom: The Liberty Party in the Old Northwest, 1838–1848*. Kent, OH: Kent State University Press, 1990.

Walker, Peter F. *Moral Choices: Memory, Desire, and Imagination in Nineteenth-Century American Abolition*. Baton Rouge: Louisiana State University Press, 1978.

Walters, Ronald G. *The Antislavery Appeal: American Abolitionism after 1830*. Baltimore: Johns Hopkins University Press, 1976.

Walters, Ronald G. *American Reformers, 1815–1860*. New York: Hill and Wang, 1978.

Warbasse, Elizabeth Bowles. *The Changing Legal Rights of Married Women, 1800–1861*. New York: Garland Publishing, 1987.

Watson, Samuel. "Flexible Gender Roles During the Market Revolution: Family, Friendship, Marriage and Masculinity among U.S. Army Officers, 1815–1846." *Journal of Social History* 29 (1995): 81–106.

Wedell, Marsha. *Elite Women and the Reform Impulse in Memphis, 1875–1915*. Knoxville: University of Tennessee Press, 1991.

Welter, Barbara. "The Cult of True Womanhood: 1820–1860." *American Quarterly* 18 (1966): 151–74.

Wiebe, Robert H. *The Search for Order, 1877–1920*. New York: Hill and Wang, 1967.

Wiecek, William W. *The Sources of Antislavery Constitutionalism in America*. Ithaca: Cornell University Press, 1977.

Wilentz, Sean. *Chants Democratic: New York and the Rise of the American Working Working Class*. Oxford and New York: Oxford University Press, 1984.

Winch, Julie. *Philadelphia's Black Elite: Activism, Accommodation, and the Struggle for Autonomy*. Philadelphia: Temple University Press, 1988.

Winter, Thomas. *Making Men, Making Class: The YMCA and Workingmen, 1877–1920*. Chicago: University of Chicago Press, 2002.

Wood, Gordon S. *The Radicalism of the American Revolution*. New York: Alfred A. Knopf, 1992.

Wyatt-Brown, Bertram. *Lewis Tappan and the Evangelical War Against Slavery*. Cleveland: Case-Western Reserve University Press, 1969.

Yacovone, Donald. "The Transformation of the Black Temperance Movement, 1827–1854: An Interpretation." *Journal of the Early Republic* 8 (1988): 281–97.

Yellin, Jean Fagan. *Women and Sisters: Antislavery Feminists in American Culture.* New Haven: Yale University Press, 1989.
York, Robert M. *George Barrell Cheever, Religious and Social Reformer, 1807–1910.* Orono, ME: University Press, 1955.
Zagarri, Rosemarie. "Gender and the New Liberal Synthesis." *American Quarterly* 53 (2001): 123–30.
Zimmerman, Jonathan. *Distilling Democracy: Alcohol Education in America's Public Schools, 1880–1925.* Lawrence: University of Kansas Press, 1999.

UNPUBLISHED DISSERTATIONS

Benson, Ronald M. "American Workers and Temperance Reform, 1866–1933." Ph.D. dissertation. Notre Dame University, 1974.
Clark, Elizabeth Battelle. "The Politics of God and the Woman's Vote: Religion in the American Suffrage Movement, 1848–1895." Ph.D. dissertation. Princeton University, 1989.
Coffey, John Joseph. "A Political History of the Temperance Movement in New York State, 1808–1920." Ph.D. dissertation. Pennsylvania State University, 1976.
Dunlap, Leslie Kathrin. "In the Name of the Home: Temperance, Women and Southern Grass-roots Politics, 1873–1933." Ph.D. dissertation. Northwestern University, 2001.
Dyer, Dawn Michelle. "'Combating the Fiery Flood:' The WCTU's Approach to Labor and Socialism." Ph.D. dissertation. Auburn University, 1998.
Levine, Harry Gene. "Demon of the Middle-Class: Self-Control, Liquor and the Ideology of Temperance in Nineteenth-Century America." Ph.D. dissertation. University of California at Berkeley, 1978.
Newman, Richard. "The Transformation of American Abolition: Tactics, Strategies and the Changing Meanings of Activism, 1780's-1830's." Ph.D. dissertation. State University of New York Buffalo, 1998.
Turner, James R. "The American Prohibition Movement, 1865–1897." Ph.D. dissertation. University of Wisconsin, 1972.

Index

A
Abolition movement 26, 30, 45–46, 48–57
Adair Law 99
Alcohol: as cause of domestic violence 15, 19–20, 24, 39, 41–42, 83, 99, 133 n. 39; as cause of poverty 8–11, 52, 67; consumption of 7–8, 16, 35, 60; consumption of among African Americans 69–70, 118–120; consumption of among Native American 72; consumption of among soldiers 62–64, 149 n. 6; consumption of among women 16, 35, 61, 67, 73, 74–75, 96; as destroyer of masculinity 14–15, 26, 32–36, 47; sale and manufacture of 11–13, 23, 68, 99, 116; social use of 18, 60, 67; and slavery 28; as threat to the nation 8–9, 48, 64–68, 71, 116–117
American Temperance Society 8, 16, 22, 48, 50
American Temperance Union 16, 22, 30, 48–49, 58, 62–64
Anthony, Susan B. 38–44, 53, 105, 106, 161 n. 103

B
Baxter Law 96
Blackwell, Antoinette Brown 41, 55–56
Bloomer, Amelia 37–41, 43–44

C
Cheever, George Barrell 20–21, 48
Civil War: *see* Temperance movement
Civil War Amendments 69, 70, 77, 78, 119
Comeouter movement 51, 146 n. 121
Coverture 24, 42, 44; *see also* domesticity, patriarchy, separate spheres
Crosby, Howard 61, 65, 105, 114, 115
Crusades: and Christianity 86–90; and confrontations with saloonkeepers 85–86, 88–90, 93–94; context of in disappointment with prohibition 80–82; ethno-cultural aspect of 94–96, 160 n. 86; and female morality 86–90; male involvement in 85–86, 90–93, 159 n. 61; methods employed in 86; and motivations of participants 83–84, 86–90, 100–101; political function 92–95, 96–98

D
Daughters of Temperance 38
Delavan, Edward C. 23, 49, 59
Dike, Samuel 109–110
Dix, John 81
Domesticity 14, 104, 107, 109, 116, 118, 121; *see also* coverture, patriarchy, separate spheres
Douglass, Frederick 45–47
Dow, Neal 68

E
Evangelical Temperance Association 106

F
Fraternal orders 15, 66, 134 n. 41, 151 n. 51

G
Gage, Francis Dana 41

187

Garrison, William Lloyd 46, 48, 50
Good Templars 66–67, 70, 74, 77, 115, 116, 119, 153 n. 79, 154 n. 96
Goodell, William 48, 50–53, 146 n. 120
Grant, Ulysses S. 63–64, 78, 81, 92
Greeley, Horace 9, 80

H
"Home Protection" 105, 107–110, 112, 114, 115, 121; see also Woman's Christian Temperance Union
Hooker, Joseph 63

I
Immigration 60, 66, 68, 69, 71, 94–96, 120–122, 152 n. 65
Internal Revenue Act of 1862 61

K
Knights of Labor 115

L
Labor movement 5, 68, 81, 112, 115, 116
Lewis, Dio 79, 82–83, 85, 90–91, 97, 100, 105
Liberty Party 49, 51, 146 n. 120, 147 n. 124 and 125
Livermore, Mary 38, 105, 106, 109

M
Maine Law 23–25, 40, 41, 47, 54
Market revolution 8–9, 11, 12–15, 130 n. 6
Marsh, John 25, 49, 58, 62, 67
Martha Washingtonians 34–36, 140 n. 26

N
National Temperance Society and Publication House 58, 66, 68, 69, 70, 74, 81, 82, 90, 93, 114, 116, 118–119
New York Women's State Temperance Society 40, 43

P
Panic of 1837 31
Paternalism 28, 100 n. 138
Patriarchy 14–15, 21–24, 28–29, 44–45; see also coverture, domesticity, separate spheres
Phillips, Wendell 56, 68
Prohibition: see Temperance movement
Prohibition Party 66, 68, 70, 77, 80–82, 105, 121

R
Republican Party 57, 80, 81, 92
Republicanism 11, 13, 131 n. 21

S
Second Great Awakening 2, 8
Separate spheres 13, 24, 75, 132 n. 27; see also coverture, domesticity, patriarchy
Smith, Gerrit 22, 23, 48, 49, 51, 58–59, 70, 81, 146 n. 120, 147 n. 123 and 125, 157 n. 12
Smith, James McCune 55–56
Sons of Temperance 41, 66, 67, 70, 74, 77, 91, 115, 116, 154 n. 96
Stanton, Elizabeth Cady 2, 40–43, 48, 98, 106, 108
Stewart, Eliza 86, 92, 94, 95, 97–100, 105, 113, 117
Stone, Lucy 30, 43, 53
Swisshelm, Jane Grey 42, 44, 161 n. 103

T
Temperance movement: and African Americans 45–48, 69–71, 77–78, 118–120, 122; and the abolitionist movement 26, 30, 45–57; and Christianity 8, 15, 32, 88, 108, 115–116; and the Civil War 50–59, 60–78, 120–123, 150 n. 35; and feminist reform 37–45, 54–57, 98, 105–106, 108–109, 117; and immigration 60, 66, 68, 69, 71, 94–96, 120–122, 152 n. 65; and industrialization 8–9, 11, 12–15, 66, 115, 130 n. 6; and marriage and divorce reform 21–25, 41–44, 109–110; and masculinity 13–15, 20–29, 32–34, 37, 61–66, 71–72, 129 n. 2; and middle class identity 7–13, 67, 130 n. 9; and moderate drinking 8, 60–61, 65, 67, 73–75; use of moral suasion 22, 33, 40, 65–66, 82–83, 86, 88, 93, 103–104; and Native Americans 26, 71–72, 154 n. 87; and patriarchy 14–15, 21–24, 28–29, 44–45; and prohibition 22–25, 40, 41, 47, 54, 65–66, 68, 70–72, 77, 80–82, 97, 104–105, 116, 118–119, 121;

Index

and race 14, 26–29, 45–48, 55, 69–73, 78, 117–120, 122; and slavery 14, 26–29, 45–53, 55–57, 58, 65, 69–70, 117–119; in the South 26–29, 46, 48–50, 53, 56–57, 69–71, 105–106, 111, 113, 116–123; and total abstinence 7–9, 16, 22, 29, 31, 47, 50, 59–61, 64–67, 72, 82, 103, 105, 114–115; and women's participation 16–20, 25, 34–45, 54–57, 58, 73–78, 141 n. 58, *see also* Crusades and Woman's Christian Temperance Union; and working classes 5, 31–37, 38, 50, 68, 74, 81, 112, 115, 116

Thompson, Eliza Jane 83–85, 90, 99, 102, 112–114

U

United States Brewer's Association 60
United States Christian Commission 62

W

Washingtonian movement 31–37, 38, 50, 74, 138 n. 3 and 4, 139 n. 16
Wells, Ida B. 121
Whig Party 23
Willard, Frances: election as WCTU president 106; and divorce reform 109–110; "Do everything" strategy 111–112; feminist reform 107–109; and home protection program 107–108; and prohibition 104–105; views on labor 115–116; views on race 120–121, 168 n. 119; views on woman suffrage 105–108; use of crusader image 112–114; *see also* Woman's Christian Temperance Union

Wittenmyer, Annie 86, 95, 96, 103, 104, 105, 106

Woman suffrage 40–43, 74, 77–78, 80, 103–109, 114, 115

Woman's Christian Temperance Union: cooperation with male movement 114–115; and feminist reform 103–104, 105–109, 126 n. 5, 163 n. 31; ideological diversity of 110–112; inclusion of minorities 120–121; origin of in the Crusades 102–104; and prohibition 104–105; relationship with labor movement 115–116, 166 n. 83; in the South 116–119; splits in 105, 106; and woman suffrage 105–108; *see also* Willard, Frances

World's Temperance Convention (1853) 53–57